Daily Devotions for Grandmothers

By Donna-Marie Cooper O'Boyle

Pauline
BOOKS & MEDIA
BOSTON

Library of Congress Control Number: 2024945547

ISBN 10: 0-8198-1916-6

ISBN 13: 978-0-8198-1916-1

Cover design by Tisa Muico

Published by Pauline Books & Media, 50 Saint Pauls Avenue, Boston, MA 02130-3491

Printed in the U.S.A.

www.pauline.org

Pauline Books & Media is the publishing house of the Daughters of St. Paul, an international congregation of women religious serving the Church with the communications media.

1 2 3 4 5 6 7 8 9 30 29 28 27 26 25

Lovingly for my children:
Justin, Chaldea, Jessica, Joseph, and Mary-Catherine
and my grandchildren: Shepherd and Leo
For my dear Grandmother: Alexandra Uzwiak
with a grateful heart to the Blessed Virgin Mary
and loving thanks to the great Saint Anne,
Patroness of Grandmothers

Contents

Acknowledgments

I am deeply grateful to my parents, Eugene Joseph and Alexandra Mary Cooper, for bringing me into the world and raising me in a large Catholic family. To my brothers and sisters—Alice Jean, Gene, Gary, Barbara, Tim, Michael, and David—thank you for being a wonderful part of my life. And to my dear grandmother, Alexandra Uzwiak, thank you for your loving guidance that has helped to shape me.

My heartfelt gratitude goes to my dear husband, Dave, and my beloved children—Justin, Chaldea, Jessica, Joseph, and Mary-Catherine—for their continued love and support, and to my precious grandsons, Shepherd and Leo. I love you all dearly!

Special thanks to my Sisters in Christ: United Under Mary's Mantle, for their continual prayers, and to my friend Father John Hardon, SJ, who spiritually directed and encouraged me. I believe he continues to do so from Heaven! An exuberant thank you to my mother, dear Mother Teresa, for playing a huge role in shaping me spiritually, which I know she continues to do even now. Thank you to my sister and friend Saint Faustina. And to dear Saint Anne, Jesus' grandmother, whom I ask to pray for all grandmothers!

I owe special thanks to Pauline Books and Media, and to Sister Maria Grace Dateno, FSP; Sister Allison Regina Gliot, FSP; and all of the wonderful team that helped get this book out to you!

Finally, I am extremely thankful for my readership, viewership, and listenership, and to all those I meet in my travels. I pray for you every day. Thank you for being part of my fascinating journey through life! Please pray for me, too. I pray that God will continue to bless you in great abundance!

Introduction

Is your name "Grandma"? Or are you "Nonna," "Grammie," "Granny," or "Mimi"? Are you "Nana," "Gram," "Abuela," "Yamma," or "Yaya"? Perhaps you are "Lola," "Meme," or "NaiNai." The list for the many endearing names for grandmothers goes on and on. Sometimes, the grandchild chooses the name for his or her grandmother. One day, he or she expresses it—and it sticks!

I'll never forget meeting and holding my first grandchild, Shepherd, on the day he was born. My heart was filled with a special love I had never experienced. I find it almost too precious to express. This same experience happened with my second grandchild, Leo, a few years later. My heart was bursting with grandmotherly love when he came into the world. The remarkable blessing of grandmother love grows as I grow with Leo and his big brother Shepherd.

I chose the name "Grandma" when my oldest daughter, Chaldea, asked me what I would like my grandchildren to call me. I didn't hesitate in telling her. My own grandmother was named "Grandma," and I desired to be like her!

My heart holds vivid memories of my own grandmother, the only one of my grandparents I knew, since the others had passed on before I was born. My grandmother's vibrant faith and inspiring trust in God certainly stirred the embers of faith in my little heart as a child. Watching her finger her rosary beads and experiencing the joie de vivre expressed through her sparkling eyes and beautiful smile proved to me that my Grandma was indeed an integral part of my life. Her example of love and grace nourished my heart then, and it still does now as I recall her love and care. I am sure that she prays for me from Heaven.

A grandmother's love is so incredible and unique. I have no doubt that God blesses grandparents with an exceptional and even heroic love for their grandchildren. As I explain to others when they ask about it, "There is nothing like it!"

Grandmothers fill such a significant role in their grandchildren's lives. In addition to the many things that grandparents do for their grandchildren—loving them, caring for them, and perhaps even helping raise them—their unique loving relationship provides a sense of security and support for the grandchildren. Children who are close to their grandparents tend to have fewer behavioral and emotional problems. They become resilient and are better able to deal with trauma and stress. Adult grandchildren also benefit from advice and the life experiences shared by their grandparents. At the same time, studies show that grandparents become healthier too! Years are added to their lives when they are lovingly involved with their grandchildren.

In addition, there is something else that is so amazing to consider about grandmothers, mothers, and grandchildren: every single egg that a woman will ever have in her reproductive system was developed when she was a fetus residing inside her mother's uterus. This means that while your mother was in your grandmother's womb, the egg that would later be you resided inside there too. You started your life inside of your grandmother! This also means that, if you have given birth to a daughter, then your grandchildren were just eggs inside of her when she was inside of you! It is pretty incredible to ponder.

As wonderful as this close biological bond may be, it's important to acknowledge that the vocation of being a grandmother can be challenging. A grandmother I know shared with me that she has shed many tears over her role. She thought it would be very different from what she experienced. With time and prayer, she now views her role in a new light. My friend began to understand that there was a whole lot more involved in being a grandmother. For instance, sometimes, there's the challenge of not interfering with the way in which the parents are raising the grandchildren. Here is where continual prayer for her grandchildren's spiritual well-being comes into play.

Another challenge grandmothers may face is that not everyone has the blessing of seeing her grandchildren regularly because they might live far from one another. My grandchildren live about a three-hour drive from me. I wish they were next door! When we cannot get together in person, we do videoconferencing. I thank God for modern technology.

Some grandparents may not be able to see their grandchildren at all. They may be estranged in some way—perhaps because of broken families or because the adult children have left the Church and don't want their churchgoing parents (the grandparents) to influence their children. Or, if the grandchildren are older, they themselves may be in conflict with their grandparents. In these or many other scenarios, grandmothers may hold intense pain in their hearts because they cannot see their grandchildren. For example, I met a woman at one of my speaking engagements who was sorrowful over her dilemma and asked my advice. Her son's Hindu wife prevented a relationship between her and the grandchildren. I suggested to this woman that she earnestly appeal to her son and let him know how much she desires to be a part of her grandchildren's lives. In such sad situations when a grandmother cannot be directly involved with her grandchildren, however, she can rely on the spiritual aspect of her vocation and keep her family in prayer.

This spiritual aspect of being a grandmother can even extend to women who do not have grandchildren of their own. For example, I know a grandmother who is not a biological grandmother. She was chosen as an honorary grandmother by a priest at her parish so that a little girl would not be alone on Grandparents' Day. They have continued their relationship into the girl's adult life. Whether "official" or honorary, every grandmother is exceptional and perhaps even tailor-made!

I wrote *Daily Devotions for Grandmothers* to provide a daily devotional for Catholic grandmothers of all kinds and in all situations, knowing that they will greatly benefit from encouragement, affirmation, and Church teaching, as well as many tips, anecdotes, and compelling stories. I am praying that the reflections will uplift weary hearts while offering a great big dose of hope to grandmothers who might not fully realize how important their unique vocation is in the eyes of God, or those who might be anxious about the well-being of their grandchildren. I pray as well that this book will help those grandmothers who already know of their God-given vocation but would welcome the daily inspiration to strengthen their journey. Not every reflection specifically pertains to being a grandmother, but all can be assured that this book will be infused with much nourishment for their spiritual journey.

Enjoy *Daily Devotions for Grandmothers*. May it stir your heart and nourish your faith! Perhaps you'll pour yourself a soothing cup of hot tea to sip as you do your daily reflections. Envision Mother

Mary with you and allow the reflections to "steep" in your heart as you "savor" throughout the day, giving thanks to God for such a sublime vocation.

What an amazing gift to be part of a family in which parents, grandparents, and children all help one another to get to Heaven! May God bless your beautiful and unique vocation as a grandmother. Rejoice in every moment, knowing that God hears your prayers for your grandchildren.

Yours in Jesus, Mary, and Joseph,

Donna-Marie Cooper O'Boyle

July 26, 2018, Feast of Saint Anne and Saint Joachim,
Parents of the Blessed Virgin Mary
and Grandparents of Jesus

How to Use This Book

Each part of the book (or month) has a specific theme based on popular Catholic tradition. Each month is introduced with a pertinent quote from Scripture or Church tradition.

Every day of the year, *Daily Devotions for Grandmothers* will offer the opportunity to meditate upon Scriptural verses, quotes from the saints, or some aspect of Church teaching, as well as to ponder an inspiring story, to pray a suggested prayer that matches the theme of that day, and to savor a special takeaway throughout the day.

Each of the 366 reflections (or days) will have these five elements:

- An inspiring quote or verse from Scripture or Catholic teaching, which will correspond with the theme of the month.
- *Steep:* The short story, anecdote, or teaching to ponder.
- *Act:* A suggestion for a way to put the day's reflection into action.
- *Pray:* A short original prayer to pray that day.
- *Savor:* A takeaway "spoonful of honey" to savor in your heart that day.

Though each day's reflections cover a lot of territory, it should only take about five to ten minutes to read, steep, act, pray, and savor (or you can carry out the "Act" at another time during the day when you are able). Hopefully, you can savor each theme all throughout the day.

Enjoy every day!

JANUARY

The Holy Name of Jesus

Let each of you look not to your own interests, but to the interests of others. Let the same mind be in you that was in Christ Jesus. . . .

Therefore God also highly exalted him
    and gave him the name
    that is above every name,
so that at the name of Jesus
    every knee should bend,
    in heaven and on earth and under the earth,
and every tongue should confess
    that Jesus Christ is Lord,
    to the glory of God the Father.

PHILIPPIANS 2:4–5, 9–11

January 1

> [This is] a fitting occasion for renewing adoration of the newborn Prince of Peace, for listening once more to the glad tidings of the angels (cf. Lk 2:14), and for imploring from God, through the Queen of Peace, the supreme gift of peace.[1]
>
> SAINT PAUL VI

STEEP While still in the heart of the Christmas season, we celebrate the Solemnity of the Mother of God, Mary's greatest title (and she has many!). We are reminded of Mary's significance in the life of her Son, Jesus. On this day set aside to celebrate Mary's motherhood, we can also consider the significance of our own role and importance in the lives of our grandchildren.

Mary's grand solemnity may be drowned out by noisy New Year's celebrations. While celebrating the New Year, we must not neglect our dearest Mother in Heaven on her special day of honor.

ACT Include Mother Mary in your New Year's celebrations. Express your love to her and ask her for "the supreme gift of peace" in your heart and in the world.

PRAY Dear Mother Mary, thank you for being my Mother. Please guide me and watch over my grandchild(ren).

Our Father, Hail Mary, and Glory Be.

SAVOR Mary is my Mother! I should call upon her often.

January 2

Very truly, I tell you, if you ask anything of the Father in my name, he will give it to you.

JOHN 16:23

STEEP January is traditionally dedicated to the Holy Name of Jesus. His is indeed a holy name. The second commandment instructs, "You shall not take the Name of the Lord your God in vain." Yet sadly, many abuse it.

As a grandmother, you can teach your grandchildren to show reverence to Jesus. Bowing our heads upon hearing His Name, making the Sign of the Cross when passing a church, and offering a prayer when someone uses the Lord's name in vain are all ways we can set an example for them to follow.

ACT Pray the Litany of the Holy Name of Jesus (page 409) throughout this month to grow in reverence for Jesus and His Holy Name and to make reparation for sins against His Name.

PRAY Dear Jesus, I love You. Forgive me for all the times I have not loved You and when I do not love You as I should. Please transfigure my heart so I may be a grace-filled grandmother.

Our Father, Hail Mary, and Glory Be.

SAVOR Jesus is the Name above all names!

January 3

Grandchildren are the crown of the aged,
and the glory of children is their parents.

PROVERBS 17:6

STEEP Grandchildren are an integral part of the family. The love that my own aged grandmother poured out on me and her many grandchildren, as well as the seeds of faith that she planted in my soul, made an unforgettable impression on my little heart as a child, and still do now that I am a grandmother myself.

Grandparents' love and prayers for their family are powerful! We might not see the fruits of the prayers we pray day in and day out. However, we must believe that our Lord certainly hears the prayers of a faithful grandparent.

ACT Tell God that you trust His holy will regarding your grandchildren. Pray for families who do not experience real love and care.

PRAY Jesus, I trust in You! Dear Mother Mary, please guide me and protect my grandchild(ren) from all evil.

Our Father, Hail Mary, and Glory Be.

SAVOR God hears my prayers. Prayer changes things!

January 4

> Let there be thanks to you, my sweetness, my honor, my trust, my God, let there be thanks to you for your gifts.[2]
>
> SAINT AUGUSTINE

STEEP I remember waking up from my afternoon naps as a toddler. My grandmother was sitting right next to me, holding some sort of sweet confection. Waking up to her smiling face and cheerful demeanor was always a happy surprise and a sure comfort to my little heart. In addition, I was filled with eagerness to partake in her tasty treat!

A grandmother's presence speaks volumes, and its sweetness can remind us this month of the sweetness of the Name of Jesus. My grandmother did "small things with great love," as Mother Teresa often preached. Little things aren't so little when, by God's grace, the beautiful power of love is transported through them!

ACT Call upon the "sweet Name of Jesus" often today, and do your best to be present to your family.

PRAY Dear Jesus, I love You. Please help me each day to be a faith-filled grandmother.

Our Father, Hail Mary, and Glory Be.

SAVOR Jesus strengthens virtue in my heart, sparks good works through me, and nourishes pure affection.

January 5

But they urged [Jesus] strongly, saying, "Stay with us, because it is almost evening and the day is now nearly over."

LUKE 24:29

STEEP I'll never forget saying goodbye to my grandson Shepherd and hearing him utter the sweetest one-word statement. I had gently prepared him for my departure. Yet when it was time to leave, two-year-old Shepherd squeezed me tighter. He stuttered, trying to come up with just the right word. Then, he blurted out an urgent appeal: "Stay!"

That single word completely melted my heart. The exceptional love of a little grandson for his Grandma can be almost too precious to express!

ACT "Stay" present to your grandchildren today in a visit, a phone call, videoconferencing, or in prayer. If you can, "stay" a bit longer in prayer with God today.

PRAY Dear Jesus, Blessed Mother Mary, and Saint Anne, please watch over me and my family. Thank you, dear Lord, for the gift of my distinctive vocation!

Our Father, Hail Mary, and Glory Be.

SAVOR God strengthens my vocation as a grandmother with His joy.

January 6

Jesus, Strength of Martyrs, have mercy on us.

LITANY OF THE HOLY NAME OF JESUS

STEEP In the early Church, beginning with the apostles, martyrs suffered excruciating persecution. Some were stoned to death, crucified, or burned at the stake. In our own day, Christians continue to be persecuted.

There also exist the quiet martyrs who offer their sufferings to God as a form of reparation for sin. While we might not face physical martyrdom in our daily lives, we may sometimes experience this quiet martyrdom of suffering in our role as grandmothers. But we can have hope that our suffering will bear fruit! When meditating on the suffering of Jesus, Saint Faustina lamented that she did "next to nothing for the salvation of souls." Jesus assured her that her "silent day-to-day martyrdom" ushered many souls into Heaven.[3]

ACT Offer your daily difficulties and sufferings to Jesus. Ask Him to redeem them for His glory and the good of others.

PRAY Dear Jesus, Strength of Martyrs, please grant me courage and strength. Holy martyrs, pray for me.

Our Father, Hail Mary, and Glory Be.

SAVOR When offered lovingly, my day-to-day martyrdom of monotony and "pin pricks" can help to save souls.

January 7

All the works of My hands are crowned with mercy.

Jesus to Saint Faustina, *Diary*, 301

STEEP We are called to be merciful people, taking after our Lord Jesus Christ. Yet it's not always easy to be merciful, especially when someone harms us in some way. But God bids us to holiness and mercy—to choose the high road. This doesn't mean that abuse should be tolerated, but rather that we should respond with charity instead of retaliation.

Within the family setting, mercy and forgiveness should become common practices. Each day we can choose to grow in holiness or to go the other way—not to be merciful and loving. Some days are harder than others, but by imitating Jesus in His great mercy, we can be amazing examples to our grandchildren.

ACT Choose to be merciful today.

PRAY Dear Jesus, I am not always a merciful person. Yet I want to be, to please You and to help others. Please help me.

Our Father, Hail Mary, and Glory Be.

SAVOR Jesus is all about mercy. I should always imitate Him.

January 8

Our Lady of Prompt Succor, for observing perseverance in virtue and good works, pray for us.

LITANY OF OUR LADY OF PROMPT SUCCOR

STEEP How often we need to call on Mama Mary, whom we celebrate today as Our Lady of Prompt Succor. Yet we might hesitate, thinking she is too far removed, too busy, or perhaps wouldn't understand our suffering. Certainly, Mary knows about joys, sorrows, and the deepest pain. After all, she stood by the Cross of her Son and held His lifeless Body after He died.

Jesus gave us the beautiful gift of His own Mother when He was hanging on the Cross: "Here is your mother" (Jn 19:27). Our Lady is prompt to give us aid. We can be sure of it.

ACT Share your joys and your sorrows with Mary today.

PRAY Jesus, thank You for the amazing gift of Your Mother! Mother Mary, please mother me. Help me to mother others.

Our Father, Hail Mary, and Glory Be.

SAVOR Mother Mary teaches endless wisdom. I don't need to fear calling upon her.

January 9

And blessed is she who believed that there would be a fulfillment of what was spoken to her by the Lord.

Luke 1:45

STEEP During the war between Russia and Ukraine, more than a million Ukrainians fled their home country, crossing the three-hundred-mile border to Poland after Russia invaded. My heart was deeply touched by the numerous news stories about compassionate Polish mothers and grandmothers leaving their baby strollers on the platform at train stations, along with photojournalist Francesco Malavolta's viral photo of the strollers. The strollers were stuffed with blankets and baby items in order to help the Ukrainian parents who had fled their war-torn country. I can only imagine the feelings of the desperate mothers with babes in arms coming upon the gifts of strollers awaiting them.

ACT Talk with your family about ways to help those who are unfortunate in some way. Endeavor to carry out your plans.

PRAY Dear Lord Jesus, thank You for the gift of life and the opportunity to help others in need. Mother Mary, please give me a compassionate heart like yours.

Our Father, Hail Mary, and Glory Be.

SAVOR How blessed I am to believe in our Lord and to help others believe.

January 10

> I tell you, whatever you ask for in prayer, believe that you have received it, and it will be yours.
>
> Mark 11:24

STEEP Are we asking enough in prayer? Do we trust that God will answer our prayers? The answers are really quite simple—spelled out succinctly in our verse above.

Our prayers are always answered. Yes, you read that correctly. The thing is, prayers might not be answered in the manner we had hoped. We don't always get what we want. We might not understand it, but there is always a perfect reason. After all, God only wants what is best for us so that we make it to Heaven one day. Sometimes, God allows us to wait, or to wonder, or to perhaps suffer a bit longer to earn graces for ourselves and others. We have to hang in there and trust God!

ACT Make many Acts of Trust: *Jesus, I trust in You.* And wholeheartedly trust Him as the Divine Physician Who knows exactly what you need and when!

PRAY Dear Jesus, I trust in You!

Our Father, Hail Mary, and Glory Be.

SAVOR So much happens in the waiting when we surrender our hearts to God. He knows what is best for our souls.

January 11

Jesus, our Way and our Life, have mercy on us.

LITANY OF THE HOLY NAME OF JESUS

STEEP I love my family and my faith! If you visited my home, you would observe lots of family photos all around but also many sacred images and statues. God calls us to teach the faith and make our homes a domestic church—a blessed place where we learn and grow together in holiness. Adding sacred art, spiritual music, and times for quiet are a few examples of ways you can set the tone in your own domestic church. These additions to our environment can uplift our own spirits, reminding us to pray and make wise decisions, but they also can inspire our visitors.

ACT Ponder ways you can make your home more welcoming and holy.

PRAY Dear Jesus, I want to be holy! Please help me inspire others with Your love.

Our Father, Hail Mary, and Glory Be.

SAVOR It doesn't matter if we live in a cave, a palace, or an apartment. Every home can thrive in the love of God.

January 12

I can do all things through him who strengthens me.

PHILIPPIANS 4:13

STEEP When my kids were little, they loved building tall towers of wooden blocks—higher and higher—and then watching them tumble down, perhaps not at the time they had hoped! Many times, we are like little children, earnestly trying to build those high towers on our own instead of depending on God in our lives. Our endeavors and plans topple and fall. Why? Because we have tried with our own strength—not with God's strength. We think we can do it on our own. We simply cannot.

Thankfully, God promises to share His own strength with us. All we need to do is ask.

ACT Get into the habit of starting every day with a heartfelt morning offering to God, asking Him to help you every step of the way. Pray the formal Morning Offering prayer or a prayer in your own words.

PRAY Dear Lord Jesus, I need You. I cannot do everything on my own. Please help me.

Our Father, Hail Mary, and Glory Be.

SAVOR "I can do all things through him who strengthens me."

January 13

And whatever you do, in word or deed, do everything in the name of the Lord Jesus, giving thanks to God the Father through him.

Colossians 3:17

STEEP The Name of the Lord Jesus is powerful! We shall learn the full extent in Heaven. We are called to do everything in His Name. Do we speak every word, do every action, think every thought with Jesus' Holy Name in mind?

God knows that we are all works in progress. Nonetheless, He calls us to more—to strive for holiness and become united with Jesus. We can endeavor to do all in His mighty Name. We can certainly thank God the Father through Him.

ACT Throughout January, think about all your words and deeds. Are they words you would say, or things you would do, in front of Jesus? Consider also how your words and deeds can be a holy example to help your grandchildren strive to be good and holy too. They are always watching!

PRAY Dear Jesus, help me to be mindful of my words and actions. Help me persevere in my prayers. Please pick me up when I fall.

Our Father, Hail Mary, and Glory Be.

SAVOR This brand new day is a gift from God. I will use it wisely—striving to be more like Jesus.

January 14

Strive first for the kingdom of God and his righteousness, and all these things will be given to you as well.

Matthew 6:33

STEEP It seems that everywhere we turn, myriad opinions or demands are vying for our consideration. Whether it is messages from the advertising world, the demands of our daily duties as grandmothers, or the deep struggles we experience in our lives, our attention is yanked in various directions. We can get exhausted and dizzy trying to keep up with what we think we should do.

Our Christian faith teaches us to first strive for the kingdom of God. When we get our priorities straight, everything else will fall into place—with prayer, of course—and we will be better able to live out our vocation.

ACT Today, find a space with few distractions to spend five minutes of quiet time with God. In addition, offer prayers for families in distress.

PRAY Dear Lord Jesus, I want to put You first in my life. Help me, please.

Our Father, Hail Mary, and Glory Be.

SAVOR I am blessed with the exquisite gift of life and God's amazing promises.

January 15

Jesus, Model of virtues, have mercy on us.

LITANY OF THE HOLY NAME OF JESUS

STEEP Saint Faustina, a modern saint (1905–1938), learned of the importance of Jesus' mercy. He is full of mercy and wants to impart His mercy to us—even and especially to the greatest sinners. We pray that Jesus will have mercy on us and our families, especially when we have fallen.

Do we show mercy to others? It is essential to be merciful people. This work of mercy must begin in the family—our domestic church. Tenderness, forgiveness, and mercy should be doled out in great abundance. It's exactly how we grow in holiness, right in the heart of our home.

ACT Call on Jesus for His great mercy. Ask Him to shower it on your family. Be a merciful daughter of God by being virtuous and showing God's mercy to all.

PRAY Dear Jesus, Your great example of virtue and mercy stirs my heart. Please help me to be holy. Saint Faustina, pray for me.

Our Father, Hail Mary, and Glory Be.

SAVOR Jesus wants me to seek His great mercy and impart it to others.

January 16

Jesus, Good Shepherd, have mercy on us.

LITANY OF THE HOLY NAME OF JESUS

STEEP We women can sometimes act like sheep. We pursue various attractions, act on impulses, and follow false shepherds we hope will lead us to our desired destination. We might be inclined to simply follow the crowd to fit in. We get lost in the herd of sheep, becoming numb to the ill effects of the misleading parts of our culture that dictate to women how we "should" act.

But we must not lose the way to our true Shepherd—Jesus. He seeks us and is waiting to rescue us from the cliff or the brambles like the lost sheep (see Mt 18:10–14). Jesus rejoices when He finds us, as well as when we lead our families to follow Him too. Just as Jesus is the Shepherd who guides us, we as grandmothers are called to guide our grandchildren toward Him.

ACT Seek out the Good Shepherd by raising your heart to Him.

PRAY Dear Jesus, You are my God, my Shepherd, and my Friend. I love You!

Our Father, Hail Mary, and Glory Be.

SAVOR Jesus is my loving Shepherd who leads me to Heaven.

January 17

And he said to them, "Follow me, and I will make you fish for people."

MATTHEW 4:19

STEEP Shortly after Jesus began His public ministry in Galilee, He set out to select His first disciples. Coming upon brothers Simon and Andrew casting their nets, Jesus told them to follow Him. Without hesitation, they abandoned their nets. The same happened with the next two chosen disciples—brothers James and John—who were mending nets with their father. Jesus called, and they immediately stopped working and followed Jesus.

Our daily tasks and responsibilities as grandmothers can keep us busy. Jesus may not ask us to literally drop everything in order to follow Him, but it's important for us to remember to listen for His call amid the busyness of our daily lives.

ACT Do everything in a spirit of prayer today, paying attention to how Jesus might be asking you to follow Him.

PRAY Dear Jesus, I choose to follow You and become a fisher of people. Please show me how.

Our Father, Hail Mary, and Glory Be.

SAVOR Whether busy or mundane, today is a very good day to be more attentive to Jesus' whispers to my heart.

January 18

Jesus, joy of Angels, have mercy on us.

LITANY OF THE HOLY NAME OF JESUS

STEEP Grandchildren can seem like sweet angels! Especially when they are small, we might even think that they couldn't possibly do anything wrong. After all, they are just too cute and precious. Does this sound familiar?

While we are certainly aware that our grandchildren are special, we also know they will make mistakes. For example, they might fall under the influence of peers and go down the wrong path. Grandmothers can be such an integral part of their journey through life, whether in prayer or in the flesh (or hopefully both!). Doing things such as gifting them an inspirational book, sending a spiritual card (even if you live next door!), or discussing some aspect of a saint's life with them can help form their consciences no matter how old they are. Don't underestimate how important your influence on your grandchildren is!

ACT Ponder ways to be more involved in your grandchild(ren)'s spiritual journey.

PRAY Jesus, please show me how to guide my grandchildren through my examples in deed, word, and prayer.

Our Father, Hail Mary, and Glory Be.

SAVOR Jesus is the joy of angels. I will delight in the love of Jesus today and share it with my grandchildren!

January 19

Therefore God also highly exalted him
and gave him the name
that is above every name,
so that at the name of Jesus
every knee should bend,
in heaven and on earth and
under the earth,
and every tongue should confess
that Jesus Christ is Lord,
to the glory of God the Father.

PHILIPPIANS 2:9–11

STEEP As grandmothers, we have the amazing role of spiritually looking after our grandchildren. Whether through earnest prayers and holy influence from afar (through letters, spiritual gifts, video conferencing) or by lovingly teaching them while in their presence, grandmothers have a role like none other.

The road to Heaven is difficult at times, especially when making decisions about good and evil. When tempted, our grandchildren need our help to learn to be strong. We can pray for them, and we can also pray that our teachings bestowed upon them will remain etched on their hearts forever.

ACT If you are able to, pray with your grandchildren today. Tell them that Jesus loves their prayers.

PRAY Dear Jesus, help me to be a spiritual guide to my grandchildren.

Our Father, Hail Mary, and Glory Be.

SAVOR I will give my grandchildren loads of heavenly encouragement!

January 20

Each time we say, "Jesus," we give God infinite joy and glory, for we offer Him all the infinite merits of the Passion and Death of Jesus Christ.[4]

Father Paul O'Sullivan

STEEP Sadly, some grandchildren might not learn the Holy Name of Jesus. Their parents might have left the Church or chosen to not teach the faith to their children. What do we Catholic grandmothers do in that case? We can't overstep our bounds, or we might get cut off from our precious relationship. We can pray our hearts out and beg God to work on the parents' hearts, making sacrifices, doing penances, and praying earnestly for their conversion. God will hear our prayers for our grandchildren, and with His grace, they may come to see the light in our eyes and come to know Him through us.

ACT Pray for the conversion of anyone you know who has left the Church.

PRAY Jesus, please help my family and all families to turn to You.

Our Father, Hail Mary, and Glory Be.

SAVOR I won't ever give up praying and being a holy Christian example.

January 21

Each time we say, "Jesus," it is an act of perfect love, for we offer to God the infinite love of Jesus.[5]

Father Paul O'Sullivan

STEEP As we go about our day, whether it's busy or calm, we can always whisper the name of Jesus. We can get our day started off right when we turn to our Lord first thing in the morning, praying for His will to be done in our life and asking Him to use us to help our grandchildren and others. What will today bring? Whatever it is, we should call upon the name of Jesus. He will surely assist us.

ACT Even if today is a busy day, try to fill it with the name of Jesus.

PRAY Dear Jesus, I love You! Stay with me, please. I want to face the day with You at my side.

Our Father, Hail Mary, and Glory Be.

SAVOR Today is special. It's another opportunity to show Jesus that I love Him.

January 22

Un-forgiveness is a poison that kills us from inside out.[6]

Father Seraphim Michalenko

STEEP Everyone is wounded in some way or another. It's not likely we will get through life unscathed. For that reason, we often carry around baggage that can have detrimental effects on our hearts and souls. Holding on to grudges and pain that has been inflicted on us holds us in bondage. Our attitude of unforgiveness can also affect our relationships with others, including our families and even our grandchildren.

To free ourselves from the pain of past wounds, we can give our hurts to God, the great healer. We can trust that He will heal both our personal wounds and any wounds in our relationships. We are better able to nurture our precious grandchildren when we are whole and healed.

ACT When you are tempted to dwell on a wound, offer it to God and ask for His help to heal from it.

PRAY Dear Jesus, help me to let go of any pain I am holding on to.

Our Father, Hail Mary, and Glory Be.

SAVOR Life is an incredible gift. I desire to live it fully without chains on my heart.

January 23

The soul of a child does not emanate from the mother's soul or body, but is freshly created by God Himself, Who infuses it into the body of the unborn child.[7]

Venerable Fulton Sheen

STEEP Every single human life, born or unborn, is a unique and unrepeatable gift. Human life is sacred! How blessed we are to be grandmothers—our very life exudes the profound and intrinsic dignity of human life. We are certainly blessed to be part of a human family. Yet, there exists much division in our world due to the abortion debate. Though the arguments can get very ugly—and unfortunately, even violent—we must keep in mind that this argument won't be won with fighting, but rather with love and persevering efforts to care for women and children. We must lovingly provide help, resources, and choices, such as adoption, that will encourage women to choose life.

ACT Spend time praying and pondering how you can help to protect human life from conception until natural death.

PRAY Dear Jesus, thank You for my life. Please help me to help others make the right choices.

Our Father, Hail Mary, and Glory Be.

SAVOR Human life is sacred and unrepeatable. I am truly blessed!

January 24

Jesus, most patient, have mercy on us.

LITANY OF THE HOLY NAME OF JESUS

STEEP Patience is a beautiful virtue that is somewhat difficult to acquire. I've heard from sincere Christians that the more they strove to be patient, the more they lost their patience! Perhaps this is because when we pray for patience, God gives us more opportunities to practice it.

I used to think I was a patient person. Then I married my dear spouse, whose particular personality and teasing at times has tried my patience! One day, I playfully grabbed a nearby object to pretend I'd hit him. When I looked at it, I realized it was a plaque inscribed with the words, "Love is patient; love is kind." God has a wonderful sense of humor!

Even the sweetest of grandchildren can try the patience of a grandmother! Practicing patience helps our own souls and makes an impression on others too.

ACT Look for ways you can practice patience with your loved ones today.

PRAY Dear Jesus, help me to be more patient. I want to be a beautiful example of Your love.

Our Father, Hail Mary, and Glory Be.

SAVOR Opportunities abound for me to respond with love.

January 25

The Holy Name of Jesus saves us from innumerable evils and delivers us especially from the power of the devil, who is constantly seeking to do us harm.[8]

Father Paul O'Sullivan

STEEP Today's quote mentions the evil one "seeking to do us harm." Certainly, this is not a happy thought. Yet we can't live with blinders on. We need to know the truth so that we can be safe from the devil's grasp. Calling on the Holy Name of Jesus saves us. Calling upon the Blessed Virgin Mary and Saint Michael, praying, frequenting the sacraments, and using blessed sacramentals—such as holy water, blessed salt, or blessed medals—are all strong protections. While we might not want to think about the devil, we can protect ourselves and our families by being vigilant and prayerful.

ACT Call on Jesus' Holy Name often. Ask Him, His Mother, and the angels to spiritually protect your family. Put any or all of the above suggestions (prayers, sacraments, sacramentals) into practice.

PRAY Dear Jesus, teach me not to be tricked by the devil. Please protect my family and me.

Our Father, Hail Mary, and Glory Be.

SAVOR The Name of Jesus is a powerful protection against evil.

January 26

Parents hold the place of God in the house.[9]

Venerable Fulton Sheen

STEEP Parents and grandparents are heroes in their children's and grandchildren's lives. But not every home life is a happy one. Illness, separation, or other stressors in the family can affect our grandchildren. Sometimes, because of our fallen human nature, parents and grandparents do not live up to our role of reflecting God to those in our household.

We can all pray that every child will be loved and cherished by parents and grandparents who can share virtues and set examples that will hopefully be handed down to future generations. As grandparents, we can find ways to help struggling families, even our own families. Most importantly, we can try to live a virtuous life to give an example and encouragement to others.

ACT Find a way to reach out to a family you know who is struggling and help alleviate their stress.

PRAY Dear Jesus, please help my family and families everywhere.

Our Father, Hail Mary, and Glory Be.

SAVOR The family is the vital cell of society.

January 27

The Name of Jesus gradually fills our souls with a peace and a joy we never had before.[10]

Father Paul O'Sullivan

STEEP We don't always experience God's abiding peace and joy. When things don't go our way in life or in our family's lives, we might doubt God's generosity and goodness. We might think we know what's best for ourselves and for our loved ones. But when we stray from God and His commandments, we hurt ourselves and others too.

Our Divine Physician knows exactly what we need and when we need it. He knows what is best for our souls. We have to trust God in everything. Entering into communion with Him will give us true happiness, fulfillment, and peace.

ACT If you feel discouraged about an undesired outcome, pause and ask God to help you to rely on Him.

PRAY Jesus, You know every hair on my head and every desire of my heart. Please help me experience Your abiding peace and joy. *Our Father, Hail Mary, and Glory Be.*

SAVOR God knows what is best for me and for my family.

January 28

Jesus, our Refuge, have mercy on us.

LITANY OF THE HOLY NAME OF JESUS

STEEP Why did God create babies to be so darn cute? It surely must be so that we remember their cuteness in the wee hours of the morning when their persistent loud cries wake us up to feed them, or when they grow older and do not-so-cute things!

Babies are totally dependent upon adults to meet their needs. In those moments when they need us, we can be their refuge. They have complete trust in our abilities. We should have the same sort of trust in Jesus—our refuge—that our grandchildren have in us when they are small. We should call out His Holy Name often, even in the night when we are called to duty with little ones or older ones. Jesus has our back.

ACT Endeavor to trust Jesus more wholeheartedly. Make Acts of Trust to Him often.

PRAY Dear Jesus, I trust in You!

Our Father, Hail Mary, and Glory Be.

SAVOR A simple Act of Trust voiced to Jesus changes everything!

January 29

We must forgive the unforgivable.[11]

FATHER SERAPHIM MICHALENKO

STEEP Forgiveness is a tough subject. Nonetheless, we must ask ourselves a few questions. Is there someone whom you cannot forgive? Perhaps you have experienced an unspeakable trauma or tragedy caused by someone—maybe even someone in your family. Do you stuff it down somewhere in the back of your mind so that you won't have to deal with it?

Dealing with painful situations can be very difficult, but truth be told, we only hurt ourselves when we refuse to forgive others. Unforgiveness wraps us in chains. If we don't forgive, we won't have peace. We must try to forgive others in the same way we ask God to forgive us. We must pray for the grace to forgive.

ACT Ponder what you can you do today to offer forgiveness to someone or to accept the apology of someone. In addition, make a point of getting to the sacrament of Reconciliation very soon. God grants helpful graces in this sacrament.

PRAY Dear Jesus, I need to be more forgiving. Please forgive me of my sins—past and present. Teach me how to forgive wholeheartedly.

Our Father, Hail Mary, and Glory Be.

SAVOR When I forgive someone, my imitation of Jesus radiates out to others and sets an invaluable example.

January 30

So let us not grow weary in doing what is right, for we will reap at harvest time, if we do not give up.

Galatians 6:9

STEEP A woman I know was close to her granddaughter Grace as she grew. Recently, my friend lamented, "Sorry to say, we do not have a warm and fuzzy relationship."

Because of distance and the pandemic, this grandma couldn't attend Grace's wedding. She also shared that Grace holds some resentment toward her father, who provided very well for her. She added, "Grace is very well educated, with a master's degree in Family and Children Counseling, which I hope and pray will help her understand the ups and downs of life. I also pray that she learns about forgiveness. I love her very much and wish her the best of everything that life brings."

ACT List blessings you recognize in the members of your family, especially those you see in your grandchildren.

PRAY Dear God, please heal all family divisions.

Our Father, Hail Mary, and Glory Be.

SAVOR Family life is a tremendous blessing that brings both challenges and joy.

January 31

Knowledge is in the mind; character is in the will.[12]

VENERABLE FULTON SHEEN

STEEP One day, my grandson Shepherd ate his lunch while his younger brother Leo continued to play, coming late to the table. My daughter had secretly handed Shepherd a small treat after he finished eating. She didn't want Leo to see it and decide not to eat his lunch. Shepherd tried to be discreet, but he had difficulty being sneaky.

Soon, Leo discovered the secret. Eventually, Shepherd said, "It's too hard being sneaky, but much more fun sharing!" He opened his hand and gave part of his treat to Leo. My daughter and I both smiled. Though we wanted Leo to eat lunch first, it was delightful to hear Shepherd's declaration and to see the sharing take place. What a joy it was to see how he had begun to develop a precious spirit of giving.

ACT Share something with your grandchildren today that will help them grow in virtue.

PRAY Dear Jesus, please help me help my grandchildren to build character to move their wills to do good.

Our Father, Hail Mary, and Glory Be.

SAVOR Every day is an opportunity to pray, to teach, and to love.

FEBRUARY

The Holy Family

Christ chose to be born and grow up in the bosom of the holy family of Joseph and Mary. The Church is nothing other than "the family of God."[13]

Catechism of the Catholic Church

February 1

> The Christian home is the place where children receive the first proclamation of the faith. For this reason the family home is rightly called "the domestic church," a community of grace and prayer, a school of human virtues and of Christian charity.
>
> *Catechism of the Catholic Church*, 1666

STEEP What a privilege it is to be part of a human family. Our Church calls us to make our home a special "domestic church" where we work out our salvation in and through the family. Some days, however, it might seem like we are all going to Hell in a handbasket! I know that might seem blunt, but we are all works in progress and not every home will mirror the holiness of the Church all the time. We all need to pray and continue to put one foot in front of the other in faith.

ACT Think of a way you can be a virtuous example and model for other families; then put it into practice.

PRAY Jesus, Mary, and Joseph, please help my family to imitate yours!

Our Father, Hail Mary, and Glory Be.

SAVOR With God's help, my home can be a community of grace and prayer.

February 2

Then Simeon blessed them and said to his mother Mary, "This child is destined for the falling and the rising of many in Israel, and to be a sign that will be opposed so that the inner thoughts of many will be revealed—and a sword will pierce your own soul too."

Luke 2:34–35

STEEP Conforming to custom, Jesus, being the firstborn, had to be presented in the Temple. Certainly, Jesus' presentation was a momentous occasion at which all members of the Holy Family were present.

It's a blessing to be in the presence of our family at the beginning of our lives but also at the end. I visited my sister Barbara in the final days of her fight with cancer. I vividly recall her desire to stay awake, to take everything in. She told me she "didn't want to miss it." She also insisted that her grandchildren could visit her, though her daughter was unsure of it. Even in her last days, Barbara wanted to be present to her grandchildren.

ACT Have candles blessed to use on a prayer table in your home this year.

PRAY Jesus, Mary, and Joseph, pray for all families!

Our Father, Hail Mary, and Glory Be.

SAVOR The presence of family is a gift!

February 3

> To pour knowledge into the mind of a child, without disciplining his will to goodness, is like putting a rifle into the hands of a child.[14]
>
> VENERABLE FULTON SHEEN

STEEP As Catholic grandmothers, we know that our teaching role is not simply to impart information, or as Venerable Sheen put it, to "pour knowledge" into children's minds. There are countless things they will learn from us while observing our actions and listening to our words.

Perhaps one of the most important things we will teach them is to move their will to do good. Children greatly benefit from learning this essential aspect of the spiritual life early. Let us teach them to share, to love, to care for others' feelings, and to offer kindness and compassion.

ACT Ponder ways that you can impress upon your grandchildren the loveliness and importance of caring for others.

PRAY Dear Jesus, Mary, and Joseph, help me to guide my grandchildren well!

Our Father, Hail Mary, and Glory Be.

SAVOR My role and influence in my grandchildren's life is unique and unrepeatable. With God's grace, I can make a beautiful difference!

February 4

Enter through the narrow gate; for the gate is wide and the road is easy that leads to destruction, and there are many who take it.

MATTHEW 7:13

STEEP Where is the narrow gate? Do our grandchildren know where it is? Grandmothers have the ability to lead their grandchildren to that narrow gate—to Heaven! We are their first and most important educators in the faith. We can set wonderful, dynamic examples by choosing to head toward that narrow gate throughout their lives. We can lovingly teach them the importance of choosing friends who will nurture their faith and help them not to veer off the path. We can let them know that our choices bring about consequences. Our whole life can be a vibrant example of lively faith.

ACT Look for opportunities to teach the glories of Heaven, its rewards, and the importance of striving to get there one day.

PRAY Dear Jesus, Mary, and Joseph, help me to be the best Christian example to my grandchildren that I can be. Please pray for my family!

Our Father, Hail Mary, and Glory Be.

SAVOR With God's grace, I can make a tremendous difference in my family and the world!

February 5

And be kind to one another, tenderhearted, forgiving one another, as God in Christ has forgiven you.

EPHESIANS 4:32

STEEP Words can pierce the heart. In good ways and in painful ways, words can make an impact. As Catholic women, we can choose to look for occasions to do good through kind and loving words and actions.

We should also consider how we treat people with whom we don't agree. Being kind to people we dislike is certainly a way we can be a good example to our families and others. Seemingly simple sentiments and gestures can be the beginning of transformation in someone's life—including our own lives or the lives of our families!

ACT Think of someone with whom you disagree. Resolve to treat that person with kindness the next time you interact with him or her.

PRAY Dear Jesus, Mary, and Joseph, help me to be attentive to the needs around me and put works of mercy into action.

Our Father, Hail Mary, and Glory Be.

SAVOR I will listen to the inspiration of the Holy Spirit urging my loving actions.

February 6

But now in Christ Jesus you who once were far off have been brought near by the blood of Christ.

Ephesians 2:13

STEEP A special season is approaching, in which you will embark upon a new Lenten journey. The scriptural words above remind us of Christ's Passion and love for every single soul. It's not too early to think about living the Lenten season with a holy gusto!

We can pray, fast, and offer alms in some way. We might not have to look very far for sacrifices and penances, because they often visit us unexpectedly. We can strive to live each day immersing ourselves in the present moments as they unfold, asking for God's holy will to be done and wholeheartedly accepting it in our life.

ACT Choose a Lenten practice or activity to do with your grandchildren (even from afar). Pray for God's help to come closer to Him this Lenten season.

PRAY Dear Jesus, Mary, and Joseph, help me to accept God's holy will in my life and my family's lives.

Our Father, Hail Mary, and Glory Be.

SAVOR Jesus draws me to Himself. He saves me.

February 7

How many difficulties there are also today in family relations and how many mothers are in anguish at seeing their children setting out on wrong paths! Monica, a woman whose faith was wise and sound, invites them not to lose heart but to persevere in their mission as wives and mothers, keeping firm their trust in God and clinging with perseverance to prayer.[15]

Pope Benedict XVI

STEEP No family is perfect except for the Holy Family. Yet, we can be encouraged knowing the earnest prayers and tears of Saint Monica for her wayward son Augustine brought about rich graces for him and for the entire world. Saint Ambrose told her not to fear, that it was impossible for a child to perish after so many prayerful tears were shed for him. Augustine repented and became a great saint—even proclaimed a Doctor of the Church.

Oh, the power in a mother's prayers! Grandmothers' fervent and loving prayers certainly affect their offspring and grandchildren too.

ACT Place all your discouragement, concerns, and fears before the throne of God—begging, pleading, trusting.

PRAY Dear Holy Family, and Saints Monica and Augustine, please pray for families everywhere!

Our Father, Hail Mary, and Glory Be.

SAVOR I must never give up on prayer. My prayers as a mother and grandmother are powerful!

February 8

Begin all kinds of prayer, whether mental or vocal, by placing yourself in the presence of God. Observe this rule without exception, and you will find the great advantage of it.[16]

Saint Francis de Sales

STEEP There is no doubt about it. Prayer is necessary for our spiritual survival. I would go so far as to say it's necessary even for our physical survival. If we don't have a prayer life, we will suffer in many ways. On the other hand, if we get into the habit of putting ourselves in the presence of God when we speak to Him, our prayers will become more meaningful.

Numerous saints, such as Saint Thérèse, expressed that prayer should rise from our hearts. A great number of saints, much of Church teaching, and our own life experiences have demonstrated the absolute need for prayer.

ACT Read and ponder what the *Catechism of the Catholic Church* teaches about prayer.

PRAY Jesus, Mary, and Joseph, teach me how to pray more effectively.

Our Father, Hail Mary, and Glory Be.

SAVOR I want to pray unceasingly!

February 9

My brothers and sisters, whenever you face trials of any kind, consider it nothing but joy, because you know that the testing of your faith produces endurance; and let endurance have its full effect, so that you may be mature and complete, lacking in nothing.

James 1:2–4

STEEP Our faith is tested on a regular basis. Yet we can learn and grow so much through the troubling times. Through trials and challenges, we have endless opportunities to turn to God and to do our best to respond to Him with love rather than complaints. Certainly, we ask for relief and solutions, but when we keep our eyes fixed on God and offer our sufferings lovingly to Jesus, uniting them to His Passion, we can help to save souls!

ACT Try to view any suffering and challenges you face today as opportunities to grow in holiness and even to help save souls. Ask for the graces to do so.

PRAY Dear Jesus, Mary, and Joseph, help me when my faith is tested.

Our Father, Hail Mary, and Glory Be.

SAVOR Life can be very difficult at times, yet many blessings are woven throughout. I will pray and focus on the good.

February 10

This day is holy to our LORD; and do not be grieved, for the joy of the Lord is your strength.

NEHEMIAH 8:10

STEEP Mother Teresa, whom I was blessed to know personally, professed that it was joy that sent the Blessed Mother to travel in haste over the Judean hills to help her cousin Saint Elizabeth. Mother Teresa often spoke about striving to be a handmaid of the Lord like Mary, to cheerfully travel the hills of difficulties in our lives.

The petite saint of the gutters instructed her sisters that if they didn't have joy in their hearts, they shouldn't be serving God's poor, who had troubles enough of their own to endure. The Sisters needed to be a joyful spark of light and love. Likewise, with God's grace, it is possible for us to share the joy of the Lord with our families and others even amid our own suffering.

ACT Ask Mother Mary, who was full of joy—even as she was called to do many difficult things—to inspire and teach you.

PRAY Dear Jesus, Mary, and Joseph, pray for us! Saint Teresa of Calcutta, pray for me.

Our Father, Hail Mary, and Glory Be.

SAVOR I will let the joy of the Lord be my strength. I want to exude His joy!

February 11

I was afraid. I stepped back. I wanted to call the younger ones but I wasn't brave enough . . . Thinking it was an illusion, I rubbed my eyes but to no avail, I kept seeing the same Lady.[17]

SAINT BERNADETTE
(UPON SEEING THE BLESSED MOTHER)

STEEP Today, the feast of Our Lady of Lourdes, is a good day to contemplate our Lady's life and ask for her help. We can thank her for her faithfulness to her Son's mission—always guiding us to Heaven. Out of love for all of her children, at Lourdes, Mary called for penance and prayers for the souls of sinners.

Responding to the call to prayer and penance can help sinners (ourselves included!) to transform their lives. Catholic grandmothers can pray for God's grace for sinners in need of prayer and penance.

ACT Choose a way to perform some form of penance for sinners today (such as giving up a pleasure, a treat, or extra time in the shower or bath). Encourage your grandchildren to make a prayerful sacrifice to help others.

PRAY Jesus, Mary, and Joseph, pray for my family! Saint Bernadette, please pray for me.

Our Father, Hail Mary, and Glory Be.

SAVOR My prayers and penance can help convert sinners.

February 12

For I, the LORD your God,
hold your right hand;
it is I who say to you, "Do not fear,
I will help you."

ISAIAH 41:13

STEEP Most people hesitate to talk about the devil unless they are blaming him for something. Countless others don't believe that he or Hell exists. Yet we know from Scripture that the devil tempted Jesus in the desert (see Mt 4:1–11). Temptations are inevitable. However, God is ready and waiting to protect us and our loved ones. He will not fail us. If we ensure our souls are in order and call upon our Lord continuously, the devil cannot ensnare us in his traps.

ACT Even when it seems like Hell is being unleashed, turn wholeheartedly to God and make an Act of Trust in Him.

PRAY Dear Jesus, Mary, and Joseph, please pray for the spiritual safety of my family!

Our Father, Hail Mary, and Glory Be.

SAVOR God is here to protect us and our families.

February 13

[God] has a special affection for the young, who delight Him.[18]

SAINT JOHN BOSCO

STEEP Children are very observant! Once when my grandchildren were visiting, three-year-old Leo exclaimed, "We have that in our room!" I had to look closely to see what he meant. He pointed to an image of The Divine Mercy in my office. I had forgotten that a tiny image of Divine Mercy was also on an upstairs night table. Little Leo had observed it and was excited to see two pictures of Divine Mercy.

Kids don't miss a thing!

ACT Display a sacred image somewhere in your home; it will help draw hearts to the Divine, as well as start wonderful conversations!

PRAY Dear Jesus, please have mercy on our family. Holy Mary and Saint Joseph, please pray for us!

Our Father, Hail Mary, and Glory Be.

SAVOR With God's grace, I can have a positive influence on my grandchildren.

February 14

But the steadfast love of the LORD is from everlasting to everlasting
on those who fear him,
and his righteousness to children's children.

PSALM 103:17

STEEP "Grandma! Mommy hided my candy, and I can't find it!" That was the first thing my three-year-old grandson blurted out to me during a video call. It melted my heart, seeing his forlorn little face and body language and hearing his precious declaration, complete with incorrect grammar! My daughter and I both smiled. It was hilarious to hear Leo tattle on his mother.

As grandmothers, we can commiserate to a point, but we should avoid interfering with Mom's (or Dad's) decisions and rules in the care of the children. We wouldn't want someone meddling when we raised our children. We show respect to our grandchildren's parents when we trust that they know what to do to keep their children healthy and safe.

ACT Ponder how you can support the parenting styles of the parents of your grandchildren.

PRAY Dear Jesus, Mary, and Joseph, please pray for my family!

Our Father, Hail Mary, and Glory Be.

SAVOR Life in the family, though crazy at times, is filled with smiles, giggles, and lots of love!

February 15

Love is patient; love is kind; love is not envious or boastful or arrogant or rude. It does not insist on its own way; it is not irritable or resentful; it does not rejoice in wrongdoing, but rejoices in the truth. It bears all things, believes all things, hopes all things, endures all things.

1 Corinthians 13:4–8

STEEP The Bible tells us that love is the greatest virtue. It never ends! Love is certainly a precious gift. Yet, how many times we might take love for granted, even in the course of a day. How would we survive without love? We were created by God (Who is love!) to receive love and to give love. Love is what a grandmother's vocation is all about. My grandmother's loving presence spoke volumes to my heart when I was a little girl. Her love was a comfort to me. Certainly, God's love exudes from a faith-filled grandmother and radiates to her family.

ACT Read today's verses about love slowly and prayerfully, and then make a conscious effort to impart love in myriad ways.

PRAY Dear Jesus, Mary, and Joseph, pray for me. Show me how to truly love!

Our Father, Hail Mary, and Glory Be.

SAVOR Love bears all things, believes all things, hopes all things, endures all things. It never ends!

February 16

The LORD is near to the brokenhearted,
and saves the crushed in spirit.

PSALM 34:18

STEEP Many a grandmother grieves the loss of grandchildren. She may have lost her precious grandchild due to a fatal illness, miscarriage, or even abortion. Grief can feel crippling, sometimes for a long while. Some well-meaning friends and loved ones might scramble to find the right words or may not say anything, fearing they will add pain. Some say, "Don't worry; she'll have another baby."

Truth be told, she might not have another child—but even if that is the grandmother's only grandchild, she is still a grandmother, and we should still acknowledge the blessed uniqueness of that particular child, as well as the painful loss. Let's wholeheartedly support grieving parents and grandparents with hugs, kind words, and prayers. God will heal our wounds.

ACT Reach out to the grieving. Ponder ways to help when the time may come.

PRAY Dear Jesus, Mary, and Joseph, please pray for grieving families!

Our Father, Hail Mary, and Glory Be.

SAVOR My compassion through God's grace can help heal wounds.

February 17

He said, "I looked for one to comfort me, but found none." Be that one to comfort Him, through your prayers and good works.[19]

SAINT TERESA OF CALCUTTA

STEEP Jesus loves us and seeks us out. Mother Teresa points out that He looks for comfort from those He loves. We can endeavor to comfort Jesus during our eucharistic visits. He also seeks to comfort us. So often we can feel defeated and exhausted from life's trials. Jesus calls to us. He told His "Secretary of Divine Mercy," Saint Faustina, to "**tell aching mankind to snuggle close to My merciful Heart, and I will fill it with peace**" (*Diary*, 1074).

The comfort we grandmothers find in the love of our grandchildren and family is just a small taste of the much greater comfort Jesus offers us.

ACT Endeavor to snuggle close to the Sacred Heart of Jesus in your prayers. Help others who are weary by telling them about Jesus' great love for them.

PRAY Dear Jesus, I want to draw close to Your Sacred Heart. I want to be the one to comfort You. Dear Mary and Joseph, please pray for me!

Our Father, Hail Mary, and Glory Be.

SAVOR I can visit and comfort Jesus in my prayers. He will comfort me and bring peace to my soul.

February 18

The Holy Family is the beginning of countless other holy families. The Council recalled that holiness is the vocation of all the baptized. In our age, as in the past, there is no lack of witnesses to the "gospel of the family," even if they are not well known or have not been proclaimed saints by the Church.[20]

Saint John Paul II

STEEP Are you part of a holy family? Have you thought about the kind of witness you and your family might be? The Church teaches, "Holiness is the vocation of all the baptized." Certainly, our families might not always—or ever—resemble the Holy Family. However, we can strive to walk in faith each day, following our Lord's teachings and prayerfully influencing our family for the better.

ACT Today, or sometime soon, write down a list of ways in which to grow in holiness and try to put them into practice.

PRAY Dear Jesus, please show me how to be a better example of holiness. Dear Mary and Saint Joseph, please pray for us!

Our Father, Hail Mary, and Glory Be.

SAVOR One foot in front of the other in faith each day! With God's grace, off I go!

February 19

For every believer, and especially for Christian families, the humble dwelling place in Nazareth is *an authentic school of the Gospel*. Here we admire, put into practice, the divine plan to make the family an *intimate community of life and love*; here we learn that every Christian family is called to be a small *"domestic church"* that must shine with the Gospel virtues.[21]

Saint John Paul II

STEEP Saint John Paul II tells us about the necessary ingredients for a holy family. He said, "Recollection and prayer, mutual understanding and respect, personal discipline and community asceticism and a spirit of sacrifice, work and solidarity are typical features that make the family of Nazareth a model for every home."[22]

If we are not modeling the Gospel values that radiated throughout the Holy Family's home, we can pray for the graces to do so. It will benefit our own soul, the souls of our family, and the souls of all those who know us.

ACT Close your eyes and imagine yourself inside the home of the Holy Family. Ask their help in being the grandmother you are meant to be.

PRAY Dear Holy Family, please pray for us!

Our Father, Hail Mary, and Glory Be.

SAVOR I can pray for holiness in my family.

February 20

> But, above all, I recommend to you mental prayer, and particularly that which has the life and passion of our Lord for its object.[23]
>
> Saint Francis de Sales

STEEP God is truly with us. Let us acknowledge Him. Saint Francis de Sales recommended to always place oneself in the presence of God when beginning our prayers. He also advised meditating on the life of Jesus and on His Passion. He elaborated, "By making Him frequently the subject of meditation, your whole soul will be filled with Him; you will learn His ways, and frame all your actions on the model of His."[24]

Even a busy grandmother can strive to carve out the time to meditate on Jesus' life and raise her heart to express her love to her Creator. Let's make a point to start every day prayerfully in God's presence.

ACT Put yourself in the presence of God as often as possible.

PRAY Dear Lord, I love You. I don't tell You enough. Jesus, Mary, and Joseph, please pray for us!

Our Father, Hail Mary, and Glory Be.

SAVOR I will lift my heart to God often and love Him with every breath!

February 21

Love one another with mutual affection; outdo one another in showing honor.

ROMANS 12:10

STEEP So often, we can get caught up with myriad ways in which to save the world, and we think we have to rush off and join endless committees to serve God. But when we look into the eyes of our loved ones, we can discover the need to love our family first. We must not neglect to serve our family when trying to accomplish even great things.

Sometimes, that doling out of love will be strenuous and challenging, such as in the wee hours of the morning or during painful discussions. Other times, our hearts will sail sweetly over blissful graces in our vocation of love.

ACT Whatever you do today, make time in the day to lovingly serve your family's needs.

PRAY Jesus, I love You! Jesus, Mary, and Joseph, pray for us!
Our Father, Hail Mary, and Glory Be.

SAVOR Doing great things in the world begins in my family!

February 22

Always be ready to make your defense to anyone who demands from you an accounting for the hope that is in you.

1 PETER 3:15

STEEP When we look to the Holy Family of Nazareth, we can ponder the great love among them. Their example offers much to emulate. How might we be able to set a Christian example to help families these days? We live in a culture that is often contrary to Christian virtues, and we often stand out as odd ones because we believe in the truth of the Gospel. However, we mustn't ever be embarrassed by our faith, for it forms our consciences, hearts, and souls. Our faith is a bright light in a darkened world, and our faithful example can radiate out to others.

ACT Courageously and lovingly profess your faith in a variety of gentle ways.

PRAY Dear Holy Family, please pray for my family and our world!

Our Father, Hail Mary, and Glory Be.

SAVOR My loving quiet and not-so-quiet countercultural example can make a positive difference in many lives.

February 23

Bear with one another and, if anyone has a complaint against another, forgive each other; just as the Lord has forgiven you, so you also must forgive.

Colossians 3:13

STEEP Praying the Lord's Prayer reminds us that the Lord forgives us. We pray, "Forgive us our trespasses as we forgive those who trespass against us." Do we actually forgive the people who have hurt us in some way? If we haven't, why do we expect God to forgive us? We must ponder this.

Life in a family is a spiritual journey. We are given countless opportunities to show our love, to dole out tenderness, correction, and forgiveness. We are called to forgive our family members as God forgives us.

ACT Start each day with an earnest Morning Offering to give everything over to God. Ask Him for the graces you need to be patient and forgiving.

PRAY Dear Lord, help me to forgive others as You have forgiven me. Jesus, Mary, and Joseph, please pray for us!

Our Father, Hail Mary, and Glory Be.

SAVOR God's love is powerful, and He wants me to love like He does!

February 24

Above all, clothe yourselves with love, which binds everything together in perfect harmony.

Colossians 3:14

STEEP If you visit my home, you will see family photos all over the place! My dining room wall is like a patchwork quilt of our lives. I treasure my family, so I try to capture some of the moments of our lives in photos and display them on my walls and tabletops. My children and grandchildren might not always appreciate my photo-snapping in the moment—but they will later!

Photos can help us remember many exquisite moments, yet we can't live in the past or the future. We simply have *right now* and need to fully live in the present.

ACT Live in the moment today and cherish it. Tell your family that you love them. This moment will not come again. It is unique and unrepeatable—like our lives.

PRAY Dear Lord, help me to slow down and pause to live in the moments of my life, giving glory and praise to You! Dear Holy Family, please pray for my family.

Our Father, Hail Mary, and Glory Be.

SAVOR Today, and every moment, is a great gift from God.

February 25

The devil does not bring sinners to hell with their eyes open: he first blinds them with the malice of their own sins.[25]

SAINT ALPHONSUS DE LIGUORI

STEEP It's not pleasant to discuss the devil's evil tricks to drag us to Hell. However, it is necessary. We must be aware and alert to the devil's tricks to deceive us. First, we need to acknowledge that he is indeed real and active. Secondly, it's necessary to remain in the state of grace to combat his clever temptations to lead us down the wrong path. Therefore, the sacrament of Confession is paramount on our journey. Let us keep in mind that Mary Magdalene's repentance at Jesus' feet (Lk 7:36–50) made her a saint, and that Saint Augustine not only confessed, but he published his confessions!

ACT Have great hope and learn from the saints. Teach your grandchildren the importance of prayer and the sacraments.

PRAY Lord, help me. I am often weak. Jesus, Mary, and Joseph, pray for us!

Our Father, Hail Mary, and Glory Be.

SAVOR The sacrament of Confession frees me from sin and opens the gates of Heaven!

February 26

And let the peace of Christ rule in your hearts, to which indeed you were called in the one body. And be thankful.

COLOSSIANS 3:15

STEEP I love that Saint Paul adds, "And be thankful"! Yes, let's be sure that Christ rules our hearts, and let us be thankful for the Body of Christ. Indeed, as Catholics, we possess a rich faith and are called to aspire to holiness. That's right—you and me—we are called to be saints! Mother Teresa reminded me of this often. Certainly, we might not be pondering lofty thoughts of Christ's peace or feeling thankful when changing diapers, peeling potatoes, juggling finances, or scrubbing a toilet. Still, we can be thankful for the nitty-gritty details of our vocation because they're the precise path God has given us to work out our salvation.

How will we respond to all that God gives to us? Are we thankful?

ACT Make a list of chores that you despise, or any experiences you'd rather flee from than embrace. Ask God to be with you in those moments and help you to be thankful and grow in holiness.

PRAY Dear Holy Family, pray for us!

Our Father, Hail Mary, and Glory Be.

SAVOR God calls me to become a thankful saint!

February 27

But one is tempted by one's own desire, being lured and enticed by it; then, when that desire has conceived, it gives birth to sin, and that sin, when it is fully grown, gives birth to death. Do not be deceived, my beloved.

JAMES 1:14–16

STEEP Saint James' teaching stresses the need to avoid the occasion of sin, which is to put ourselves in a situation where we are tempted to sin. Jesus gives us a rather graphic remedy in Mt 5:29—"If your right eye causes you to sin, tear it out and throw it away; it is better for you to lose one of your members than for your whole body to be thrown into hell." Jesus' words might trouble us, but it's important to know that Jesus always gives great help and grace to resist temptation.

Just as we want our grandchildren to make the right choices, Jesus lovingly wants the same for us.

ACT Teach your grandchildren to avoid the occasion of sin and resist temptation by praying and being attentive. Give examples.

PRAY Dear Lord, help me to be an exemplary teacher of the faith to my grandchildren. Dear Holy Family, help us flee from sin!

Our Father, Hail Mary, and Glory Be.

SAVOR Staying close to Jesus with prayer is the remedy for conquering temptations and avoiding sin.

February 28

Can a woman forget her nursing child,
    or show no compassion for the child of her womb?
Even these may forget,
    yet I will not forget you.
See, I have inscribed you on the palms of my hands;
    your walls are continually before me.

Isaiah 49:15–16

STEEP Mother Teresa often preached about God's great love for each one of us. Paraphrasing the words in our verses above, she was often excited to explain God's tender and unconditional love and wanted to give us encouragement, especially for the times when we will navigate troubled waters. She said God will never forget us and that we should remember that we are very precious to Him, He loves us, and we are right in His hand. Just as we could never forget our beloved grandchildren, God could never forget us!

ACT Actively teach your grandchildren about the love of God. Try to weave this teaching into many conversations.

PRAY Dear Lord, I can't thank You enough for loving me. Dear Holy Family, please pray for us!

Our Father, Hail Mary, and Glory Be.

SAVOR God will never forget me! God doesn't leave me!

February 29

How very good and pleasant it is
when kindred live together in unity!

PSALM 133:1

STEEP Today's verse speaks of living in unity. Does that really sound like a day in the life of a family? Well, it could—but it certainly takes a lot of work to make it happen. Truly, it is within the family that we work out our sanctification. We take care of each other physically, but also spiritually. It is quite amazing to know that God actually handpicks us and puts us all together to love one another and grow in holiness. Loving our family in this way can be very challenging sometimes, but it leads to a beautiful unity!

ACT Ask your grandchildren to tell you about their favorite part of being in a family. Have them draw it or write it down.

PRAY Dear Lord God, thank You for loving our family. Dear Holy Family, please pray for us!

Our Father, Hail Mary, and Glory Be.

SAVOR The human family is such a beautiful thing!

MARCH

Saint Joseph

Anyone who cannot find a master to teach him prayer should take this glorious saint [Joseph] for his master, and he will not go astray.[26]

Saint Teresa of Avila

March 1

> Joseph became the guardian, the administrator, and the legal defender of the divine house whose chief he was . . . It is, then, natural and worthy that as the Blessed Joseph ministered to all the needs of the family at Nazareth and girt it about with his protection, he should now cover with the cloak of his heavenly patronage and defend the Church of Jesus Christ.[27]
>
> Pope Leo XIII

STEEP The month of March is dedicated to Saint Joseph. Illustrious Saint Joseph was very quiet in Scripture: his words were not recorded by any of the Gospel writers. Yet the humble saint is beloved for his great love and powerful protection.

We should never hesitate to turn to Saint Joseph with any need. Many saints and popes have encouraged the faithful to do so. Saint Teresa of Avila said, "Because of my impressive experience of the goods this glorious saint obtains from God, I had the desire to persuade all to be devoted to him. I have not known anyone truly devoted to him and rendering him special services who has not advanced more in virtue."[28]

ACT Ask Saint Joseph often to take care of your family. He will!

PRAY Jesus, thank You for Your love and many blessings. Dear Saint Joseph, terror of demons, pray for my family.

Our Father, Hail Mary, and Glory Be.

SAVOR Saint Joseph can help me steer the ship.

March 2

> The family is the *original cell of social life* . . . The family is the community in which, from childhood, one can learn moral values, begin to honor God, and make good use of freedom. Family life is an initiation into life in society.
>
> *Catechism of the Catholic Church*, 2207

STEEP So much happens in the family! Additionally, according to God's plan, there's so much that is supposed to happen, as today's quote tells us.

Our world seems to be filled with everything but Christian moral values. The breakdown of the family leaves children with splinters and pieces of what should be a firm foundation in their lives. It's not the children's fault that they live in a chaotic world and perhaps even in a broken or wounded family. Grandmothers can love and nurture children in difficult family situations—whether our own grandchildren or children from struggling families we know.

ACT Write down three ways you can make a positive difference in your family and in society. Pray to the Holy Spirit for guidance. Carry out your inspirations to be a radiant example.

PRAY Dear Holy Spirit, please guide me always. Dear Saint Joseph, please pray for my family.

Our Father, Hail Mary, and Glory Be.

SAVOR My prayers and good example can help my family and others.

March 3

As the family goes, so goes the nation, and so goes the whole world in which we live.[29]

SAINT JOHN PAUL II

STEEP Saint John Paul II warns us that if the family fails, the nation and the world go down the tubes! My friend, Servant of God Father John Hardon, SJ, has stated, "The family, as we now understand it, came into existence with Christianity. Twenty centuries of history teach us that family life is only as stable and as sound as the Christian faith of a culture." He explained succinctly, "As this faith goes, so goes the family."[30]

The family is much more important than we might fully recognize. We can ask ourselves if we are modeling Christian life in our actions and words—inside and outside our home.

ACT Ponder ways to help today's families and put your ideas into action.

PRAY Dear Lord Jesus and Blessed Mother Mary, please be with me. Dear Saint Joseph, please pray for my family.

Our Father, Hail Mary, and Glory Be.

SAVOR Christian families are a brilliant light to the world!

March 4

> Parents are the principal and first educators of their children. In this sense the fundamental task of marriage and family is to be at the service of life.
>
> *Catechism of the Catholic Church*, 1653

STEEP Parents cannot rely on others to teach the faith to their children. They must learn it, live it, teach it, and step up to the plate to become the principal and first educators of their children. As grandparents, we too impart the faith to our grandchildren in so many ways—certainly by our teachings, but also by our love and actions. In some families where the parents don't teach the faith to their children, the grandparents may become the primary teachers of the faith.

My grandmother taught me the importance and power of prayer by praying the Rosary. Without words, she set a powerful example for me, simply by my observing those worn beads glide through her fingers.

ACT Be on the lookout for ways in which to teach the faith to children. Endeavor to get God into your conversations with them!

PRAY Dear Jesus and Mary, show me how to teach the faith. Dear Saint Joseph, please pray for my family.

Our Father, Hail Mary, and Glory Be.

SAVOR What a blessing to be given the task to be "at the service of life."

March 5

In the same way, let your light shine before others, so that they may see your good works and give glory to your Father in heaven.

MATTHEW 5:16

STEEP One time, Mother Teresa met a poor blind man who had been completely ignored by everyone and was unable to care for himself. The man's old oil lamp was covered in cobwebs and unused because no one visited. Mother Teresa asked if he would light the lamp for the sisters when they visited. He happily agreed. Some years later, the man got a message to Mother Teresa. He said the light she lit in his life continues to shine!

We may never know this side of Heaven how our little works of love and mercy have helped to transform someone's heart and soul, but with God's grace, we can still bring light into others' lives and trust God that our light will continue to shine even when we aren't there to see it!

ACT Be a light to someone today. Encourage your grandchildren to join you.

PRAY Dear Jesus, You flood my soul with light and life. Thank you! Dear Saint Joseph, please pray for my family.

Our Father, Hail Mary, and Glory Be.

SAVOR I can bring light into someone's life today!

March 6

She opens her mouth with wisdom,
and the teaching of kindness is on her tongue.

Proverbs 31:26

STEEP As Catholic women, we are called to use our feminine gifts to reach out to others in myriad ways. Our listening ear and a promise of prayer to someone in despair, or to someone who needs companionship or comfort, can help immensely. So does a warm, sincere smile when looking into someone's eyes.

We can put whatever else we're doing on hold for the moment to be present to another person. Time passes quickly, and we don't want to miss opportunities to make someone's life better and help that person to know God's love.

ACT Each day, as you pray a Morning Offering, ask our Lord to help you to be more attentive to the needs that unfold around you.

PRAY Jesus, please help me to help others. Saint Joseph, please pray for my family.

Our Father, Hail Mary, and Glory Be.

SAVOR I can be a bright spark of faith, hope, and love to my family and those with whom I come in contact.

March 7

You know how much Christian courage you need in order to carry out God's commands in your lives and in your families. It is the courage to be willing every day to build up love—the kind of love of which Saint Paul says: "Love is patient and kind. . . . Love never ends."[31]

SAINT JOHN PAUL II

STEEP There may be more challenging times in family life than the warm and fuzzy moments. It takes Christian courage to "build up love" in the family. Grandmothers' integral role is essential and life-giving in courageously building up this love.

Christian grandmothers point the way to Heaven through loving actions, firm beliefs, willingness to dole out forgiveness, and Saint Paul's definition of love. We plant countless wonderful seeds of faith, hope, and love!

ACT List three ways you can "build up love" in your family today.

PRAY Lord, please grant me the courage I need to build up love through my vocation. Saint Joseph, please pray for my family.

Our Father, Hail Mary, and Glory Be.

SAVOR Love never ends.

March 8

I also prayed to St. Joseph, asking him to watch over me; ever since my childhood I had a devotion for him that easily merged with my love for the Blessed Virgin.[32]

Saint Thérèse of Lisieux

STEEP As a single mother, I once felt terrorized by a very unruly upstairs neighbor who was often under the influence of alcohol and drugs. He threatened to harm me. I called the police but to no avail. They had to catch him in the act.

My friend Father Bill encouraged me to pray a thirty-day novena of prayer to Saint Joseph, assuring me the saint would help. I prayed the novena. Lo and behold, on the thirtieth day, the neighbor suddenly moved out! I've been a very close friend of dear Saint Joseph ever since, continually singing his praises.

ACT In this month of Saint Joseph, entrust one difficult situation in your life or your family's lives to Saint Joseph's intercession.

PRAY Jesus, thank You for Your great love and the gift of the saints! Dear Saint Joseph, please pray for my family.

Our Father, Hail Mary, and Glory Be.

SAVOR Saint Joseph is a powerful protector.

March 9

By his obedience to Mary and Joseph, as well as by his humble work during the long years in Nazareth, Jesus gives us the example of holiness in the daily life of family and work.

Catechism of the Catholic Church, 564

STEEP Daily routines and trying to check off endless "to-do" lists might make family life feel like a busy, never-ending whirlwind. It can seem simply very ordinary or even mundane at times. Yet, in the midst of it all, it's important to pause to take a breath and ponder the beauty and sacredness of the human family.

We absolutely need to pray—offering our hearts to Jesus, asking His help in navigating family life. After all, we become holy in the midst of pots and pans, diaper changes, and sibling rivalry. What a gift the Christian family really is—craziness and all!

ACT Pause, pray, and ponder in a deep way today. Try to observe at least three examples of growing in holiness in the daily life of family and work.

PRAY Jesus, thank You for giving us the example of holiness in daily life. Dear Saint Joseph, please pray for my family.

Our Father, Hail Mary, and Glory Be.

SAVOR My life can be a beautiful tapestry of holy prayer and work.

March 10

> May St. Joseph become for all of us an exceptional teacher in the service of Christ's saving mission, a mission which is the responsibility of each and every member of the Church.[33]
>
> SAINT JOHN PAUL II

STEEP I once heard a young expectant father express his excitement and assumptions about how his life would be after his baby was born. He said, "I don't think anything will change as far as our schedules." I was torn. Should I tell him the truth? Or let him find out for himself that babies indeed change our schedules?

There's no doubt about it. Children change our lives in ways we could never have imagined! Blessings abound and transformation occurs in parenting children—and also later on when grandparenting!

ACT Call on good Saint Joseph. He is always ready to help. Begin a novena to him today to end on his feast day (March 19).

PRAY Lord, thank You for the incredible gift of the human family! Saint Joseph, please pray for us.

Our Father, Hail Mary, and Glory Be.

SAVOR If God revealed every change and challenge ahead, we might feel overwhelmed. Family life is transforming!

March 11

> Now in what spirit did Joseph serve Jesus and Mary? In a spirit of love, because he appreciated the divinity of Jesus and the excellence of Mary.[34]
>
> SAINT PETER JULIAN EYMARD

STEEP It is wonderful that we have Mary, Joseph, and the saints to aid us. We can turn to them often to seek their powerful intercession and learn more about them from solid, approved sources. It's never too late to learn. We can discover more and more about our rich faith every day of our lives.

We can also aim to teach what we learn, even in very gentle and simple ways. We might be the only one who reaches out with a loving teaching to a particular person we meet along our journey through life.

ACT Make a point to incorporate God and prayer into your conversations. Don't be afraid! It can change a life!

PRAY Jesus, thank You for Your love. Saint Joseph, please pray for my family.

Our Father, Hail Mary, and Glory Be.

SAVOR Life is an amazing journey of discovery.

March 12

> The family should live in such a way that its members learn to care and take responsibility for the young, the old, the sick, the handicapped, and the poor. There are many families who are at times incapable of providing this help. It devolves then on other persons, other families, and . . . society to provide for their needs.
>
> *Catechism of the Catholic Church*, 2208

STEEP Our quote today seems wonderful, yet it can be difficult to carry out. Many of us are too busy with our own lives to devote attention to others' needs. This could be due to a lack of resources, urgent family crises, or any number of other reasons. We also might fear moving beyond our comfort zones to help the poor, handicapped, or sick.

Yet no matter our situations, Christian families can greatly help others. We can begin by training children to be generous through simple works of mercy. This can help establish good spiritual habits and mold their hearts and consciences—and can help our own families too!

ACT Introduce works of mercy to the children in your life. Let your Christian light shine!

PRAY Dear Jesus, open my eyes and heart to the needs around me.

Our Father, Hail Mary, and Glory Be.

SAVOR Ample opportunities to help someone unfold every day.

March 13

Make him [Saint Joseph] the patron of your family and you will soon have tangible proof of his protecting hand.[35]

SAINT PETER JULIAN EYMARD

STEEP My friend was told she couldn't conceive post-chemotherapy. She did conceive but then lost several babies to miscarriage. Her husband's heart was broken. She asked him to go to their church and sit near the statue of Saint Joseph. Within days, she found out she was pregnant and was due on March 19 (Saint Joseph's feast day)! Matteo Joseph was born a bit early, but my friend's daughter Francesca Maria was born two years later on March 19! My friend exclaimed, "Not a soul on this planet can tell me that Saint Joseph did not intercede on my behalf."

ACT Go to Saint Joseph with all of your cares and concerns. He knows all about the family and will indeed help you.

PRAY Dear Jesus, help me this day. Dear Saint Joseph, please pray for my family.

Our Father, Hail Mary, and Glory Be.

SAVOR We are immensely blessed to have the intercession of the saints!

March 14

And after taking some food, he regained his strength.

Acts 9:19

STEEP My friend was present at a luncheon for seminarians. They were delighted that Mother Teresa was going to stop by to greet them and give a little teaching. Before that happened, however, an impromptu teaching unfolded unexpectedly. Upon entering the room, Mother noticed that one of the seminarians had very little food on his plate. She leaned in, dramatically lifted a huge platter of food, and dished a hefty portion onto the young man's plate! She told him that he wouldn't be able to take care of others if he was distracted by his own hunger pains.

What a marvelous lesson for us all! We can certainly apply this to our own experience as grandmothers. As focused as we may be on caring for our families, we should also remember to take care of ourselves!

ACT Be sure to take care of yourself—eating well, taking your vitamins and any necessary medicines, and getting enough sleep at night.

PRAY Dear Jesus, Mary, and Joseph, help me to take good care of myself.

Our Father, Hail Mary, and Glory Be.

SAVOR If I am nourished, rested, and well, I can better take care of others.

March 15

With Christians, a poetical view of things is a duty. We are bid to color all things with hues of faith, to see a divine meaning in every event.[36]

SAINT JOHN HENRY NEWMAN

STEEP Today's quote challenges us to see divine meaning in every event. We can certainly try to do this by praying for discernment so that we will recognize God at work in everything.

It might be difficult to see with eyes of faith when faced with challenges. But we should firmly believe that God will grant every grace we need when we ask Him. He will reveal Himself to us. Oftentimes, He does this through very ordinary daily occurrences. God gives us "grandmother eyes" to see with the eyes of faith.

ACT Begin the habit of seeking divine meaning in the events of your everyday life. Jot down your observations. Later on, you'll be happy that you did write them down to reminisce and learn from.

PRAY Dear Jesus, help me to see You at work in the world around me. Dear Saint Joseph, please pray for my family.

Our Father, Hail Mary, and Glory Be.

SAVOR Each day unfolds in mysterious and holy ways. I will live in its present moments, seeking God always.

March 16

Devotion to St. Joseph is one of the choicest graces that God can give to a soul. . . . When God wishes to raise a soul to greater heights, he unites it to St. Joseph by giving it a strong love for the good saint.[37]

Saint Peter Julian Eymard

STEEP During this month of Saint Joseph, we can take time to ponder the humble patriarch's attributes and virtues. Regarding this, I think my friend makes a good point. She said, "Saint Joseph was truly holy. After all, he's the only person who ever lived with two people who never sinned! If something went wrong at home, well, you knew whose fault it was." She added, "No wonder Joseph is never quoted in the Bible. I, too, would probably keep my mouth shut under those circumstances."

Obviously, none of us live with sinless people, but we can still show reverence toward our family members like Saint Joseph did!

ACT Get into the habit of calling on Saint Joseph daily. Do something to show reverence to a family member today.

PRAY Saint Joseph, please pray for me to be more like you.

Our Father, Hail Mary, and Glory Be.

SAVOR I can be holy like Saint Joseph today. I'll try my best!

March 17

Christ beside me, Christ before me, Christ behind me, Christ within me, Christ beneath me, Christ above me.

Saint Patrick

STEEP "Gigi, I'm thirsty!" three-year-old Zoe would often tell her grandmother Jane when visiting. Jane suggested that her daughter get Zoe checked for diabetes. Thanks to Jane's persistence, after a month, Zoe was given tests and immediately admitted to a children's hospital. Zoe's mysterious thirst was solved, and she could be treated.

Jane shared that the doctors said Zoe was very fortunate to be diagnosed before she became too ill. Jane concluded, "All I could do was praise God and cry in thanks that He got her to the hospital to get the medical attention that she needed. And I was just His instrument."

Even during this month of Saint Joseph, known for his silence, we should trust our grandmotherly instincts and speak up about important matters, especially regarding our grandchildren!

ACT Ponder whether God is calling you to speak up about any situations in your life.

PRAY Jesus, thank You for loving me! Saint Joseph, please pray for us.

Our Father, Hail Mary, and Glory Be.

SAVOR God can use me as His instrument!

March 18

Whatever is true, whatever is honorable, whatever is just, whatever is pure, whatever is pleasing, whatever is commendable, if there is any excellence and if there is anything worthy of praise, think about these things.

PHILIPPIANS 4:8

STEEP Saint Paul encourages us to think about noble things—whatever is pleasing to God. As Christians, we answer to a higher power—that would be God! We cannot get sucked up into the devil's lies and false promises, deceptively disguised in pretty little alluring packages.

As women, we are often bombarded by societal expectations that can distract us from thinking about noble things. Staying prayerful and aware helps us a great deal to make the right choices along our spiritual journey. This is important because the way we think can affect the way we interact with others, including our grandchildren. Keeping our minds on noble things will help us better be able to share our faith and love with others.

ACT Be mindful of what you watch and take in today (media, books, television, movies, and the like).

PRAY Lord God, thank You for my very life! Saint Joseph, please pray for my family.

Our Father, Hail Mary, and Glory Be.

SAVOR God calls me to think about noble things.

March 19

The whole month of March is one long feast in honor of Saint Joseph. But the nineteenth is the great day of triumph; the other days celebrate his virtues and his special graces, but today celebrates his triumphal entry into heaven.[38]

Saint Peter Julian Eymard

STEEP Today, the feast of Saint Joseph, is a special day indeed! If you visited my home, you would see images of the illustrious saint all throughout my house: statues, icons, and paintings that have been handed down to me, or that I found along the way—even at a flea market!

We should treat Saint Joseph with the same reverence he treated Mary and Jesus. We shouldn't bury a statue of him upside down to try to buy or sell a house! Prayer is not about superstition or doing things a certain way to get certain results. Instead, we should strive to develop a close relationship with this good saint.

ACT Go to Saint Joseph with a sincere heart to seek his intercession.

PRAY Lord God, thank You for the great gift of Saint Joseph! Saint Joseph, please pray for my family and me.

Our Father, Hail Mary, and Glory Be.

SAVOR Saint Joseph is an awesome and trustworthy guardian and protector.

March 20

When you invoke Saint Joseph, you don't have to speak much. You know your Father in heaven knows what you need; well, so does His friend Saint Joseph. . . . Tell him: "If you were in my place, Saint Joseph, what would you do? . . . Well, pray for this on my behalf!"[39]

Saint André Bessette

STEEP I was moved by my experience on pilgrimage to the Oratory of Saint Joseph in Montréal, which was founded by Saint André Bessette. Brother André was initially rejected from religious life for frail health, considered unintelligent, and given the lowly role of doorkeeper. Yet it was there at the door where he welcomed thousands of distressed people. Miracles took place through him, with Saint Joseph's intercession.

God lifts the lowly and calls them to great missions. Whether we—or our grandchildren—are facing ill health, others' low opinions of us, or anything else, God has a plan for all of us!

ACT Take another look at today's quote and put Saint André's advice into practice.

PRAY Jesus, please help me to know Your plan for me. Saint André and Saint Joseph, please pray for us.

Our Father, Hail Mary, and Glory Be.

SAVOR Every person is created for a great purpose.

March 21

St. Joseph urged me to have a constant devotion to him. He himself told me to recite three prayers [the Our Father, Hail Mary, and Glory be] and the Memorare once every day. He looked at me with great kindness and gave me to know how much he is supporting this work [of mercy]. He has promised me this special help and protection. I recite the requested prayers every day and feel his special protection.

SAINT FAUSTINA, *DIARY*, 1203

STEEP God gifted Saint Faustina the wonderful guidance and protection from Saint Joseph in her work of propagating the Divine Mercy devotion to the world. Can we even imagine being given a great saint as a personal guide? And with a promise from Saint Joseph himself!

Even if we are not called to something as far-reaching as Saint Faustina was, we all have missions from God—especially our mission as grandmothers. We can all ask Saint Joseph for his guidance and protection.

ACT Consider adding the Memorare to Saint Joseph (page 413) to your prayers today.

PRAY Jesus, Mary, and Joseph, help me.

Our Father, Hail Mary, and Glory Be.

SAVOR The saints tremendously aid us!

March 22

> Let the little children come to me, and do not stop them; for it is to such as these that the kingdom of God belongs.
>
> LUKE 18:16

STEEP My friend Linda was leaving church with her two-year-old granddaughter, Ava, when Ava ran up to an elderly man and hugged him tightly around the knees. Linda assumed that her granddaughter thought the man was someone she knew. She thought Ava would be surprised when she looked up and saw someone unfamiliar.

Instead, after hugging the stranger's legs, Ava looked up at his face and smiled. The man smiled back, and little Ava skipped away. Linda said, "We were not sure what had just occurred, but she made us both smile. I think God thought this very nice man needed a hug from one of His littlest messengers." Grandchildren are a blessing not only to their grandparents but to everyone whose lives they touch.

ACT Endeavor to give and receive love more wholeheartedly.

PRAY Jesus and Mary, thank you for the blessing of grandchildren. Saint Joseph, please pray for my family and me.

Our Father, Hail Mary, and Glory Be.

SAVOR Precious grandchildren bring love and light to the world.

March 23

In the course of that pilgrimage of faith which was his life, Joseph, like Mary, remained faithful to God's call until the end.[40]

SAINT JOHN PAUL II

STEEP Like Saint Joseph and Mary, we are invited to faithfully and prayerfully put one foot in front of the other to make our way toward Heaven—to be faithful to God's call. And I'll tell you—an awful lot happens along the way!

As Catholic women, we are also called to spiritually mother others on our journey, not only our family members. I have often felt God calling me to push beyond what was comfortable to reach out to a complete stranger and to impart truths of the Catholic faith. I have even lovingly recommended the beautiful sacrament of Confession to perfect strangers! Numerous times, I have observed amazing transformations. Taking time to listen to someone's woes and offering kind words or prayers can be just the medicine that person needs.

ACT Find one way to spiritually mother someone today.

PRAY Lord God, thank You for my Catholic faith. Dear Mary and Saint Joseph, please pray for my family and me.

Our Father, Hail Mary, and Glory Be.

SAVOR God gives me many amazing opportunities to be a spiritual mother.

March 24

The Lord is good,
a stronghold in a day of trouble;
he protects those who take refuge in him.

Nahum 1:7

STEEP Today is my mother's birthday. She weighed a minuscule one and a half pounds at birth! In a time before sophisticated incubators, when my mother was not suckling at her mother's breast or keeping warm nestled against my grandmother's body, she was kept in a little shoebox surrounded by cotton and a hot water bottle. Imagine that!

My mother was baptized in the hospital because of grave concerns about her survival. It's amazing to think about it now—that my dear mother not only survived her tiny birth weight and its complications, but grew to be a healthy, hardworking woman who married and had eight children of her own, as well as many grandchildren and great-grandchildren!

ACT Ponder your own life. Thank God for all the mother figures in your life.

PRAY Jesus and Mary, thank you for the women in my life who have taught me to be a good grandmother. Saint Joseph, please pray for us.

Our Father, Hail Mary, and Glory Be.

SAVOR The human family is exquisite and beautiful beyond measure, and I will heartily thank God for it.

March 25

The angel said to her, "Do not be afraid, Mary, for you have found favor with God. And now, you will conceive in your womb and bear a son, and you will name him Jesus."

LUKE 1:30–31

STEEP Can we imagine being visited by the Angel Gabriel as a young teen? Could we muster up a fiat? Could we trust God?

Saint John Paul II explained that Mary doesn't ask if it's possible, but how it will be fulfilled. With her fiat, "Mary shows herself the true daughter of Abraham, and she becomes the Mother of Christ and Mother of all believers."[41]

In our daily lives as grandmothers, we can prayerfully apply Mary's fiat and her trust. Obviously, none of us are as prepared (or as perfect!) as Mary. But how can we as grandmothers imitate her? Just as Mary pondered the angel's message, we can ponder in our own hearts how we can live out her virtues in the vocation God has called us to.

ACT Ponder the significance of the Annunciation.

PRAY Jesus and Mary, help me to trust in God's holy will for me. Saint Joseph, please pray for us.

Our Father, Hail Mary, and Glory Be.

SAVOR I have much to learn from Mary.

March 26

Finally, be strong in the Lord and in the strength of his power.

EPHESIANS 6:10

STEEP My friend Maria loves being a grandma. She has observed a variety of temperaments and personalities among her three grandsons and three granddaughters, and she makes an effort to get to know each of them individually by taking them out for ice cream and playing chess with them. To Maria's surprise, her fifteen-year-old grandson is now beating her at all the chess games and wants to enter tournaments.

Maria knows her role involves much more than warm fuzzies. She shared, "I find we need to pray and sacrifice for our grandchildren." Maria taught her grandchildren to pray the Rosary. Now that they are teens, she encourages them to pray it and watches movies about saints with them. She also believes it's important to give them suggestions about going to Confession, or even to bring them herself. She added, "We must love and instruct them in the faith."

ACT Near or far, be a living example of Catholic faith to your grandchildren as you take an active role in their lives.

PRAY Jesus and Mary, please watch over us. Saint Joseph, please pray for my family.

Our Father, Hail Mary, and Glory Be.

SAVOR Grandmothers have big shoes to fill!

March 27

Saint Joseph was sent to the Church much in the same way that he was sent to Jesus and Mary, in order to secure the material and spiritual good of God's family.[42]

Saint André Bessette

STEEP My friend Lisa noticed something strange poking up in her yard. She dug it up and found a statue of Saint Joseph the Worker that had been buried face down! She knew about the practice of burying the poor overworked saint when buying or selling a house. Lisa questioned the previous property owner, who explained that she had not buried the statue and had lived there for thirty years. Lisa scrubbed layers of dirt off her newly discovered statue. Upon seeing his attractive colors and design, she decided to give him a proper place of rest and honor on her night table, where he would keep watch over her husband and herself throughout the years to come.

Lisa's story reminds us that Saint Joseph is always nearby, waiting to help us.

ACT Find a way to honor Saint Joseph in your home.

PRAY Jesus and Mary, thank you! Saint Joseph, please pray for us.

Our Father, Hail Mary, and Glory Be.

SAVOR Treasures of grace are hidden in the daily details of life.

March 28

He was chosen by the eternal Father as the trustworthy guardian and protector of his greatest treasures, namely, his divine Son and Mary, Joseph's wife.[43]

Saint Bernardine of Siena

STEEP My friend Lisa recalled, "I often looked at the statue of Saint Joseph on my nightstand and thought about his prompt intercession in answer to my prayers." She decided to ask Saint Joseph to help her family, especially during trying times. Through the strains, joys, and challenges of raising a family and navigating life during the many seasons that passed, Lisa continued to beseech Saint Joseph.

Over time, Lisa developed a quiet, steady relationship with this powerful saint. Years later, Lisa realized he had truly been watching over her family. Many important relationships in our lives take time to develop, so even if we don't yet know Saint Joseph well, we can begin to get to know him better and trust that he is taking care of us!

ACT Resolve to get to know Saint Joseph better.

PRAY Jesus and Mary, I love you! Saint Joseph, please pray for me.

Our Father, Hail Mary, and Glory Be.

SAVOR Life is full of blessings!

March 29

Remember us, St. Joseph, and plead for us to your foster-child. Ask your most holy bride, the Virgin Mary, to look kindly upon us.[44]

Saint Bernardine of Siena

STEEP Perhaps the one thing that Lisa most yearned for, but didn't think possible, was for her Protestant husband to share her beautiful Catholic faith. She shared her initial doubts: "With his United Methodist roots and strong family ties, conversion to Catholicism would be near impossible." She didn't want to coerce, nag, or push him into something he didn't desire. She simply went about her days setting an example by remaining faithful to Catholic teachings—going to Mass, praying, and partaking in the sacraments.

She began a novena to Saint Joseph, which she has since kept up almost perpetually. Thanks be to God, Lisa's prayers were heard! Lisa wholeheartedly believes that Saint Joseph was responsible for her husband's conversion to the Catholic faith.

ACT Entrust one person or situation in your family to Saint Joseph today.

PRAY Jesus and Mary, be with me. Saint Joseph, please pray for us.

Our Father, Hail Mary, and Glory Be.

SAVOR The saints help us get to Heaven!

March 30

> Throughout all of history, Joseph is the man who gives God the greatest display of trust, even in the face of such astonishing news. [. . .] I would like to say: God loves you, he has not forgotten you, and Saint Joseph protects you! Invoke him with confidence.[45]
>
> Pope Benedict XVI

STEEP My friend Maria observed that her extended family had not been participating at Mass and Confession as they should. She decided to do something.

She started by lighting candles at church, asking Saint Joseph and Mary for a miracle for her family. Later that week, Maria asked her granddaughter to go with her to Confession. She agreed! Her granddaughter's mother (Maria's daughter), who rarely attends Confession, also went. Maria counted that as a miracle. She said, "I got all three of my granddaughters to go to Confession before Easter. This is amazing to me."

Some family members might have difficulty seeing the importance of the sacraments, but today's story shows that it can truly happen, especially through the help of the saints.

ACT Invite family members to join you the next time you go to Mass and Confession.

PRAY Jesus and Mary, please help all families. Saint Joseph, please pray for us.

Our Father, Hail Mary, and Glory Be.

SAVOR God works miracles every day!

March 31

As we come to the close of this month consecrated to Saint Joseph, let us look up to heaven to see his unveiled glory and to assure ourselves of his powerful protection.[46]

SAINT PETER JULIAN EYMARD

STEEP I love Saint Joseph so much that I named my son after him. I also named a religious goods store that I opened "Saint Joseph's Corner." I consider the humble saint a personal hero and have written about him in my books, often recommending his untiring intercession.

Finishing this month dedicated to the illustrious saint, I heartily encourage you, too, to take him on as a special friend and mighty intercessor, especially in your grandmotherly role. An exorcist friend has recommended that we also ask Saint Joseph's guardian angel to assist us in our urgent needs. He explained that Saint Joseph's guardian angel must be powerful in order to protect Saint Joseph so he could watch over the Holy Family!

ACT Learn about Saint Joseph and teach your grandchildren what you've learned.

PRAY Jesus and Mary, thank you for helping me. Saint Joseph, please pray for my family.

Our Father, Hail Mary, and Glory Be.

SAVOR Saint Joseph is a great gift to me as a grandmother!

APRIL

The Holy Spirit

So that you may not slacken your pace because of weakness, nor forget the blessing of the blood poured forth for you with such burning love, but may be constantly strengthened and filled with pleasure as you walk. The Holy Spirit, my loving charity, is the waiter who serves them my gifts and graces. . . . I [the Father] am their table, my Son is their food, and the Holy Spirit who proceeds from me the Father and from the Son, waits on them. You see, then, how they feel me constantly present to their spirits.[47]

God the Father to Saint Catherine of Siena

April 1

Do you not know that you are God's temple and that God's Spirit dwells in you?

1 Corinthians 3:16

STEEP As baptized Catholics, we have the Holy Spirit dwelling within us. Do we fully realize this? We tend to forget about this amazing supernatural indwelling. God gifted us with the Holy Spirit to aid us on our journey through life.

One time, my exorcist friend prayed over me over the phone and said something I'll never forget. He said, "Once you fully realize that the Holy Spirit dwells within you, the evil one won't be able to bother you as much." His words opened my mind and heart, and I suddenly felt a very clear awareness of the indwelling of the Holy Spirit! As grandmothers, we can use the grace of the Holy Spirit's indwelling to help our grandchildren recognize that he also dwells in them and that they, too, are temples.

ACT Pray to the Holy Spirit regularly. Ask for His help and protection.

PRAY Dear Holy Spirit, please enlighten me and guide me.

Our Father, Hail Mary, and Glory Be.

SAVOR God gave an amazing gift in the Holy Spirit, Whom I can call upon at any time!

April 2

For the bread of God is that which comes down from heaven and gives life to the world.

John 6:33

STEEP When my daughter Chaldea was three, she desperately wanted to receive Holy Communion—so much so that she tried to run back to the church! After Mass, as we headed home down the sidewalk, Chaldea broke loose from my hand and started to run as fast as her little legs could carry her. She wanted Jesus in the Eucharist! I caught up to her and explained that she would be old enough to receive one day, but not today.

What if we could all be as eager to receive Jesus in the Eucharist as a little child? Though we may teach the faith to our young grandchildren, we can also learn from them, striving to have the heart of a child. Jesus wants that. He wants our sincere love and devotion.

ACT The next time you go to Communion, receive Jesus like a child.

PRAY Dear Jesus, I want to love You with childlike innocence. Dear Mary, please assist me.

Our Father, Hail Mary, and Glory Be.

SAVOR Jesus comes to me fully in Holy Communion.

April 3

O Blessed Host, in whom is contained the Body and Blood of the Lord Jesus as proof of infinite mercy for us, and especially for poor sinners.

SAINT FAUSTINA, *DIARY*, 356

STEEP Many saints preached about the necessity of Holy Mass and the sacraments in our lives. Saint Faustina penned in her *Diary*, "The courage and strength that are in me are not of me, but of Him who lives in me—it is the Eucharist" (*Diary*, 91). Saint Teresa of Calcutta often explained that she and her sisters absolutely needed to receive the broken Body of Jesus in Holy Communion every morning to receive the necessary strength, graces, and courage to go out into the streets to care for the broken bodies of the poor. Similarly, we should strive to prioritize Mass and the sacraments in our lives so we can be strengthened to better live out our vocation of love as grandmothers.

ACT Visit Jesus in the Blessed Sacrament the next chance you get. While there with Him, ponder how He is absolutely essential nourishment for your soul.

PRAY Dear Jesus, may I long to receive You in Holy Communion with a sincere and contrite heart!

Our Father, Hail Mary, and Glory Be.

SAVOR Without Jesus in the Eucharist, my soul will die.

April 4

It was as a child that I myself first heard about the message of Our Lady of Fatima . . . it left an impression on me. . . . I never forgot it.[48]

FATHER ANDREW APOSTOLI

STEEP Children are never too young to learn about prayer. My dear friend of happy memory, Father Andrew Apostoli, CFR, was an expert on Fatima. In the foreword to my children's book, he explained that little Jacinta, "probably the most zealous of the visionaries . . . was only seven when Our Lady appeared to them."

He said, "It has been said that if an idea is impressed on the mind and heart of children before the age of seven, they will never forget it."[49] Because of this, it's so important to teach our children and grandchildren about the faith as young as possible. That said, if they haven't been catechized in their youth, there is always time to do so, but perhaps with added fervent prayers for their acceptance and growth in the Catholic faith.

ACT Introduce the youngest children in your life to the saints and approved apparitions.

PRAY Dear Holy Spirit, please open me to the treasure of Your grace. Saint Jacinta, please pray for us.

Our Father, Hail Mary, and Glory Be.

SAVOR I will continually pray for the treasure of grace from the Holy Spirit.

April 5

O Blessed Host, I trust in You when everything conspires against me and black despair creeps into my soul.

Saint Faustina, *Diary*, 356

STEEP Jesus entrusted Saint Faustina with the mammoth task of propagating the devotion of Divine Mercy. She endured serious struggles, including two dark nights in the spiritual life, and many times she was not believed—even by her superiors. When word about her visions got out in the convent, she was mercilessly ridiculed. The young saint-in-the-making battled periods of doubt, and later, ill health. Jesus in the Eucharist helped to sustain her.

Saint Faustina put her trust fully in Jesus. Instead of defending herself against others' questioning, she begged Jesus for a spiritual director. Eventually, Father Michael Sopocko (now a Blessed) came on the scene. He guided Sister Faustina to propagate the devotion of Divine Mercy.

Whatever struggles and trials we experience as grandmothers, we can follow Saint Faustina's example and earnestly trust God with our lives.

ACT The next time you receive Jesus in the Eucharist, entrust a current difficulty in your life to Him.

PRAY Dear Jesus and Mary, please help me. Saint Faustina, please pray for me.

Our Father, Hail Mary, and Glory Be.

SAVOR Jesus, I trust in You!

April 6

You knit me together in my mother's womb.

PSALM 139:13

STEEP My friend Fran shared that she "made a special pact" with her first grandson, Jayden, when he was still in his mother's womb. Fran was at the sonogram appointment for the announcement of the sex. The parents hoped for a daughter. Fran already had three sons and a step grandson and thought it would be nice to buy frilly pink dresses, but she was not disappointed the baby was a boy. She shared, "I saw this as my opportunity to reach Jayden through God and assure him that he would always be very special to me."

Now, Jayden is ten years old, and he and Fran are very close. Fran said, "He knows that he can always count on me, and he holds a very special place in my heart."

ACT Find opportunities to tell your grandchildren how very special they are to you.

PRAY Dear Jesus, Mary, and Joseph, please help our family. *Our Father, Hail Mary, and Glory Be.*

SAVOR Life is a wonderful gift!

April 7

Peace I leave with you; my peace I give to you. I do not give to you as the world gives. Do not let your hearts be troubled, and do not let them be afraid.

John 14:27

STEEP One day I visited a flea market with my daughter and saw a little girl and her mother notice a little red wagon. They approached the elderly vendor, who offered the girl the wagon for free and said they could keep it with him until they were ready. "But what if you forget me?" the little girl asked.

Smiling endearingly at her, the man asked, "How could I ever forget you, sweetheart?" It was a precious moment to watch. They headed off; within minutes, another child came along. We were flabbergasted when the man asked, "Would you like this wagon for your very own?" My heart sank as I watched the new child take the wagon.

We will always have disappointments in our lives and sometimes in our vocation as grandmothers. Yet we can take heart knowing that despite these disappointments, God does not forget our needs.

ACT Trustingly ask God for something you need today.

PRAY Dear Lord Jesus, thank You for Your love!

Our Father, Hail Mary, and Glory Be.

SAVOR My Lord will never forget me!

April 8

Let your steadfast love, O Lord, be upon us,
even as we hope in you.

Psalm 33:22

STEEP My grandsons, Shepherd and Leo, are the lights of my life. I suspect you can tell that I love being a grandmother! They live far from me, so it is not a quick trip to visit. I'd rather we lived next door! During the Covid-19 pandemic, we were separated for more than a year. We used videoconferencing to visit, but we deeply missed one another. One time, two-year-old Leo reached his hand toward the phone's camera and said, "Grandma, I want to touch you!"

When we finally visited, we were beside ourselves with crazy happiness. Shepherd and Leo kept hugging me. Shepherd said, "I never want to stop hugging you!" What a gift! My heart melted.

Near or far, we love our "grand-blessings." We must remember that our prayers and presence to them, even through technology, can help to form their consciences and comfort their hearts.

ACT Engage with your grandchildren and show them your love in a creative way, like sending them a letter in the mail—even if they live next door!

PRAY Dear Jesus and Mary, please watch over us.

Our Father, Hail Mary, and Glory Be.

SAVOR God gifts my heart with abiding love.

April 9

Holy Spirit, clothe us with love for our brethren.

LITANY OF THE HOLY SPIRIT

STEEP "Love for our brethren" means praying for their salvation. How many times, even in the course of a day, do we get requests for prayers? For me, it is constant. Just today, my friend contacted me to say that her friend's baby was rushed to the hospital! My heart jumped, and I began to pray immediately and got the word out to my fellow prayer warriors.

It's a beautiful blessing when others entrust us with their prayer requests. We can hope that if our grandchildren witness how we promptly and lovingly respond to others who ask for our prayers, then they, too, will know that they can turn to us with any prayer request or need they have, trusting that we will always intercede for them.

ACT Set aside a specific time today for intercessory prayer.

PRAY Jesus, Mary, and Joseph, give me the grace to be willing to offer generous prayers for those in need.

Our Father, Hail Mary, and Glory Be.

SAVOR The Holy Spirit clothes us with love!

April 10

The LORD is good to those who wait for him,
to the soul that seeks him.

LAMENTATIONS 3:25

STEEP Waiting can be hard. It tests our patience. Grandmothers wait during the day and the night. It might be for the arrival of their unborn grandchild. It could be for their older grandchild to get home from a date one evening, or to get in touch.

Waiting for God is tough too. We might pray earnestly but not see results—that is, results that we hope for. In times when God asks us to wait for something, we can take comfort knowing that our dear Lord is indeed the Divine Physician Who knows not only what we need, but also when we need it. We should seek God with patience and wholehearted trust. He is here. He is listening to our prayers. Sometimes, the answer is not "no." Rather, it is "wait."

ACT If possible, steal away to an empty church and sit at Jesus' feet to pour out your heart and just be with Him.

PRAY Jesus, Mary, and Joseph, please help me to grow in patience and trust.

Our Father, Hail Mary, and Glory Be.

SAVOR I will wait for the Lord and always seek Him.

April 11

I looked for pity, but there was none;
and for comforters, but I found none.

PSALM 69:20

STEEP In the Garden of Gethsemane, Jesus asked His disciples to remain with Him, staying awake, while He cried out to His Father in prayer. Three times, Jesus found them sleeping when He most needed them to "stay awake" (see Mt 26:36–46).

How often we have felt alone and abandoned. As grandmothers, we might feel alone if our families don't visit. At such times, we wish someone would comfort us. More than once, Mother Teresa told me to "be the one." She meant that I should stay close to Jesus and not "fall asleep." She encouraged me to comfort Him with my "many prayers and visits to Him in Adoration." Grandmothers can also "be the one" to the people in our lives who need a caring friend or a spiritual grandmother. All the while, the love and comfort we pour out to others comes back to comfort our own hearts. God is so beautiful like that!

ACT Stay with Jesus today by comforting someone in need.

PRAY Jesus, please allow me to be the one.

Our Father, Hail Mary, and Glory Be.

SAVOR I can be the one to comfort Jesus and others.

April 12

Holy Spirit, teach us to pray, and Yourself pray with us.

LITANY OF THE HOLY SPIRIT

STEEP What a gift it is to be a Catholic grandmother! The Holy Spirit truly lives within us. In addition to our own prayer lives, we have many opportunities to set a loving Christian example for our grandchildren, whether they are near or far from us—or near or far from the Church. Even if the grandchildren have not been baptized or their parents are against religion, we can still help to form our grandchildren's consciences and lovingly guide them on the right path.

Remember that we are not in this alone! The Holy Spirit works through our loving prayers and actions to have amazing effects on our grandchildren's hearts and souls. He will guide us and even pray with us!

ACT As you go about your day, try to be aware of the Holy Spirit living within you.

PRAY Dear Holy Spirit, please teach me to pray and please pray with me.

Our Father, Hail Mary, and Glory Be.

SAVOR God has gifted me with the extraordinary role of a Catholic grandmother!

April 13

O Blessed Host I trust in You when the practice of virtue will appear difficult for me and my nature will grow rebellious.

SAINT FAUSTINA, *DIARY*, 356

STEEP There are many seasons in our lives. Some are easy, bright, and cheery, while others might be arduous, dark, and scary. The spiritual life is both mysterious and fascinating. One thing is certain—we absolutely need to aspire to holiness. We have to pray and move our wills away from a spirit of rebellion and complacency. If we lie back, haphazardly let go of the oars, and let the current take control of our boat, the evil one will stealthily race in and steer our boat off course toward rocky cliffs or deadly waterfalls.

But even if this happens, the Holy Spirit is always ready to rescue us! Even when we struggle to stay on course in the spiritual life, we can trust that God will always lovingly reach out to help us.

ACT Be careful not to overfill today with busyness and neglect prayer. Set aside time to pray, and then pray with sincerity.

PRAY Dear Father, Son, and Holy Spirit, help me to pray.

Our Father, Hail Mary, and Glory Be.

SAVOR I will trust God to steer my boat.

April 14

> If our wills are on the side of God, we cannot be discouraged, for the side which we have chosen is always victorious, is never flouted.[50]
>
> VENERABLE FULTON SHEEN

STEEP "Kids these days!" How many times have we heard that expression? Kids are always surprising us, making us smile or think. One of my second-grade faith formation students surprised me with a vulnerable yet profound statement during a class about their upcoming First Holy Communion. She rose suddenly from her seat and hurried to the front of the class. Motioning for me to bend down, she whispered, "I believe, but I want to believe MORE!" She desired an increase in faith. It was amazing to hear from a seven-year-old.

We can learn from "kids these days," even our own grandchildren. We, too, can choose to ask God for an increase in faith. We can choose to go the right way. But we need to move our wills. That begins with an earnest desire of our hearts.

ACT Choose to follow God in all your actions today.

PRAY Dear Jesus, increase my faith.

Our Father, Hail Mary, and Glory Be.

SAVOR God wants me to believe more.

April 15

From the Eucharist comes strength to live the Christian life and zeal to share that life with others.[51]

Saint John Paul II

STEEP One day, my friend Father Bill entered a seemingly empty church. He genuflected reverently and prayed quietly before opening the tabernacle door to retrieve the Blessed Sacrament. Meanwhile, a man quickly hid in the confessional when Father Bill entered and clandestinely watched him. The following day, the man knocked on the rectory door. He wanted to know what he could do to possess the same love and reverence for the Eucharist that Father Bill displayed the day before. He desired to become a Catholic.

The man was converted by my friend's example, and Father Bill hadn't said a word! This story can give us great hope as grandmothers that our daily actions and witness can move our grandchildren's hearts toward God.

ACT Do something to show your love for God today. You never know who's watching!

PRAY Dear Jesus, help me bring my grandchildren closer to You.

Our Father, Hail Mary, and Glory Be.

SAVOR My example can change a life!

April 16

> The Christian family is a communion of persons, a sign and image of the communion of the Father and the Son in the Holy Spirit. In the procreation and education of children it reflects the Father's work of creation. It is called to partake of the prayer and sacrifice of Christ. Daily prayer and the reading of the Word of God strengthen it in charity.
>
> *Catechism of the Catholic Church*, 2205

STEEP The quote above sounds marvelous. Yet, when we observe our family on any given day, we may not see the image of the Blessed Trinity. Is that because it is hidden or because we are not living up to our potential? We can ask ourselves that question. And while we can't control our family members' choices or actions, we can ask ourselves what we, as grandmothers, can do to help our families better image the Trinity.

The *Catechism* also teaches that through our procreation and education of our children, we actually reflect God the Father's creation. That is an awesome statement!

ACT Make an effort to see the image of the Trinity in your family today.

PRAY Most Blessed Trinity, please help my family.

Our Father, Hail Mary, and Glory Be.

SAVOR I can help my family reflect the Trinity.

April 17

O Blessed Host, our only hope in the toil and monotony of everyday life.

SAINT FAUSTINA, *DIARY*, 356

STEEP The Eucharist should be the absolute center of our lives because Jesus should be at the center of our life of worship. He is, after all, THE ONE Who started the Catholic Church. Scripture teaches, "The cup of blessing that we bless, is it not a sharing in the blood of Christ? The bread that we break, is it not a sharing in the body of Christ? Because there is one bread, we who are many are one body, for we all partake of the one bread" (1 Cor 10:16–17).

Saint Faustina considered the Eucharist "our only hope" in navigating daily monotony. Grandmothers can be deeply devoted to Jesus in the Blessed Sacrament each day even amid daily monotony or on days we can't go to daily Mass due to other obligations, illness, or scheduling conflicts. We can make spiritual Communions when we are not able to receive sacramentally.

ACT Ponder Jesus' great love for you in making Himself available in the Eucharist.

PRAY Dear Jesus, thank You for the gift of Yourself!

Our Father, Hail Mary, and Glory Be.

SAVOR Jesus Christ is as present with us here in the Eucharist as He was when He walked the earth.

April 18

When you approach the tabernacle remember that *he* has been waiting for you for twenty centuries.[52]

Saint Josemaría Escrivá

STEEP The saints have modeled a deep love of Jesus in the Eucharist—when receiving Holy Communion and when adoring Him in the Blessed Sacrament. They firmly believed that He was their strength and essential nourishment for their souls. Without Him, they suffered.

Having lived through a worldwide pandemic, many faithful Catholics suffered a painful longing for Jesus in the Eucharist because their churches were closed. Jesus awaited our visits as we awaited our churches to reopen. Many Catholics—perhaps even you—showed their deep love for Him by visiting quiet or empty churches to be near their Beloved. Much patience, earnest prayer, and spiritual Communions helped get us all through until we were able to return to Mass and receive our Eucharistic Lord again.

ACT Talk to Jesus today about your love for Him. Carve out special time for Him.

PRAY Dear Jesus, I love You! Please strengthen my faith.

Our Father, Hail Mary, and Glory Be.

SAVOR I need the Bread of Life!

April 19

Or do you not know that your body is a temple of the Holy Spirit within you, which you have from God, and that you are not your own? For you were bought with a price; therefore glorify God in your body.

1 Corinthians 6:19–20

STEEP Do we live and act according to the truth that the Holy Spirit dwells within us? This matters not only for our own souls, but also because sincerely and humbly living and acting as if the Holy Spirit dwells within us will radiate out to others. With God's grace, what we say or do can help to transform other souls, beginning within our own families and extending to each and every person with whom we come in contact. The Holy Spirit dwelling within a grandmother's heart sparks holy flames amid the embers of faith in her grandchildren. These holy flames can't help but reach the hearts of all around them!

ACT Invite the Holy Spirit to live more robustly in your life—to guide your prayers, words, and actions.

PRAY Holy Spirit, please enlighten me and shower me with Your gifts!

Our Father, Hail Mary, and Glory Be.

SAVOR The Holy Spirit dwells within me!

April 20

Jesus said to them, "I am the bread of life. Whoever comes to me will never be hungry, and whoever believes in me will never be thirsty."

JOHN 6:35

STEEP The world promises to satisfy our hunger and thirst. We can get deeply lost in the tangled web of false promises from the world and the evil one. Other times, we witness people we know—sadly, perhaps even our own children or grandchildren—falling into the same trap.

Jesus calls to all of us and promises that it is He Who will satisfy our hearts. He wants to nourish us and our loved ones with the Bread of Life. When we turn away due to sin, He wants us to seek Him with a contrite heart. He will allay our fears and give us strength each day to battle the world's false promises and to try to protect our loved ones as well.

ACT Make an examination of conscience, considering how you can better avoid the world's false promises and be a spark of bright hope to others who have lost their way.

PRAY Dear Jesus, please continue to nourish me with Your Bread of Life!

Our Father, Hail Mary, and Glory Be.

SAVOR Only Jesus can truly satisfy my hunger and thirst.

April 21

> O Blessed Host, I trust in You when the burdens are beyond my strength and I find my efforts are fruitless.
>
> SAINT FAUSTINA, *DIARY*, 356

STEEP Sometimes, all seems lost. Whether it's a problem in our personal spiritual lives or a family crisis that affects us and our grandchildren, we might feel like it's the absolute end of the world. Taxed beyond measure by the battle at hand, we might have trouble mustering up the necessary strength to address the problem. Or, when we try, we might feel that our efforts are pitiful and weak at best. I have certainly felt this way on many an occasion.

Saint Faustina penned in her *Diary* that she knew exactly where to turn when the burden was beyond her strength and she felt her own efforts were fruitless. Jesus is THE One! He endured the weight of the cross, and He can also help us carry our burdens. Whatever we're facing, we can always trust in Him and seek His help.

ACT Jot down your concerns and fears on a piece of paper or journal, then give them to God in prayer.

PRAY Dear Lord, I surrender everything to You!

Our Father, Hail Mary, and Glory Be.

SAVOR Jesus, I trust in You!

April 22

Let us therefore approach the throne of grace with boldness, so that we may receive mercy and find grace to help in time of need.

HEBREWS 4:16

STEEP Why is it so hard to completely trust God? Sometimes it might feel like we're perpetually waiting for the proverbial other shoe to drop—always worrying about how a situation will turn out, perhaps especially when we're concerned about our grandchildren! But even if we struggle to approach God with sincere faith, we can ask God to grant us graces to be able to trust Him more wholeheartedly.

Jesus promises that He will reward our sincere trust in Him. It's important for us to remember that He is the Divine Physician and because He is, He knows exactly what is best for our souls and our grandchildren's souls. He is trustworthy!

ACT When challenges present themselves and your day gets rearranged, try hard to trust Jesus. Ask His help and tell Him, "Jesus, I trust in You!"

PRAY Lord Jesus, I love You and want to trust You more!
Our Father, Hail Mary, and Glory Be.

SAVOR Jesus is always ready to answer my prayers.

April 23

As often as you eat this bread and drink the cup, you proclaim the Lord's death until he comes.

1 Corinthians 11:26

STEEP In order to worthily receive our Lord Jesus in the Eucharist, we need to repent of our sins and receive forgiveness through the sacrament of Reconciliation. A priest friend recently shared that he is always delighted to hear the first confessions of little children because they are precious and innocent. Not only that—he added, "They always skip back to their parents! It is the joy of forgiveness." And it's the same for us. At times, we might feel nervous or timid about going to Confession, or even feel we just don't have time. However, it's essential that we do participate in this life-transforming sacrament in which joy and peace enter our hearts. We can feel like a child again with our new clean slate!

ACT If your grandchildren are old enough, encourage them to go to Confession this Easter season. If they're still too young, reflect on their innocence and what it can teach you.

PRAY Jesus, I am sorry for all of my sins. I want to receive You worthily.

Our Father, Hail Mary, and Glory Be.

SAVOR The joy of the Lord's forgiveness is my strength!

April 24

Those who eat my flesh and drink my blood abide in me, and I in them.

John 6:56

STEEP When baptized Catholics do not partake in the Eucharist, they are not being fed spiritually. Their souls are dying. That might sound severe, or exaggerated; however, it is true.

My friend Sally helped John, who had been away from Confession for sixty years, to return to the life-transforming sacrament. John didn't know where to start. Sally suggested writing his sins on a piece of paper he could take into the confessional. Sally waited outside while John was in the confessional. When John was finished, Sally rejoiced with him that all his sins were forgiven!

As grandmothers, we can help our family members return to Confession too, especially if they've been away for a long time. Like Sally, we can set a good example by encouraging and assisting them in whatever way they need.

ACT Think of a relative or someone else you know who is away from the sacraments. Pray for that person, and then take the next opportunity to invite them to return to Confession.

PRAY Jesus, help me to help others turn to You.

Our Father, Hail Mary, and Glory Be.

SAVOR God is full of mercy!

April 25

For we walk by faith, not by sight.

2 CORINTHIANS 5:7

STEEP Newborns rely on caregivers for everything they need to survive. As babies grow, they require guidance every step of the way. Seeing or remembering our grandchildren at these early stages reminds us of this. The world is an awfully big place for a little one who needs constant protection and continual life lessons. Each and every thing is totally new.

God wants us to become like children in our trust in Him. The world is a big place for us too, especially in an ever-changing culture whose ideologies often conflict with our faith. God wants us to pray so that He may guide and teach us to follow His Commandments.

ACT Stretch your mind back to your own childhood. How were you taught—for better or for worse? Do you have special stories that you can impart to your grandchildren?

PRAY Dear Lord God, thank You for creating me!

Our Father, Hail Mary, and Glory Be.

SAVOR I will lay myself in God's hands.

April 26

For the Son of Man came to seek out and to save the lost.

Luke 19:10

STEEP God wants our hearts for sure. If we try to avoid Him, He seeks us out. When we do encounter God in prayer, He wants our love, humility, and full abandonment. Our desire to be with Him will grow as we get to know Him through spending time adoring Him in the Blessed Sacrament, participating at Holy Mass, and lifting our hearts to Him at any time.

Similarly, growing in our vocation as grandmothers stirs our hearts to desire to be with our grandchildren. Our love for them and our love for God combine in our desire to encourage them to develop a relationship with Jesus.

ACT Make a list of the things that distract you from encountering God in prayer. Try to avoid those things today. Make a list of the things you think will help you to become more attentive to His whispers to your soul. Try to incorporate those things into your prayer time.

PRAY Dear Jesus, I love You and want to be with You!

Our Father, Hail Mary, and Glory Be.

SAVOR Jesus wants my wholehearted and humble surrender.

April 27

Cast all your anxiety on him, because he cares for you.

1 PETER 5:7

STEEP My friend Father Luke Mary Fletcher, CFR, told me about a time the friary doorbell rang as Benediction was about to begin. Father Luke ran down to tell the man that they could serve him in five minutes, but then a sudden, uneasy feeling came over him. Rushing upstairs, he concluded Benediction, faced the monstrance toward the front door, and made the Sign of the Cross with it. Father Luke asked Jesus to bless the man. The man started to howl and curse.

Father and another friar rushed outside to speak with him, but he ran away. "As we started to pursue him, a large number of rats seemed to come out of nowhere and blocked our path. We prayed for his deliverance that night." Father Luke added, "I went to bed reminded of the power of the Presence of Jesus in the Blessed Sacrament."

ACT Ask Jesus in the Eucharist to spiritually protect your family.

PRAY Jesus, please bless me and all who need You right now.

Our Father, Hail Mary, and Glory Be.

SAVOR Jesus is truly with us!

April 28

Commit your way to the LORD;
trust in him, and he will act.

PSALM 37:5

STEEP Today is a brand new day. What will we do with it? Every single morning, we arise afresh. We might not *feel* refreshed due to not enough sleep or aches and pains in our older age. Nonetheless, we will encounter many new opportunities for grace in our day ahead. Perhaps we will even experience a special healing.

Starting our days in a prayerful mindset helps us better live out our vocation as grandmothers. Blessings are waiting, hidden in the mundane or the difficult. God is with us. Mother Mary is with us too. Our guardian angel is by our side. Let's not forget about him. He wants to help us. All these spiritual helpers are guiding us toward Heaven through our daily lives.

ACT Talk to your guardian angel more often, starting today. Ask him for his protection and guidance.

PRAY Dear Jesus, Mary, and Joseph, please take care of my family and me.

Our Father, Hail Mary, and Glory Be.

SAVOR How blessed I am to be a Catholic woman!

April 29

I am the living bread that came down from heaven. Whoever eats of this bread will live forever; and the bread that I will give for the life of the world is my flesh.

John 6:51

STEEP When leading a youth retreat in Brooklyn, my friend Father Luke had a beautiful experience during Adoration. He said, "I looked up to see that the priest was being led by a young altar server who looked identical to the eight-year-old me. I was astounded!" As the priest incensed the Blessed Sacrament, Father Luke recalled happenings in his life from the time he was a young altar boy in Indiana until the present. Unexpectedly, the incense smoke "bellowed through the holes in the thurible and formed a perfect heart shape right in front of my face!"

Similarly, we might see our own younger selves reflected in our grandchildren. We can be assured that God will surely lead their lives too!

ACT Consider how you've seen Jesus lead you and your grandchildren throughout your lives so far.

PRAY Dear Jesus, I love You! Please continue to guide my grandchildren and me.

Our Father, Hail Mary, and Glory Be.

SAVOR I want Jesus to guide my entire life.

April 30

But ask the animals, and they will teach you;
  the birds of the air, and they will tell you;
ask the plants of the earth, and they will teach you . . .
Who among all these does not know
  that the hand of the LORD has done this?

JOB 12:7–9

STEEP One spring morning, I arose to the sound of birds singing their little hearts out. A variety of melodies pierced the air, as if the different species of birds were letting me know that they were happy to be alive. It was immensely lovely. I have become a bit of a bird watcher, and I snap away to capture pictures of them every chance I have.

What can we learn from the birds? We can at least pause to listen to the beautiful gift of marvelous music from God in every way He shares it with us. Admiring God's gifts can give us grandmothers cause to remember how good God is to us and thank Him for it.

ACT Today, take in every single thing! Everything has its purpose. Be extra attentive to the many gifts from God throughout today.

PRAY Dear Jesus, You love me so. Thank You for all of Your gifts!

Our Father, Hail Mary, and Glory Be.

SAVOR I will relish the goodness of the Lord!

MAY

The Blessed Mother

Here am I, the servant of the Lord; let it be with me according to your word.

Luke 1:38

May 1

> Mary is the Lord's humble servant, prepared from eternity for the task of being the Mother of God. Joseph is the one whom God chose to be the "overseer of the Lord's birth", the one who has the responsibility to look after the Son of God's "ordained" entry into the world.[53]
>
> SAINT JOHN PAUL II

STEEP May is dedicated to our Blessed Mother. However, she shares today with her husband, Saint Joseph, because today is the feast of Saint Joseph the Worker!

John Paul II said, "Human work, and especially manual labor, receives special prominence in the Gospel . . . At the workbench where he plied his trade together with Jesus, Joseph brought human work closer to the mystery of the Redemption."[54] As Catholic grandmothers, whether our work is a job outside the home or the daily labor of caring for our families, we can look to Saint Joseph as our model.

ACT Ponder how you can serve God through your work today.

PRAY Lord, I offer You today's work. Saint Joseph, pray for me.

Our Father, Hail Mary, and Glory Be.

SAVOR Saint Joseph, caregiver of Jesus and Mary, has much to teach me.

May 2

Then he said to the disciple, "Here is your mother."

JOHN 19:27

STEEP When her mother died, twelve-year-old Saint Teresa of Avila asked the Mother of God to be her mother. She said, "When I began to understand what I had lost, I went, afflicted, before an image of Our Lady and besought her with many tears to be my mother. It seems to me that although I did this in simplicity, it helped me. For I have found favor with this sovereign Virgin in everything I have asked of her, and in the end she has drawn me to herself."[55]

Just as Mary mothered Saint Teresa, we as grandmothers can apply this same spiritual motherly love to others: to our grandchildren, but also to anyone else in need!

ACT Mary is the great Mother of God, gifted to you by Jesus Himself! Ask her to mother you.

PRAY Mary, thank you for being my mother. Please help me to spiritually mother others, especially my grandchildren.

Our Father, Hail Mary, and Glory Be.

SAVOR Mother Mary helps me in my vocation of grandmotherly love!

May 3

His mother treasured all these things in her heart.

LUKE 2:51

STEEP Our world is fast-paced. Unless our personal "world" has slowed down in this stage of life, it's sometimes difficult to escape the whirlwind. Mary's life was surely also busy, but she kept the word of God by receiving it with humility and love, reflecting upon it, and living it with unambiguous fidelity. She took time to prayerfully ponder God's word. She sat still, she knelt, she listened.

It's essential to schedule specific times for daily prayer in order to form the good habit of lifting our hearts toward Heaven every chance we have. In this way, our lives can become a beautiful conversation with our Creator. Taking time to ponder God's word will bear great fruit in our life and vocation, and this fruit can nourish our families because of God's grace radiating through it.

ACT Pause to ponder God's word today, whether by reading the Bible or by simply listening to His whispers to your heart and soul.

PRAY Jesus, please speak to my heart. Mary, teach me to ponder the truths of the faith. Please guide me to your Son!

Our Father, Hail Mary, and Glory Be.

SAVOR Mary can show me how to reflect on God's word.

May 4

> When you hastened with holy joy across the mountains of Judea to see your cousin Elizabeth, you became the image of the Church to come, which carries the hope of the world in her womb across the mountains of history.[56]
>
> Pope Benedict XVI

STEEP What was Mary thinking as she hurried over one hundred miles of rough terrain to Elizabeth's home? The young Jewish teen must have been overflowing with joy, knowing of her elderly cousin's pregnancy. Mary wholeheartedly embraced the task to go "in haste" to aid Elizabeth. Through each and every mile, history was in the making, as Mary made her way with Jesus residing in the tabernacle of her womb.

We also may be asked in haste to help loved ones, whether by physically traveling to them or by our prayers and loving advice. Whenever we are called upon for help, let us imitate Mary and "hasten with holy joy!"

ACT Find one way today to run in haste to help your family members.

PRAY Jesus, thank You for the gift of womanhood. Mary, please show me how to go in haste to help others.

Our Father, Hail Mary, and Glory Be.

SAVOR The Visitation teaches me how to serve others joyfully.

May 5

But alongside the joy which, with your *Magnificat*, you proclaimed in word and song for all the centuries to hear, you also knew the dark sayings of the prophets about the suffering of the servant of God in this world.[57]

Pope Benedict XVI

STEEP Mary's role was a mix of joy and suffering intertwined. Yet when she uttered her fiat, she wholeheartedly accepted every bit of it and whatever was to come. We certainly aren't the Blessed Mother, but we can relate to this part of her experience! A grandmother's life is also filled with a mix of joys and sufferings. In all the ups and downs, we can take comfort in knowing that our Blessed Mother understands our hearts, and we can seek to emulate her by embracing the full range of our life experiences in our vocation: both the sufferings and the joys.

ACT Get close to Mary. Talk to her about your joys and sorrows. She understands because she herself has endured deep sorrows and joys.

PRAY Dear Lord, help me to accept whatever joys or sufferings come my way today. Mother Mary, please pray for me.

Our Father, Hail Mary, and Glory Be.

SAVOR I am gifted to have Mary as a mother who understands my heart.

May 6

> Shining over his birth in the stable at Bethlehem, there were angels in splendor who brought the good news to the shepherds, but at the same time the lowliness of God in this world was all too palpable.[58]
>
> POPE BENEDICT XVI

STEEP Surely, while holy angels watched and adored, Mary and Joseph basked in the miracle of their Son's birth and the great gift that He was to them and to the whole world. However, it wouldn't be too long before Mary would feel her heart pierced through when their little baby was presented in the Temple, and again when they were suddenly uprooted to take flight into Egypt because of the grim threat to their baby's life.

Our lives may not be as intensely dramatic as the Holy Family's. Yet, we too have moments when our lives or vocations do not go the way we planned or hoped. In such moments, we can remember the Holy Family's dramatic beginnings and pray for their intercession.

ACT Spend time today meditating on the Christ Child's birth and the life of the Holy Family as well as your own family's story.

PRAY Dear Holy Family, please guide and guard my family. *Our Father, Hail Mary, and Glory Be.*

SAVOR I am immensely blessed with the Holy Family as my guide.

May 7

The old man Simeon spoke to you of the sword which would pierce your soul, of the sign of contradiction that your Son would be in this world.[59]

Pope Benedict XVI

STEEP The Blessed Mother knows well the sword of suffering. On what should have been a happy occasion—presenting her precious baby in the Temple—she heard Simeon prophesy the division her Son would cause, and then heard him say, "A sword will pierce your own soul too" (Lk 2:35).

Mary remained faithful to God's will even when she knew she would suffer deeply at the side of her suffering Son. Hers was a holy, mysterious, and sometimes sorrowful vocation. Mary's acceptance of holy suffering can teach us how to respond to suffering in our own roles within our families. We don't have to piously pretend the sword of suffering does not hurt, but rather, we can follow Mary's example of trustful surrender to God.

ACT Lovingly surrender your sorrows and struggles to Jesus. Ask Him to make them redemptive for your own soul and others'.

PRAY Dear Mary, show me, teach me, help me to imitate your trustful and loving surrender to God.

Our Father, Hail Mary, and Glory Be.

SAVOR I should never fear going to Mary with any need.

May 8

From the Cross you received a new mission. From the Cross you became a mother in a new way: the mother of all those who believe in your Son Jesus and wish to follow him.[60]

Pope Benedict XVI

STEEP If we have ever watched a loved one suffer, we know how painful an experience it can be. We can try to imagine what Mary went through, standing at the foot of the Cross, watching her only Son die a most cruel death. Yet even as the dark shadow of the Cross towered over her, Mary was given a special mission from her Son. Scripture tells us Jesus told His Mother that she became the mother of all, right there beneath the Cross.

Knowing of Mary's great sufferings can help to comfort our own sorrowful hearts when enduring grief, suffering, and sadness in our own families. In addition, speaking from experience of my own grandmother, we grandmothers can be such a comfort to our grandchildren. With God's grace, our sufferings can become redemptive, and we can discover that we are called to comfort the suffering even as we may suffer ourselves.

ACT Acknowledge Mary as your Mother.

PRAY Jesus, thank You for the great gift of Your own Mother! *Our Father, Hail Mary, and Glory Be.*

SAVOR Mary understands my suffering.

May 9

Mystical Rose, pray for us.

Litany of Loreto

STEEP My friend Father Luke begins each day with Mary by taking morning Rosary walks. He stops first in front of the friary at the simple statue of Our Lady of Grace, nestled in a recessed niche surrounded by a white cage and rose bushes. He loves watching "as random people, like passerby pilgrims, stop and say a prayer." But one particular May morning, he had to rub his eyes—"To make sure that I was seeing what I was seeing!"

At the feet of Our Lady, a single fully bloomed rose came forth from a branch below. "There was not a single bud on any of the other rose bushes," he recalled.

Like Father Luke, let's take time for Mary and honor her. With our grandchildren, we can learn more about Mary, visit a Marian shrine, pray Marian prayers, participate in Marian devotions, raise our hearts to her in thanksgiving, and ask for her graces. When we honor Mary, we will see signs of her presence and love in our lives and families.

ACT Look for signs of Mary in your life today.

PRAY Dear Mystical Rose, thank you for your love!

Our Father, Hail Mary, and Glory Be.

SAVOR Mary deserves our love and honor!

May 10

> The mother eagle gets her young to fly by pecking away pieces of the nest bit by bit, until finally the young have to leave the temporary security.[61]
>
> Venerable Fulton Sheen

STEEP In the case of today's quote, I don't think I would be the one pecking away at the nest bit by bit! I want my children and grandchildren to grow into the amazing human beings they were created to be, but it's bittersweet to let them go.

Mothers and grandmothers lay down that essential foundation of faith, hope, and love. We nourish the gifts that God has given to our children and grandchildren at their Baptisms, and we continue to guide and guard them until that day comes when they learn to fly. We will always be their steady anchor in life, but once they're fully grown, our loving guidance will be carried out differently. We may patiently await their requests for advice, all while continuing to set a prayerful example.

ACT Schedule a special activity or visit with your child or grandchild.

PRAY Lord, thank You for Your blessings! Mary, Star of the Sea, please help us!

Our Father, Hail Mary, and Glory Be.

SAVOR Life is a precious gift!

May 11

The month of May is . . . a month which the piety of the faithful has long dedicated to Mary, the Mother of God. . . . The moving tribute of faith and love . . . will soon be paid to the Queen of Heaven in every corner of the earth.[62]

SAINT PAUL VI

STEEP My friend Linda's granddaughter Ava is four years old. Linda shared, "Her entire little life, Ava has played with my Miraculous Medal, which I never take off. She's gotten to know Mary through this medal."

One day, Ava discovered a picture of Mary in Linda's bedroom and asked, "Can Mary stay with me in my room?" Linda was thrilled to hear her precious request. Ava chose a place to hang Mary's picture. Ever since, "Ava sings and talks to Mary and hangs different things on the picture she feels Mary might like."

Even our small displays of faith can help our grandchildren develop a relationship with God and His Mother!

ACT Make a moving tribute of faith and love to Mary.

PRAY Dear Mother Mary, Star of the Sea, please shine upon my grandchildren and guide their way to your Son!

Our Father, Hail Mary, and Glory Be.

SAVOR I can approach Mary with a childlike innocence.

May 12

Holy Mary, Mother of God, our Mother, teach us to believe, to hope, to love with you. Show us the way to his Kingdom![63]

POPE BENEDICT XVI

STEEP Whenever I watch children ceremoniously place a crown on a statue of the Blessed Mother, I start to tear up. It's so precious to watch them show love and honor to Mary. This month is a perfect time to participate in a May crowning. It does not have to be a formal event. It can be carried out at home in your own domestic church. You can speak to your grandchildren about Mary's role as Queen of Heaven and Earth and how we can pray that she will be the queen of our hearts. You can explain to them that we crown Mary to show honor to her. Then, give them the honor of honoring Mary by letting them crown her!

ACT Make plans to crown a statue or image of Mary. Gather the children and pray to Mary, sing to Mary, and crown her!

PRAY Jesus, we love You. Mary, Star of the Sea, please shine upon my family and guide our way to your Son.

Our Father, Hail Mary, and Glory Be.

SAVOR Mary is the Queen of my heart!

May 13

Fatima is a call to live by Faith. The Fatima message strengthens us to have trust in times of trial.[64]

FATHER ANDREW APOSTOLI

STEEP Today is the feast of Our Lady of Fatima. On May 13, 1917, the Blessed Mother appeared to three shepherd children to reveal her plan for the world's peace. She asked for people to turn from sin, pray a daily Rosary, offer penance, and fulfill the Five First Saturday devotion. Mary also stressed the need to pray for sinners who are in danger of Hell because there is no one to pray for them. The three young shepherds wholeheartedly embraced the call from Heaven. We, too, can strive to fulfill Mary's requests, teach our families about her message, and invite them to join us in prayer.

ACT Tell your grandchildren about Our Lady of Fatima. Pray the Rosary with them—even a decade—for the conversion of sinners.

PRAY Dear Lord, thank You for Mary. Our Lady of Fatima, protect me and guide my way to your Son!

Our Father, Hail Mary, and Glory Be.

SAVOR Our Lady's message strengthens me and calls me to a holy life.

May 14

> The point is this: the one who sows sparingly will also reap sparingly, and the one who sows bountifully will also reap bountifully.
>
> 2 Corinthians 9:6

STEEP When I think of sowing and reaping, I can't help but recall my own gardening experiences. No matter how much I weed and how much mulch I put down, inevitably, the stubborn weeds sneak their way through. If I don't pluck them out by the roots, before long they invade the entire garden.

In our spiritual lives, we must be careful about what we allow to take root in our hearts. The effects of a little temptation that we fall for can multiply until they threaten to take over. We need to rely on God's grace to eradicate the "weeds" in our hearts. And just as an experienced gardener teaches a novice, we can use our spiritual experiences to teach our grandchildren how to sow bountifully and avoid the "weeds."

ACT Pull up the "weeds" in your soul by scheduling a time to go to Confession.

PRAY Jesus, You are my Savior! Mary, Star of the Sea, guide my way to your Son!

Our Father, Hail Mary, and Glory Be.

SAVOR I should sow bountifully and be careful of "weeds" so that I may reap bountifully!

May 15

Hail, O Star of the ocean, God's own Mother blest,
ever sinless Virgin, gate of heav'nly rest. . . .
Keep our life all spotless, make our way secure,
till we find in Jesus joy for evermore.

FROM "HAIL STAR OF THE SEA" PRAYER

STEEP We will never fully comprehend the great gift of Mother Mary this side of Heaven. She is our guiding light! She always leads us to her Son. "Our Lady, Star of the Sea" is an ancient title given to Mary in the fourth century by Doctor of the Church Saint Jerome. Later, Saint Bernard of Clairvaux also beautifully exalted Mary in this role. Today, this devotion is popular throughout the world. Seafarers call upon her; churches are named after her.

When we need direction or guidance in our vocation as grandmothers, or are in danger of capsizing in the storms of life, let us turn to Mary, our steadfast guiding star.

ACT Imagine Mary guiding your steps today.

PRAY Jesus, thank You for Your Mother! Mary, Star of the Sea, "show thyself a Mother, may the Word divine, born for us, thine Infant, hear our prayers through thine."[65]

Our Father, Hail Mary, and Glory Be.

SAVOR God's own Mother helps me in my vocation of grandmotherly love!

May 16

During this beautiful month of Our Lady, let us crown her with fragrant flowers—the flowers of love, gentleness, meekness and humility for one another, and ask Jesus to be truly a cause of joy to her as He was.[66]

Saint Teresa of Calcutta

STEEP Mother Teresa, the humble saint of the gutters, was very devoted to the Mother of God. In today's quote, she suggests a way to crown Mary with the "fragrant flowers" of virtues.

Even if we are unable to participate in a May crowning ceremony or to invite our grandchildren to join one, we can teach and model for them the way to crown Mary that Mother Teresa describes. Each day, we can work at being virtuous, and we can "crown" Mary with all those virtuous works of mercy.

ACT Crown Mary with one virtue today. Encourage your grandchildren to think of one virtue with which they can crown Mary today too.

PRAY Jesus, help me to be a cause of joy to Your Mother. Dear Mary, please help me.

Our Father, Hail Mary, and Glory Be.

SAVOR Prayerfully working to become more virtuous is a gift to our Mother Mary.

May 17

A cheerful heart is a good medicine,
but a downcast spirit dries up the bones.

PROVERBS 17:22

STEEP My friend Father Luke has walked the streets of New York City to minister to needs and to pray. He shared with me, "I can't tell you how many grace-filled encounters I've experienced in the streets." One story he shared was of a man he met who used a walker because he was missing a leg. They said hello and smiled at one another each time they crossed paths. One day, Father Luke said to his new friend, "Do you know how to get to Heaven? One step at a time!" The man laughed and replied, "Brother, that's all I can do!"

The man's cheerful heart helped him to laugh and joke even though his situation appeared difficult. At times in our lives when we or our families are facing difficulties, it may be challenging to cultivate a cheerful heart. However, we can do so by seeking the joys in our vocation and connecting with others.

ACT Take time to smile, laugh, and joke!

PRAY Dear Jesus, I love You! Dear Mother Mary, help me to find joy.

Our Father, Hail Mary, and Glory Be.

SAVOR A cheerful heart is a good medicine!

May 18

In the days that followed the Lord's Resurrection, the Apostles stayed together, comforted by Mary's presence, and after the Ascension they persevered with her in prayerful expectation of Pentecost.[67]

Pope Benedict XVI

STEEP Can we even imagine how the apostles and Mary felt after Jesus' death and resurrection? They believed in His promises that the Holy Spirit would be sent to them. Still, they sorely missed Him. As they waited and prayed together, Mary's holy presence was a deep comfort. With great tenderness, Mary mothered them. Yet she leaned on them too, especially Saint John.

Similarly, as grandmothers we have the God-given gift of being a comforting, tender presence to our families. But God also gives us the gift of our loved ones to lean on during difficult times. And during times when we feel alone, God's gift of His Mother can comfort us!

ACT In any struggles you face today, imitate the apostles and Mary and lean on those who will help.

PRAY Jesus, thank You for Your blessings! Mother Mary, Star of the Sea, please guide my way to your Son!

Our Father, Hail Mary, and Glory Be.

SAVOR God gives us to each other to lean on.

May 19

[It is useful for us to] rediscover the maternal role that she plays in our lives so that we may always be docile disciples and courageous witnesses of the Risen Lord.[68]

Pope Benedict XVI

STEEP Many women have shared with me that they have suffered from a deep "mother wound." Their own mothers were unable to provide love and care to them as they should have. The women had learned survival techniques when young, and later in life discovered that they were severely emotionally wounded, which helped them to understand why they partook in certain unhealthy behaviors along the way.

As grandmothers, we recognize the importance of providing maternal love for every child, but even grandmothers need to experience a mother's love! If you suffer from a mother wound, you can seek healing through psychological help, but also by turning to Mother Mary. She can help to heal hearts and become a sorely needed mother figure.

ACT Give your wounds to Jesus and Mary. Seek other help if necessary. Strive to be attentive to the women or girls in your life who have suffered.

PRAY Jesus, open my eyes and heart. Mother Mary, help me to help others.

Our Father, Hail Mary, and Glory Be.

SAVOR Mary is my amazing Mother!

May 20

We believe that the Holy Mother of God, the new Eve, Mother of the Church, continues in heaven to exercise her maternal role on behalf of the members of Christ.

Catechism of the Catholic Church, 975

STEEP Can we imagine the pure love between Mary and her Son? Perhaps our experiences with our own children and grandchildren can give us a glimpse! We can ponder when Jesus was a tiny babe in her arms and at her breast as she cradled Him close to her Immaculate Heart, or when He was a little toddler sitting upon His Mother's lap and learning to pray. Mary surely stroked His soft hair and sang to Him. The unity between Mother and Son continued in Jesus' mission for the salvation of the world.

Perhaps our relationships with our children and grandchildren aren't always close or perfect—after all, we aren't sinless like Jesus and Mary! But however our relationships develop and change over the years, we can take comfort in uniting ourselves to Jesus and Mary too.

ACT Throughout this whole day, call Mary your own Mother.

PRAY Dear Jesus, thank You for Your Mother. Dear Mother Mary, guide my way to your Son!

Our Father, Hail Mary, and Glory Be.

SAVOR Mary is waiting to help—to mother me!

May 21

This is the month during which Christians, in their churches and their homes, offer the Virgin Mother more fervent and loving acts of homage and veneration; and it is the month in which a greater abundance of God's merciful gifts comes down to us from our Mother's throne.[69]

Saint Paul VI

STEEP What comforting words we read in today's quote! I love what Saint Paul VI said about this special month dedicated to Mary. I'll be honest, I want to be sure that I don't miss out on God's great mercy coming down from Mary's throne! I love the thought of the graces being more abundant this month. But we need to remember to ask for them! As we continue to make our way through this special month, let's be mindful of Mary in our lives.

ACT Don't miss opportunities to raise your heart and mind to Mother Mary, requesting her many graces for yourself and your family.

PRAY Jesus, I love You! Mother of God, thank you for your love!

Our Father, Hail Mary, and Glory Be.

SAVOR Mother Mary awaits my love and prayers.

May 22

I do not promise to make you happy in this world but in the other.[70]

Blessed Mother to Saint Bernadette Soubirous

STEEP Jesus doesn't promise us a "rose garden" in this life. In fact, He said we need to deny ourselves, pick up our cross, and follow Him. His Mother Mary also spoke of the treasures of Heaven as compared to this sometimes-arduous life on earth.

As our grandchildren grow, they will also learn about the difficulties of this life. When this happens, we can use both our faith and our life experiences to teach them to look forward to Heaven as their ultimate goal. Our encouragement and wisdom can help them to persevere on their pilgrimage toward Heaven no matter what this earthly life brings.

ACT No matter how old your grandchildren are, encourage them to talk to Mother Mary at any time and remind them that our earthly journey leads to Heaven.

PRAY Dear Jesus, have mercy on us. Virgin Mary, Star of the Sea, please shine upon us and guide us to Heaven!

Our Father, Hail Mary, and Glory Be.

SAVOR The joys of Heaven are worth the sufferings of this world.

May 23

I fly unto thee, O Virgin of virgins, my Mother.

FROM THE MEMORARE

STEEP Mother Teresa was once given a statue of the Blessed Mother for a chapel at one of her convents. After receiving it at the train station, she boarded the train, carrying the tall statue wrapped in brown paper, and set it on the seat next to her. The conductor asked for a freight charge for the large parcel. The petite nun explained, "Oh no. You see, I have a pass." And she read aloud to him: "Mother Teresa and companion ride for free." Mary was her companion every day. But this day, she was in statue form! The conductor did not argue with her. Who would argue with Mother Teresa?

This story might bring a smile to our faces, but it can also encourage us to consider Mary as our companion. We can take comfort in her presence when we are lonely, and we can ask her to accompany our grandchildren when we are unable to be with them ourselves.

ACT Find a way to honor Mary in your home and try to include your grandchildren.

PRAY Dear Mary, be my constant companion!

Our Father, Hail Mary, and Glory Be.

SAVOR Mary is always with me and leads me to her Son, Jesus.

May 24

Be only all for Jesus through Mary.[71]

SAINT TERESA OF CALCUTTA

STEEP Many of us know, whether from childhood devotions or from learning Catholic teaching, that Mary is an important part of our tradition. Not some obscure character from ages past, Mary is very much alive, loves us dearly, and is always ready to help.

We may hear the misguided objection that Catholics focus too much on Mary. We may hear this even from our own family members, or perhaps our grandchildren will hear it from other people they encounter. However, we can respond that we don't worship Mary: we love and honor her. After all, if it wasn't for that young, faithful Jewish Mary giving her fiat, we wouldn't have Jesus!

ACT Write down at least three ways you can bring Mary into others' lives.

PRAY Father God, thank You for Mary! Dear Mary, Star of the Sea, please guide my way to your Son!

Our Father, Hail Mary, and Glory Be.

SAVOR Mary loves me very much and is always ready to help.

May 25

It was through the Blessed Virgin Mary that Jesus came into the world, and it is also through her that he must reign in the world.[72]

SAINT LOUIS DE MONTFORT

STEEP Saint Louis de Montfort was an eighteenth-century priest on fire with love for and devotion to Mary. His writings and teachings continue to have a remarkable influence on the Catholic Church. Countless folks have used his famous thirty-three-day preparation formula to consecrate themselves to Jesus through Mary.

Saint Louis believed that a true devotion to Mary would robustly establish our devotion to the Lord. He said Jesus is not known enough because His Mother is not known enough, and that God wishes for His Mother to be more known, loved, and honored. As Catholic grandmothers, we can respond to God's wishes and work to make His Mother better known to the people in our lives.

ACT Consider consecrating yourself to Jesus through Mary.

PRAY Father God, thank You for creating Mary. Dear Mary, Star of the Sea, show me the way to your Son!

Our Father, Hail Mary, and Glory Be.

SAVOR Honoring Mary helps me to better honor Jesus.

May 26

Holy Mary, cause of our joy, pray for us.

LITANY OF LORETO

STEEP My friend Linda's four-year-old granddaughter, Ava, had grown very close to her great-grandmother, Theresa. Sadly, Theresa had been diagnosed with ovarian cancer. One day, before Theresa's chemotherapy, Linda and Ava video called her. Ava, eager to give her great-grandmother a loving pep talk, looked at her on the screen. She said, "Be strong and close your eyes." Ava closed her eyes to demonstrate. As her little eyelashes fluttered, Ava said, "And think of Mary and think of things that make you happy—like Ava!"

Our grandchildren's loving words and actions can melt our hearts and possibly even help take the sting from difficulties. Let's encourage them to use their beautiful God-given gifts!

ACT Reach out to encourage someone in need today. Ask Mary to help.

PRAY Dear Blessed Mother Mary, help me to share your happiness with others.

Our Father, Hail Mary, and Glory Be.

SAVOR Opportunities abound to show God's love.

May 27

So great was [Mary's] humility that she desired nothing more upon earth than to remain unknown to herself and to others, and to be known only to God.[73]

SAINT LOUIS DE MONTFORT

STEEP Can we even imagine Mary's great humility? According to Saint Louis de Montfort, the Virgin Mary desired to remain hidden even though she had been given the extraordinary role of the great Mother of God! Venerable Mary of Agreda wrote in *The Mystical City of God* that the Blessed Mother was quick to pick up a dish cloth or a broom while she was visiting her cousin Saint Elizabeth. At the wedding feast at Cana, Jesus' humble Mother turned the wine steward's attention to Jesus: "Do whatever he tells you" (Jn 2:5).

We grandmothers can learn from each of these examples of Mary's humility: turn to Jesus, listen to Him, and willingly do the humble, hidden work of our daily lives.

ACT List ways that you can cultivate the virtue of humility. Put them into practice.

PRAY Dear Blessed Mother, please teach me your ways.

Our Father, Hail Mary, and Glory Be.

SAVOR Though Mary remains humble, she is a powerhouse of grace!

May 28

Do not be afraid, Mary, for you have found favor with God.

Luke 1:30

STEEP When my daughter Jessica was in kindergarten, she was chosen to be the Blessed Mother in a Christmas pageant at her Catholic school. And Baby Jesus was a real live baby! My heart was in my throat, watching intently and praying that Jessica would not drop Baby Jesus. Eventually, I let go of my fears and trusted God. Jessica did just fine!

As grandmothers, we will experience many a time when we worry about our grandchildren, in matters big or small. No matter what the situation or our fears may be, the best thing we can do for our grandchildren is to pray and trust in God. After all, we are not in control of our grandchildren's lives. We should certainly do what we can to help them, but in the end, we must do our best to entrust all to God.

ACT Try to let go of your fears today and wholeheartedly trust God. Ask Mary to help.

PRAY Dear Mother Mary, please help me to trust God as you did.

Our Father, Hail Mary, and Glory Be.

SAVOR I can trust God with my life each and every day.

May 29

Let us pray that each family becomes another Nazareth where prayer, joy, love, and peace come, and if there is peace, joy, love, prayer in the family, there will be holiness.[74]

Saint Teresa of Calcutta

STEEP Mothers and grandmothers have a lot to do with setting the tone in the family. First of all, I am recalling that saying, "If Mama ain't happy, ain't nobody happy!" But beyond that, we women "feather the nest." We can invite Mama Mary into our domestic churches and ask her to help us set the tone. If, as Mother Teresa suggests, we ask her to help us make our family another "Nazareth," then joy, peace, love, and unity will reign.

This might seem almost impossible. Peace? Unity? In a busy family? But I say, "Yes!" We are all works in progress, but seeking heavenly assistance can sanctify our homes.

ACT Invite Mary into your home through images of her, songs, prayers, and spiritual reading.

PRAY Our Lady, please help me set the tone!

Our Father, Hail Mary, and Glory Be.

SAVOR With divine help I can lead my family to Heaven!

May 30

Thus, far from creating distance between her and us, Mary's glorious state brings about a continuous and caring closeness. She knows everything that happens in our life and supports us with maternal love in life's trials.[75]

Saint John Paul II

STEEP Life in the family is filled with busyness and sometimes a bit of chaos too. We can become so involved in checking off our to-do lists and attending to the needs at hand that we might lose sight of Mary's role in our lives. According to Saint John Paul II, Mary lovingly supports us through our trials. She knows all about us. This should give us great comfort and a cause to pause and acknowledge her as our loving mother.

For those grandmothers who live a quieter life, knowing that Mary is lovingly attentive to everything about our lives also gives great comfort and can alleviate any loneliness.

ACT Carve out times throughout your day to pause and remember Mary's loving closeness.

PRAY Jesus, I love You. Mary, please guide me.

Our Father, Hail Mary, and Glory Be.

SAVOR Mary knows everything that happens in my life and supports me with maternal love in my trials.

May 31

In those days Mary set out and went with haste to a Judean town in the hill country, where she entered the house of Zechariah and greeted Elizabeth.

Luke 1:39–40

STEEP Today, we celebrate the feast of the Visitation, in which Mary sets the beautiful example of giving generously. Even though she had just found out she would be the Mother of God, Mary went "in haste" to be of loving service where she was most needed.

One day, I set out to visit my elderly, grieving friend Elizabeth on the first anniversary of her son's death. It happened to be on the feast of the Visitation! I couldn't help but think of Mary visiting her cousin Elizabeth that day. Whatever is going on in our own lives, we Catholic women can imitate Mary by practicing our gift of loving generosity and hospitality to help others who need it.

ACT Sometime soon, deeply ponder the Blessed Mother traveling across hill country while her unborn Jesus resided in His first tabernacle. Imitate Mary by reaching out to someone in need.

PRAY Dear Jesus, please help us. Mother Mary, please teach me to be more generous.

Our Father, Hail Mary, and Glory Be.

SAVOR Mary is a perfect example of generosity.

JUNE

The Sacred Heart

O Sacred Heart of Jesus, living and life-giving fountain of eternal life, infinite treasury of the Divinity, and glowing furnace of love, Thou art my refuge and my sanctuary. O adorable and glorious Savior, consume my heart with that burning fire that ever inflames Thy Heart. Pour down on my soul those graces that flow from Thy love. Let my heart be so united with Thine, that our wills may be one, and mine may in all things be conformed to Thine. May Thy will be the rule of both my desires and my actions.[76]

Saint Gertrude the Great

June 1

And so even now, in a wondrous yet true manner, we can and ought to console that Most Sacred Heart.[77]

Pope Pius XI

STEEP The devotion to the Sacred Heart of Jesus predates but is connected to the devotion to Divine Mercy. This connection can be seen in an image that Jesus revealed to Saint Faustina. Jesus is shown with His left hand opening His garment, exposing rays of blood and water gushing from His Sacred Heart. Jesus' Heart was pierced open on the Cross after He died for our salvation (see Jn 19:31–36). His love and mercy continue for all His children.

Today's quote is from an encyclical in which Pope Pius XI discusses the extraordinary needs of his time. He wrote those words in 1928. So much has happened since then. For many Catholics, devotion to the Sacred Heart in June has become a way to strengthen or witness to our beliefs in the face of secular ideologies that contradict the faith. Jesus' love and mercy from His Sacred Heart help us to lovingly reach out to those who believe in problematic secular messages.

ACT Pray the Litany of the Sacred Heart (page 417).

PRAY Dear Jesus, thank You for Your great love and mercy.
Our Father, Hail Mary, and Glory Be.

SAVOR I will pray and stay close to Jesus' Sacred Heart.

June 2

Truly I tell you, unless you change and become like children, you will never enter the kingdom of heaven.

MATTHEW 18:3

STEEP My friend Linda shared that, other than on holidays, her family had stopped saying grace before meals. One weekend, while her granddaughter Ava was staying at her house, Linda's son and his girlfriend stopped over and ended up staying for dinner. They all sat down together, but before they could eat, Ava announced that they needed to pray. She began to say a prayer, thanking God for their food, but stopped her prayer to tell everyone that they needed to say it "together." Linda said, "We all did, and it took a couple of do-overs for her to think that we all got it right. We all ate together and prayed together . . . thank you, Ava!"

ACT Recall a time your grandchildren have helped you grow in holiness.

PRAY Dear Jesus, please bless every child, born and unborn. *Our Father, Hail Mary, and Glory Be.*

SAVOR Children teach us, just as we teach them!

June 3

The Heart of the Lord Jesus is the starting-point of the holiness of each one of us. From the Heart of the Lord Jesus let us learn the love of God and understanding of the mystery of sin—*mysterium iniquitatis.*[78]

SAINT JOHN PAUL II

STEEP One day I spent time with a sweet four-year-old boy. At one point, I quietly prayed, "Oh, Lord." The precious young man quickly turned to me and asked, "What is that word?" My heart sank. I knew his formerly Catholic parents had not raised him with religion. His curious statement drove that home further.

Let us never tire of praying for children around the world whose parents do not teach them about God—perhaps, sadly, even our own grandchildren. In addition, we should pray for parents and grandparents to learn about God themselves, and then to come back to the faith and teach the children.

ACT Seize every opportunity to be a loving Christian witness. It will never be wasted!

PRAY Dear Jesus, help me to help others.

Our Father, Hail Mary, and Glory Be.

SAVOR I can lovingly introduce others to God.

June 4

We see the hand of God, not only in the wonders of nature, but also in our experience of work and effort. Work thus becomes prayer and thanksgiving.[79]

Saint Josemaría Escrivá

STEEP My friend lamented that she couldn't find much time to spend with God due to family responsibilities and time she spends on Catholic media. She often goes to bed at night disappointed that she didn't have enough quiet time in prayer. I suggested that sometimes, instead of listening to a recording while washing the dishes, she spend that time offering her heart in prayer to our Lord.

Perhaps many of us are busy grandmothers who can relate to this! We are all called at times to reexamine our priorities. We can strive to make prayer a priority by inviting God into the ordinary moments of daily life—amid pots and pans and the stuff that makes up our days!

ACT Lift your heart to God throughout your day.

PRAY Lord Jesus, I wish to meet with You in prayer.

Our Father, Hail Mary, and Glory Be.

SAVOR I will seek the Lord in daily prayer.

June 5

> My eyes have gazed in recollection upon the host and the chalice, where time and space in some way *merge* and the drama of Golgotha is re-presented in a living way.[80]
>
> Saint John Paul II

STEEP My friend Father Luke shared that he was trying to deepen his understanding of what happens during Mass. One day, just before the consecration, he looked down and noticed the image of the crucifix above reflecting in the red wine. The white, round host reminded him of the stone that secured Jesus' tomb, just as he had seen during Masses he had said on Calvary and in Christ's tomb. This reminded Father Luke that the Cross and Resurrection are mystically made present again at every Eucharist.

In all of our lives, we encounter the cross of Christ, which visits us through sickness, hardship, or sadness. We can also experience the resurrection of Christ in receiving our Lord's Body and Blood in the Eucharist, which helps to sustain us and gives us holy fuel for our journey.

ACT If you can, receive the Eucharist today. If not, make a spiritual Communion.

PRAY Jesus, please nourish my soul.
Our Father, Hail Mary, and Glory Be.

SAVOR My Lord Jesus Christ gives to me the unfathomable gift of Himself in the Eucharist. I will let Him know of my gratefulness.

June 6

> Behold this Heart which has so loved men that it has spared nothing, even to exhausting and consuming itself, in order to testify its love.[81]
>
> JESUS TO SAINT MARGARET MARY ALACOQUE

STEEP Saint Margaret Mary Alacoque was born in France and entered the Visitation convent at Paray-le-Monial in 1671. She experienced several mystical revelations about Jesus' Sacred Heart. Jesus allowed her to rest her head upon His Heart. He told her that He chose her for this work and desired to make this devotion known throughout the world and to diffuse the treasures of His goodness.

Today, many Catholics of all ages are drawn to this devotion. We can honor Jesus' Sacred Heart by making frequent Communion when possible, including Communion on the first Friday of each month, and by observing Holy Hours. Finally, we should be sure to share the love of Jesus' Heart with our beloved grandchildren in any way possible!

ACT Learn more about the Sacred Heart devotion, or teach your grandchildren about it.

PRAY Jesus, please help me to know Your love for me and to come closer to Your Sacred Heart.

Our Father, Hail Mary, and Glory Be.

SAVOR Jesus has spared nothing to show His love for me.

June 7

To a great extent the world is what we make it. We get back what we give. If we sow hate, we reap hate; if we scatter love and gentleness, we harvest love and happiness.[82]

VENERABLE FULTON SHEEN

STEEP Today's simple, poignant quote is an excellent rule for life—a golden rule that we can share with our family and others. We must teach the young ones with words and examples. When they are older and out of the nest, our lessons are mostly imparted by how we live our lives.

Yet many times, even after we have sown the seeds of faith, the kids wander from the Church, or what seems worse, they break away completely. Though this is discouraging, parents and grandparents can't give up. Instead, we can put our energies into continuing to sow love and gentleness, trusting that our efforts will bear fruit in God's perfect timing.

ACT List three ways you can be a loving example of the Catholic faith to your family.

PRAY Jesus, help me to sow love and gentleness.

Our Father, Hail Mary, and Glory Be.

SAVOR I am continually gifted with opportunities to sow and harvest love and kindness.

June 8

> Here is the most magnificent, the most profound gift of the Heart of Jesus that we find in creation: man born of God, man adopted as a son in the Eternal Son, humanity given the power to become children of God.[83]
>
> Saint John Paul II

STEEP Tragedy and love made a family. Sylvia's daughter and her husband decided to take in a three-year-old boy, Mason, after his mother was killed in a car accident. "I was happy, scared, nervous, and excited to have a grandson," Sylvia shared. "My daughter said it would be temporary. I knew in my heart that it was going to be forever."

The day arrived for Sylvia to meet her new grandson. "Standing in front of me was a gorgeous, blue-eyed baby boy. When he first hugged me, I felt the bond between us that I knew could never be broken. Every day, I thank the Lord for bringing him into our lives."

Whatever circumstances may have led to us becoming grandmothers, we can all thank God for the families He has given us!

ACT Take time to pray for every family, especially adoptive and foster families.

PRAY Dear Holy Family, guide my family.

Our Father, Hail Mary, and Glory Be.

SAVOR Love grows in families!

June 9

Now faith is the assurance of things hoped for, the conviction of things not seen.

HEBREWS 11:1

STEEP My friend Jane shared, "One of my fondest memories of my dear grandmother Frances was of her kneeling down at the side of the bed to pray her prayers in Polish." Jane felt deeply impacted by her grandmother's loving faith, and it surely stirred the embers of faith in her own heart. She said, "She taught me so much by her witness of love and humility."

As grandmothers, we hope that our grandchildren will say the same about us someday! The gift of faith is such an integral part of a Catholic's life. We can pray that God will increase the virtue of faith that we were given at our Baptism so that we may help increase it in others.

ACT Find at least one way to help someone grow closer to God today.

PRAY Jesus, please increase my faith and help me help others grow closer to You.

Our Father, Hail Mary, and Glory Be.

SAVOR Jesus provides every comfort, help, and refuge.

June 10

> This feast [of the Sacred Heart] is a day of salvation and eternal blessings for all those who honor it with a sincere and humble heart. So let us love this divine Heart, and try to conform ours to It in everything.[84]
>
> SAINT MARGARET MARY ALACOQUE

STEEP Heavenly blessings abound! Saint Margaret Mary Alacoque reassures us so in her words above. Are we attentive to these blessings? Do we seek them even in times of difficulty? Do we trust that God is blessing us even when we don't feel blessed? Are we sure to thank God for the many amazing blessings He bestows upon us even in the course of one day?

As I just typed those words, something caught my eye through the slider kitchen door. A huge owl flew right by! God knows that I love birds. God's blessings are manifest in many ways.

ACT Try to notice all the blessings God gives you today. Write down as many as you can.

PRAY Jesus, thank You for Your many blessings. Help me to be more attentive to them, on good days and bad.

Our Father, Hail Mary, and Glory Be.

SAVOR God continuously blesses me!

June 11

Praise to the divine heart that wrought our salvation; to it be glory and honor forever. Amen.[85]

Pope Leo XIII

STEEP I once spoke with a very talented artist who felt discouraged because her religious art, as beautiful as it was, had not been received well in the past. She was venturing out to begin a new project but felt very weighed down with doubt. I tried to encourage her to not worry about the past but to live in the present moment instead.

It is sometimes difficult to shake off our cares and concerns, especially when negativity from our past is weighing us down. Yet, with Jesus, we can boldly move forward. We must surrender everything to Him and pray for a joyful new beginning. God will certainly supply the graces we need to move forward with courage and trust in Him.

ACT Consider whether you are holding on to anything from your past. Give this to God in prayer and resolve to move forward.

PRAY Dear Jesus, I need You! I trust in You!

Our Father, Hail Mary, and Glory Be.

SAVOR I can give all of my cares and concerns to Jesus.

June 12

It is altogether impossible to enumerate the heavenly gifts which devotion to the Sacred Heart of Jesus has poured out on the souls of the faithful, purifying them, offering them heavenly strength, rousing them to the attainment of all virtues.[86]

Pope Pius XII

STEEP Many years ago, I found an old, framed black-and-white image of the Most Sacred Heart of Jesus—in a thrift shop, of all places! I instantly knew that I had to buy it and bring it home. It has graced the wall of my living room in every apartment and house I have lived in since. I can't tell you the number of hours or even quick moments I've stood or knelt before it, speaking to our Lord—many times moved to tears over consolations when gazing into Jesus' eyes and listening to Jesus' loving whispers.

Sacred images lift our hearts to heavenly realities. Parents or grandparents can make these beautiful holy images available for their families.

ACT Spend time today praying before an image of the Sacred Heart.

PRAY Dear Jesus, please draw me closer to Your heart.

Our Father, Hail Mary, and Glory Be.

SAVOR Meditation before the Sacred Heart image will bring peace to my soul.

June 13

> [Saint Anthony] is one of the most popular saints in the whole Catholic Church, venerated not only in Padua . . . but also throughout the world. Dear to the faithful are the images and statues that portray him with the lily a symbol of his purity or with the Child Jesus in his arms.[87]
>
> Pope Benedict XVI

STEEP When Suzanne was seven years old, her grandparents brought her a gift from the Vatican: a special rosary in a silver case. "I think it was the most precious and beautiful thing I had ever owned," she said. "So, of course, I took it to school to show my friends"—and she lost it!

Devastated, she confessed to her grandmother, who calmly told her not to worry, but to ask Saint Anthony to find it. "What struck me at the time was she was not angry with me," Suzanne recalled.

Suzanne found her treasured rosary and still has it today. She ended up taking Anthony for her Confirmation name because they became great friends, thanks to her grandmother's calm and wise example of trust in the saints.

ACT Consider gifting your grandchildren a blessed religious item.

PRAY Jesus, thank You for Your love. Saint Anthony of Padua, please pray for us.

Our Father, Hail Mary, and Glory Be.

SAVOR I can be a vibrant example of God's love to my grandchildren.

June 14

Since there is in the Sacred Heart a symbol and a sensible image of the infinite love of Jesus Christ . . . therefore is it fit and proper that we should consecrate ourselves to His most Sacred Heart.[88]

Pope Leo XIII

STEEP As a single mother, I received temporary financial assistance. One day, a woman arrived to search my humble apartment for evidence of a man living there. If so, my benefits would cease. I was very uncomfortable with the stranger in my home. However, something came over me. I pointed to the Sacred Heart image on my wall. I declared, "That's the Man I am living with!" Truth be told, when we consecrate ourselves to the Sacred Heart, we are "living with" Jesus every day in a deeper way, even more closely than we live with our families.

As we are making our way through the month of June, we might consider making an act of consecration to the Sacred Heart of Jesus as Pope Leo XIII suggests above.

ACT Pray the Act of Consecration by Pope Leo XIII (page 413). Ponder the words.

PRAY Dear Jesus, please take my consecration to Your Sacred Heart.

Our Father, Hail Mary, and Glory Be.

SAVOR Jesus' love for everyone is like a grandmother's love for grandchildren, but even stronger.

June 15

I need a heart burning with tenderness
Who will be my support forever,
Who loves everything in me, even my weakness . . .
And who never leaves me day or night.[89]

Saint Thérèse of Lisieux

STEEP As a young girl and later as a nun, Saint Thérèse knew Who her true friend was and Whom she could count on at any time of day or night. She was absolutely sure that Jesus' Sacred Heart burned with tenderness. He loved and supported her as He does for each of us, no matter our weaknesses and failings.

Jesus beckons to us to love Him back and consider Him our true friend. Just as we want close relationships with our families and want our grandchildren to know they can count on us day or night, God wants us to have the same kind of closeness with Him.

ACT Write a poem to Jesus, your true Friend.

PRAY Jesus, help me be a friend to You.

Our Father, Hail Mary, and Glory Be.

SAVOR Jesus is my true Friend.

June 16

Whoever becomes humble like this child is the greatest in the kingdom of heaven. Whoever welcomes one such child in my name welcomes me.

Matthew 18:4–5

STEEP One day, my first-grade faith formation student brought a huge smile to my face and pierced my heart with his precious innocence and love. We were discussing prayer, and little Anthony shot up his hand like a rocket, eager to share.

He lovingly clasped his hands in prayer and said, "When I pray, I just say, 'God! I love You SO much!'" His facial expression and body language brimmed with joy. We can surely learn from Anthony! Our verses today can be considered a gentle and loving message from Jesus. After all, we are called to be humble, trusting, and childlike in prayerful surrender to our Lord. And we know that God is love and loves us very much.

ACT Imagine yourself as a little girl and with arms outstretched to Jesus, show Him that you love Him very much. Draw closer to Him in full surrender.

PRAY Jesus, help me to get to know You more deeply. Thank You for being my true Friend.

Our Father, Hail Mary, and Glory Be.

SAVOR Jesus is my gentle Friend.

June 17

You heard me, only Friend whom I love.
To ravish my heart, you became man.
You shed your blood, what a supreme mystery! . . .
And you still live for me on the Altar.
If I cannot see the brilliance of your Face
Or hear your sweet voice,
O my God, I can live by your Grace,
I can rest on your Sacred Heart![90]

SAINT THÉRÈSE OF LISIEUX

STEEP Saint Thérèse loved our Lord with a tender, yet intense, pure love. In today's quote, she tells Him that no matter what—even if she fails to see Him or hear Him, perhaps when going through dark times—she can and will rest against His Sacred Heart.

If even great saints went through dark times, it's inevitable that we will as well. When those times come, whatever is happening in our spiritual lives, our families, or the world around us, we can take comfort in knowing that Jesus is there in the darkness, waiting to be our refuge.

ACT Lay your head on Jesus' Heart in prayer.

PRAY Jesus, I love You. Thank You for Your love.

Our Father, Hail Mary, and Glory Be.

SAVOR Jesus' Sacred Heart is my refuge.

June 18

Tell aching mankind to snuggle close to My merciful Heart, and I will fill it with peace.

JESUS TO SAINT FAUSTINA, *DIARY*, 1074

STEEP How we love to be comforted by a trusted friend or loved one, especially when we have heavy hearts. Life can be difficult and many things can tug at our hearts. As women, we are naturally very concerned for others, especially for the welfare of our own families. Because of this, we can suffer in empathy when we see our loved ones suffering, or when we see the pains of "aching mankind." At these times, we can pray and offer penance, asking God to help us.

Jesus told Saint Faustina to make known that all should draw near to His merciful Heart—He knows we ache, and He used the words "snuggle close." That should be tender music to our ears. Jesus wants us to become vulnerable and lay our head against His Sacred Heart—to trust Him with our lives and the lives of our family members.

ACT Take comfort in Jesus by bringing a situation or a suffering loved one close to His Heart today.

PRAY Dear Jesus, please comfort my loved ones and me.

Our Father, Hail Mary, and Glory Be.

SAVOR I can snuggle close to Jesus' Heart.

June 19

He who did not withhold his own Son, but gave him up for all of us, will he not with him also give us everything else?

ROMANS 8:32

STEEP Jessie's late grandmother once told her, "What is yours will be yours, Jessie." What Jessie couldn't understand then, she realized later in life.

When reflecting on a past heartbreak, Jessie said, "Later, in His time, God gave me graces and gifts beyond anything I'd ever imagined. He gave me my husband and children. He knew me before I was born; He knew the plans He had for me. Now I understand: 'What *is* yours *will be* yours!'"

When reflecting on the death of her youngest child, Jessie continued, "I gave back that which was given to me." Her loving grandmother, too, knew the same loss. Jessie shared that she can say to her grandmother, "I look up to Heaven where you are with your daughter and mine, and together we can say, '*What is Yours, Dear Lord, will be Yours.*'"

ACT Make a list of the blessings throughout your life. Share that list with God in gratitude.

PRAY Jesus, help me to grow in understanding.

Our Father, Hail Mary, and Glory Be.

SAVOR Jesus knows my heart and what I need for salvation.

June 20

Since the Heart of Jesus appears to us as the sensible sign of His love, the visible wound in the Heart will naturally recall the invisible wound of this love.[91]

JEAN BAINVEL

STEEP Connected to the Sacred Heart devotion is the mystery of the blood and water that flowed from Jesus' pierced Heart on Calvary. This image is the central aspect of the devotion to The Divine Mercy. From this image comes a powerful prayer: "O Blood and Water which gushed forth from the Heart of Jesus as a fount of mercy for us, I trust in You" (see *Diary* 84, 187, 309). Jesus promised the grace of conversion when we pray this prayer for sinners with a contrite heart. I love to pray this prayer for many folks I know every evening before falling asleep.

ACT Pray for the conversion of sinners using the powerful prayer above. Try to do so during specific times of the day of your choosing.

PRAY Jesus, please have mercy on me and on the whole world.
Our Father, Hail Mary, and Glory Be.

SAVOR Jesus is full of love and mercy!

June 21

Only love, revealed by the Heart of Christ, can transform the human heart and open it to the whole world, making the world more human and more divine.[92]

SAINT JOHN PAUL II

STEEP My elderly neighbor Cynthia claimed to be an atheist and wanted nothing to do with God. In fact, when we first met, she said, "Don't preach at me." She didn't want me to be like her "fire and brimstone" Christian friends who thought they were helping her turn to God before it was too late.

I reassured Cynthia that I would not preach. I brought homemade chicken soup and goodies to her, doing my best to cheer her up, as she was often depressed. One day, out of the blue, she took my hands into hers, looked into my eyes, and said, "Please don't ever stop praying for me." My heart was pierced through.

Grandmothers often have a special gift for sharing God's authentic love through what I call "chicken soup evangelization!"

ACT Ponder whom God wants you to serve today.

PRAY Dear Jesus, send me forth.

Our Father, Hail Mary, and Glory Be.

SAVOR Authentic love comes from God.

June 22

For this child I prayed; and the LORD has granted me the petition that I made to him. Therefore I have lent him to the LORD; as long as he lives, he is given to the LORD.

1 SAMUEL 1:27–28

STEEP In the early 1950s, Jane's Aunt Doris was having trouble conceiving. Doris' mother, Frances (Jane's grandmother), made a pilgrimage to the Shrine of Saint Anne de Beaupré in Canada, where she climbed the steps on her knees, asking Saint Anne to pray that Doris may conceive a child. She even asked God to let her own severe migraines get worse if they had to, as long as her daughter could have a child.

Six months later, Doris was on a cruise and felt seasick. When she returned home, she found out that she was pregnant. Doris now has five grown children. Jane said, "The real miracle is that my grandmother never experienced a migraine again!"

When we grandmothers pray for our families, God certainly hears our petitions for them, but He also makes sure to take care of our own needs!

ACT Ask God to grant the petitions closest to your heart.

PRAY Jesus, please grant me the graces I ask for.

Our Father, Hail Mary, and Glory Be.

SAVOR Faith moves mountains!

June 23

Elderly people help us to see human affairs with greater wisdom, because life's vicissitudes have brought them knowledge and maturity.[93]

SAINT JOHN PAUL II

STEEP Jessica bundled up her five small children and took them to surprise Grandma in the nursing home. When they arrived, Grandma was quietly sitting in her room, dressed nicely and listening to polka music that reminded her of Grandpa.

Grandma turned and beamed with surprise when she heard the children in her doorway, but she also seemed like she had been expecting them. Grandma explained, "When Auntie Mary wasn't coming today, I prayed God would send someone, and here you are—ask and you shall receive!"

All throughout the visit, Grandma smiled while tears twinkled in her eyes. Later, in the dining room, the children gave her goodbye kisses. The ladies nearby said, "How many kisses you get, Millie; how lucky you are!"

"The look of happiness and love on Grandma's face," Jessica said, "told me we were the lucky ones."

ACT If you can, surprise someone with a loving visit today or soon.

PRAY Jesus, please let me be Your love to others and please comfort the lonely.

Our Father, Hail Mary, and Glory Be.

SAVOR A loving family is the most exquisite gift.

June 24

If life is a pilgrimage towards our heavenly home, then old age is the most natural time to look towards the threshold of eternity.[94]

SAINT JOHN PAUL II

STEEP My elderly friend Josephine became bitter and depressed in her later years. After her husband passed away, she lived alone and her adult children eventually stopped visiting.

"I don't understand it," she lamented to me. "Sundays are supposed to be a day for family, and my family doesn't visit me." There was nothing I could do to change her adult children, but I visited Josephine whenever I could to keep her company and try to cheer her up.

Truth be told, God is always present to us, as is our guardian angel, and we are connected in a real way to the Communion of Saints. So, even if we can't see or hear these heavenly friends, we always have someone with us.

ACT If possible, carry out a work of mercy with your grandchildren to teach them about bringing comfort to the lonely.

PRAY Jesus, thank You for the gift of my faith, which motivates me to love others.

Our Father, Hail Mary, and Glory Be.

SAVOR Jesus' love for me sends me forth to impart His love to others.

June 25

To be a Christian is to be merciful.[95]

SERVANT OF GOD FATHER JOHN HARDON

STEEP We learn compassion, love, and mercy through the Heart of Jesus. We will never fully understand the depths of God's mercy until we reach Heaven. Still, we are distinctly called to turn to God's mercy, to help others to do so, and to be a vessel of mercy to others. This can happen in our families and with complete strangers.

I'll never forget rushing through an airport and seeing a distressed young mother on the floor, yelling at her young children. I couldn't just pass by. I offered assistance and eventually, a blessed Miraculous Medal and a hug. God's mercy pushes us forth!

To be a Christian is to be merciful because our goal is to be like Christ. When we show mercy, both to our loved ones and to strangers, we show our grandchildren what Christ is like.

ACT Pay attention to others' needs around you.

PRAY Jesus, help me to be merciful like You.

Our Father, Hail Mary, and Glory Be.

SAVOR "To be a Christian is to be merciful."

June 26

We should never again use the expression, "When Jesus was on earth" or think of Him as being only in heaven, Jesus is still on earth . . . While all the sacraments confer grace, the Eucharist contains the author of grace, Jesus Christ Himself.[96]

Servant of God Father John Hardon

STEEP The late Cardinal Nguyen Van Thuan was a prisoner of war in Communist prisons in Vietnam for thirteen years, nine of them in solitary confinement. He used the palm of his hand to contain three drops of wine sent to him for medicinal purposes, plus a drop of water, to secretly celebrate the Eucharist in his prison cell. He said, "This was my altar, and this was my cathedral! It was true medicine for soul and body."[97]

Most likely, we grandmothers will not experience grueling darkness like Cardinal Van Thuan. But when we experience other kinds of "darkness," such as illness or isolation, Jesus' Presence is our true medicine.

ACT Thank God for the blessing of freedom and the gift of the Eucharist.

PRAY Jesus, thank You for being with me always.

Our Father, Hail Mary, and Glory Be.

SAVOR "The Eucharist contains the author of grace, Jesus Christ Himself."

June 27

Mary has so great a desire to be invoked by us, that she may dispense her favors to us in greater abundance.[98]

Saint Bonaventure

STEEP Many saints preached and wrote extensively about how the Blessed Mother is our perpetual help. During a complicated pregnancy in which the doctor believed I was losing my baby, a serious heart condition and a large hemorrhage in my uterus placed me on complete bed rest. Mother Teresa told me not to be afraid and promised her prayers. She encouraged me, "Just put yourself in the hands of our Blessed Mother and let her take care of you. When you are afraid or sad or troubled just tell her so. She will prove herself a Mother to you. Pray often: 'Mary, Mother of Jesus, make me alright'; 'Mary, Mother of Jesus, be Mother to me now.'"[99]

Mother Teresa's advice has continued to aid and inspire me throughout my life since that precarious pregnancy. May we perpetually seek and invoke Mary's aid, in big things and little ones too.

ACT It's a perfect day to pray the Memorare.

PRAY Pray the Memorare (page 412).

Our Father, Hail Mary, and Glory Be.

SAVOR Our Mother in Heaven is perpetually helping us.

June 28

The price of reaching heaven is the practice of selfless love here on earth. That is why God puts into our lives so many occasions for loving people who obviously do not love us, or giving ourselves to people who have never given themselves to us.[100]

SERVANT OF GOD FATHER JOHN HARDON

STEEP How hard it is to seek the "high road" when dealing with people who are not nice to us, or even worse, who are downright cruel. It's especially difficult when this happens in the family.

I know a woman, Susie, whose mother-in-law is self-centered. Though she lives nearby, she chooses to not help Susie with her many young children. Despite this strained relationship, Susie strives to love her mother-in-law and understand her aloofness and failure to have a grandmotherly relationship with the children.

We all encounter the seemingly unlovable in our lives. The most important thing is that we pray and lovingly practice selfless love.

ACT Do something kind for a difficult person in your life.

PRAY Jesus, please help me remember Your great suffering for love of us.

Our Father, Hail Mary, and Glory Be.

SAVOR I will strive to love the unlovable.

June 29

Charm is deceitful, and beauty is vain,
but a woman who fears the Lord is to be praised.

PROVERBS 31:30

STEEP When my daughter Jessica was just five years old, her classmates at her Catholic school nominated her to be the class president. "Campaign" posters were created to announce her "run for office." As election day approached, I smiled upon seeing them displayed in the school hallways. One precious poster declared, "She cares, she's honest, she's trustworthy, and she loves Jesus!"

Could the same be said about us? Let us strive to have the simple faith and virtues of a child!

ACT Write a list of each of your grandchildren's best qualities. Praise them for them and encourage them to be virtuous.

PRAY Jesus, help me to spread Your love and do Your holy will. Mother Mary, please show me the way to your Son.

Our Father, Hail Mary, and Glory Be.

SAVOR I can be caring, honest, and trustworthy, and love Jesus.

June 30

Keep these words that I am commanding you today in your heart. . . . Write them on the doorposts of your house and on your gates.

Deuteronomy 6:6, 9

STEEP My friend Jessie went through a time of anguish in college. When asked for advice, her grandmother hurriedly wrote to her, "Say the Rosary! Say, 'Dear Lord, I have so many problems I cannot handle. Please take over. Let the greatness of God take over. I let go and let God. I am never alone. God is with me always.' Think positive!"

Three decades later, Jessie held the well-worn piece of scrap paper and lovingly unfolded it "for the millionth time to see [Grandma's] quick penmanship, knowing her eagerness to share these faith-filled words with me because she knew how they could transform a life."

We certainly hope for our own grandchildren to turn to us for advice throughout their lives. When they do, let us be quick to respond with holy wisdom, guidance, and love.

ACT Write down the advice you most want to give your grandchildren and save it.

PRAY Dear Lord, help me let go and let You take over.

Our Father, Hail Mary, and Glory Be.

SAVOR God is with me always.

JULY

The Precious Blood of Jesus

Let us fix our gaze on the blood of Christ and realize how precious it is to His Father, seeing that it was poured out for our salvation and brought the grace of conversion to the whole world.[101]

SAINT CLEMENT I

July 1

> This veneration of the Precious Blood . . . means that we have a deep sensitivity to the awfulness of sin. Sin . . . must be the most dreadful thing in the universe. Why? Because it cost the living God in human form the shedding of His Blood.[102]
>
> SERVANT OF GOD FATHER JOHN HARDON

STEEP Jesus shed His Precious Blood on the Cross because of our sins but also because of His great love for us. He desires that we enjoy eternal happiness with Him in Heaven. Because of this, it's wise to examine our consciences daily, ask God for forgiveness, and get to the sacrament of Confession regularly.

This month, let us be extra mindful of any bad habits in our life that can get out of control if not nipped in the bud. As grandmothers, we can instill good habits within our hearts, as well as in our grandchildren—teaching them the importance of working to be good with God's grace and of asking forgiveness for our sins.

ACT Schedule a time for Confession and do your best to get there.

PRAY Dear Jesus, I am sorry for the suffering You went through to save my soul. Please help me avoid sin.

Our Father, Hail Mary, and Glory Be.

SAVOR Sin is deadly, and Jesus' mercy is lifesaving!

July 2

In him we have redemption through his blood, the forgiveness of our trespasses, according to the riches of his grace.

Ephesians 1:7

STEEP Oftentimes, we may get caught up in our busy lives, keeping up with our grandchildren and loved ones, accumulating things we think we need, or seeking worldly pleasure—so much so that we might neglect to pray as we should. This can also happen during summer months when we might have a change of scenery on a vacation. We can fall into the trap of thinking we are self-sufficient. Sadly, we can end up forgetting about God.

Today's verse reminds us that we have been redeemed by the Blood of Jesus, that He forgives us—that He is merciful. Let us never fear turning to Him to get back into His graces. He is God, and we are dependent on Him! Even our busyness can be an opportunity to rely on His help.

ACT Take time today to intentionally remember God.

PRAY Dear Jesus, please take the reins. I want to follow Your holy will.

Our Father, Hail Mary, and Glory Be.

SAVOR I have been redeemed by Jesus' Precious Blood.

July 3

Devotion to the Precious Blood means . . . that we invoke Christ under the attribute of His Precious Blood . . . I honestly doubt if very many out of a thousand would know . . . the Litany of the Precious Blood.[103]

SERVANT OF GOD FATHER JOHN HARDON

STEEP It may seem daunting or even disconcerting to venerate or become devoted to blood. However, in the Precious Blood devotion, we are really stating that we love Jesus because of His sacrificial and merciful love for us, in which He went so far as to allow His own Precious Blood to be shed for our salvation.

We learn in today's quote that among the many litanies our Church has to offer, a Litany to the Precious Blood exists. In addition to praying this Litany, you can find opportunities to talk with your grandchildren about Jesus' great love and mercy for all of us to help them understand this devotion.

ACT Pray the Litany of the Precious Blood (page 415), pondering God's great love for you.

PRAY Dear Jesus, I don't appreciate You as I should. Please open my eyes and heart to Your merciful love.

Our Father, Hail Mary, and Glory Be.

SAVOR Jesus' love for me is far beyond my comprehension.

July 4

But if we walk in the light as he himself is in the light, we have fellowship with one another, and the blood of Jesus his Son cleanses us from all sin.

1 John 1:7

STEEP We can get stuck in the dark corners of life. Sometimes, the evil one allures us there by tricking us into believing it's a good place to be by making sin appear attractive. At times, we endure a dark night in the spiritual life. The evil one weighs us down with discouragement, fear, hopelessness, defeat, and eventually despair. We might be confused about a direction to take.

Today's verse encourages us to choose the light—which is God—and also to have fellowship with one another in the light. As Catholic women, we can surround ourselves with like-minded and faith-filled friends. Good friends, such as other grandmothers who can relate, can help one another strive for holiness, rescue each other from the tricks of the evil one, and guide each other out of life's dark corners.

ACT Today, or soon, seek fellowship with other Christians, including other grandmothers or those who may be lonely.

PRAY Dear Jesus, Mary, and Joseph, show me the way.

Our Father, Hail Mary, and Glory Be.

SAVOR I must consciously seek Christ's light.

July 5

No sinner, having recourse to the compassion of Mary, should fear being rejected; for she is the Mother of Mercy, and as such desires to save the most miserable.[104]

Saint Alphonsus de Liguori

STEEP Mother Mary is certainly connected to Jesus' Precious Blood. After all, she stood at the foot of the Cross as her Son Jesus shed His Blood. Jesus gifted us with His own Mother that day. Mary loves all her children and never wants any of us to go astray by choosing evil over truth and goodness. Just as Jesus shed His Blood for us out of mercy, Mary is full of mercy. Countless saints have had recourse to the great Mother of Mercy and have earnestly sung her praises, including Saint Alphonsus de Liguori, who tells us never to fear being rejected by her. We are comforted knowing that Mary is the Mother of Mercy for our families as well and wants them to be saved too.

ACT Carve out time to visit with Mary. Pray an extra decade of the Rosary for sinners.

PRAY Jesus, thank You for the gift of Your Mother!

Our Father, Hail Mary, and Glory Be.

SAVOR I can be a handmaid of Mary by praying for her children, starting with my grandchildren.

July 6

This cup that is poured out for you is the new covenant in my blood.

LUKE 22:20

STEEP At every Holy Mass, Heaven literally touches Earth. We are mystically connected to the Last Supper when Jesus instituted the Eucharist. Jesus Christ is present with us at Holy Mass! He is present in the priest who offers Mass and present in His Word at Mass. He is also present with the congregation because as we learn in Scripture, "For where two or three are gathered in my name, I am there among them" (Mt 18:20). He is present in His Body and Blood.

If we attend Mass with our families, we might be distracted at times with our children and grandchildren and have trouble focusing. But we can be reassured by remembering that even with noisy or rambunctious children in tow, Heaven touches Earth and Jesus is present at Mass, where we are transformed by His presence, love, and mercy.

ACT Endeavor to participate more fully and reverently at each Holy Mass and to encourage your grandchildren to do the same. Ask holy Mary to help you.

PRAY Dear Jesus, thank You for Your love for me!

Our Father, Hail Mary, and Glory Be.

SAVOR Jesus is present to me at Mass and in Holy Communion.

July 7

It is through the sacrament of Penance that the baptized can be reconciled with God and with the Church.

Catechism of the Catholic Church, 980

STEEP I witnessed God work a miracle in someone's heart during a retreat. That weekend, I presented five talks to a large group on the vocation of Catholic womanhood. A woman later came up to me and shared that because of my talks, she felt prodded to Confession that very day, after twenty years away! I felt incredibly grateful to God for moving that woman's heart to confess in that transforming sacrament and receive God's powerful graces.

We might not all have the experience of giving a retreat talk that changes someone's heart. Yet when we allow our own hearts to be formed by God, we can be sure that He will work through us to move others—whether our own grandchildren or complete strangers.

ACT Be vulnerable before Jesus. He's always waiting to hear our confessions. And be a bright light to others—moving hearts toward Him!

PRAY Dear Jesus, please make my heart more like Yours.

Our Father, Hail Mary, and Glory Be.

SAVOR Jesus loves a repentant heart.

July 8

Every drop of Christ's Blood in the Agony in the Garden, every drop He shed on Calvary, every drop was united hypostatically[105] with the Second Person of the Trinity. Every drop of that Blood was adorable.[106]

SERVANT OF GOD FATHER JOHN HARDON

STEEP Perhaps we would rather not focus on the horrors of Jesus' shedding of His Precious Blood. When sharing the faith with our grandchildren, we might be tempted to focus more on the pleasant or "easy" parts than on things like the Passion. However, today's quote reminds us that we should remember what Jesus suffered for us, and that He will be pleased with our prayers. Jesus told Saint Faustina that meditating on His Passion is a sure way to advance in virtue and holiness (see *Diary* of Saint Faustina, 1512 and 369). Surely, we want to share that opportunity with our grandchildren as well!

ACT Meditate on Jesus' Passion and have a conversation with your grandchildren about it, even if it is challenging.

PRAY My Lord, I am sorrowful that my sins caused You to shed Your Precious Blood.

Our Father, Hail Mary, and Glory Be.

SAVOR Jesus' merciful love for me is unfathomable!

July 9

By the tender mercy of our God,
the dawn from on high will break upon us,
to give light to those who sit in darkness and in the shadow of death.

Luke 1:78–79

STEEP "Good morning, Princess Momma." My friend Jessica opened her eyes to see her small daughter "smiling at me like an angel from Heaven." Alaina's blue eyes twinkled. The sun streamed in, glistening her blonde curls like a halo around her pretty face. Jessica said, "My breath stopped at the picture of sunlit loveliness and innocence God awakened me with."

Moments later, in the kitchen, Jessica felt perplexed. How could it be so dismal outside when the sun had just been shining so brightly? Her husband commented, "It's been overcast all morning. The sun never came out." Jessica looked at Alaina, scooped her up, kissed her, and said, "Then it must have been you!"

We are truly blessed to have grandchildren and others in our lives who brighten our days—sometimes even literally, as in Jessica's case! Even when things seem overcast or gloomy, we can be grateful for memories of moments when brightness shone through.

ACT Thank someone who has brought brightness into your life.

PRAY Dear Jesus, thank You for loving me.

Our Father, Hail Mary, and Glory Be.

SAVOR Blessings abound!

July 10

Train children in the right way,
and when old, they will not stray.

Proverbs 22:6

STEEP One of Christy's earliest memories is of visiting her grandparents at lunchtime. Daily, her grandfather, Joseph, went home to eat with his wife, Marian. After lunch, the family and anyone visiting knelt together and prayed the Rosary.

Christy's grandmother's buffet was not filled with china but with glass jars of various types of beautiful beads, crucifixes, and all sorts of fittings for making rosaries in the evenings. The grandchildren were allowed to pick beads, centerpieces, and crosses for their "special rosaries" when they received their sacraments. Marian sent the other rosaries she made to missions and monasteries.

Marian continued these traditions for over fifteen years after Joseph passed away. The rosary project then moved to Christy's father, who passed it on to Christy. She taught the skill to her children, who can now continue the family tradition her grandparents began.

ACT Start a new family tradition or help to carry out an existing one.

PRAY Dear Jesus, Mary, and Joseph, please guide my family. *Our Father, Hail Mary, and Glory Be.*

SAVOR I can help nourish rich traditions in my family.

July 11

And forgive us our debts,
as we also have forgiven our debtors.

Matthew 6:12

STEEP Forgiveness might be a hard pill to swallow. We might still be feeling the sting of rejection or pain from an injustice or abuse. This can be especially painful when the person who hurt us is a family member—perhaps even one of our beloved grandchildren.

The one who has offended us might never admit the wrongdoing nor ask to be forgiven. Why forgive someone who hasn't asked for forgiveness? Well, we are called to do so by God Who forgave us first. We need to rise above the injustice with God's grace and offer forgiveness, whether directly to that person or simply in our prayers.

Forgiving the one who has hurt us does not mean we will automatically trust him or her again. Yet, forgiveness will unlock the chains of grudge and pain wrapped around our hearts.

ACT Resolve to forgive someone today, whether directly or in prayer.

PRAY Dear Jesus, help me to forgive like You.

Our Father, Hail Mary, and Glory Be.

SAVOR Forgiving others frees us from emotional and spiritual pain.

July 12

Keep watch over yourselves and over all the flock, of which the Holy Spirit has made you overseers, to shepherd the church of God that he obtained with the blood of his own Son.

Acts 20:28

STEEP I once read an article about a woman whose husband was stranded in a collapsed coal mine. Due to his occupation, her husband used to leave trails of dirt and dust behind him. Prior to the accident, the wife felt a bit annoyed by the dirt. Afterward, she said she would give anything to see the dirt on the bottom of her bathtub again.

Many times we get annoyed by family members' messes or mistakes. Our life on this planet is short and all the more reason to strive to be patient with our loved ones, and most especially to be thankful to God that they are in our lives.

ACT Make a point to compliment your family members. Look for the good in each one of your flock and praise them for it.

PRAY Dear Jesus, help me to understand Your great love for mankind. Help me be more loving.

Our Father, Hail Mary, and Glory Be.

SAVOR Time spent with loved ones is a precious gift!

July 13

We are to study to come to a deeper understanding of what those two words . . . Precious Blood, really mean.[107]

SERVANT OF GOD FATHER JOHN HARDON

STEEP Once when the chalice was elevated in the consecration at Mass, I let out a silent gasp. I think in that moment, I was in holy awe of Jesus, present in His Precious Blood.

Today's quote recommends striving for a deeper understanding of Jesus' Precious Blood. We can do this at the feet of Jesus during visits to the Blessed Sacrament. When we are unable to get to the church, we can adore Jesus from wherever we are and ask Him to teach us.

Learning about Eucharistic miracles can help us too. Several Eucharistic miracles[108] throughout the centuries have been analyzed by different scientists, and they've all found that all the samples have the same blood type! How blessed we and our family members are that Jesus is truly present to us!

ACT Meditate on Jesus' Precious Blood by studying or learning more from trusted sources. Share your findings with your grandchildren.

PRAY Jesus, help me to have a deeper devotion to Your Precious Blood.

Our Father, Hail Mary, and Glory Be.

SAVOR Jesus loves me and urges me to share the truth about His Precious Blood with others.

July 14

Neither gifts or portraits take the place of the beloved one. And our Lord knew it well. We need Him, so He gave us Himself.[109]

VENERABLE FULTON SHEEN

STEEP Yes, indeed. We need our Lord present in the Eucharist. On the day of his ordination, Archbishop Fulton Sheen resolved to make an hourly visit to Jesus in the Blessed Sacrament every day. He called it his "hour of power," saying that by spending time with Jesus, we become more like Him.

Gifts from and pictures of our grandchildren are precious treasures, but nothing is as valuable as our grandchildren's presence. In the same way, we can teach them the value of Jesus' Presence in the Eucharist and how important it is to visit Him in the Blessed Sacrament.

ACT Spend time with Jesus whenever you can. If possible, take your grandchildren with you for a Eucharistic visit soon.

PRAY Dear Jesus, thank You for the gift of Yourself in the Blessed Sacrament.

Our Father, Hail Mary, and Glory Be.

SAVOR Jesus loves me and yearns for my visits to Him.

July 15

How awesome is this place! This is none other than the house of God, and this is the gate of heaven.

GENESIS 28:17

STEEP My friend Jessica told me that her older children set a good example for the younger ones at Mass. She smiled, adding, "Then you have one who does things her own way." She referred to how her youngest daughter sat on the kneeler, took off her shoes, and put them in the aisle before closing her eyes to pray!

How do we manage when we bring a grandchild to Mass who does things their own way or misbehaves? Perhaps he or she is not accustomed to Mass—or, if the child is older, perhaps he or she has questions or doubts about the faith. It can be difficult for children to understand what's going on, and it can be difficult for the grandparent as well. Here's where lots of patience comes into play!

ACT Practice patience with your grandchildren and find moments to teach the faith to them.

PRAY Dear Jesus, Mary, and Joseph, please take care of my family.

Our Father, Hail Mary, and Glory Be.

SAVOR Children are amazing blessings in our lives!

July 16

Flower of Carmel, / Tall vine blossom laden, / Splendor of heaven, / Child-bearing, yet maiden. / None equals thee. / Mother so tender, / Whom no man did know, / On Carmel's children / Thy favors bestow. / Star of the Sea.[110]

ATTRIBUTED TO SAINT SIMON STOCK

STEEP The Blessed Virgin and the Child Jesus appeared to Saint Simon Stock and presented him with the brown scapular. Mary promised, "This shall be to thee and all Carmelites a privilege, that whosoever dies clothed in this shall never suffer eternal fire."[111] But not only Carmelites can wear it. In fact, the brown scapular has become one of the most popular sacramentals in the Catholic Church.

The *Catechism* instructs that sacramentals are "sacred signs which bear a resemblance to the sacraments" (*CCC*, 1667). Wearing a blessed brown scapular is a tangible way to help inspire faith in our own hearts and in the hearts of others, including our grandchildren. We can explain to them that among other things, it is a protection, a gift from Mother Mary.

ACT If you aren't wearing a brown scapular already, consider it.

PRAY Our Lady of Mount Carmel, please guide my family.

Our Father, Hail Mary, and Glory Be.

SAVOR We are blessed to have sacramentals to bolster our faith and protect us!

July 17

Most Holy Trinity, Father, Son, and Holy Spirit, I adore You profoundly.[112]

ANGEL OF PEACE AT FATIMA

STEEP In 1916, the Angel of Peace appeared to the three young shepherd children: Lucia, Francisco, and Jacinta. He catechized them in the doctrine of the Eucharist, prayer, and reparation. On the Angel's third visit, he taught them a special prayer of reparation (page 414) and asked them to pray it three times. Afterward, the Angel gave the Sacred Host to Lucia and the Precious Blood to Francisco and Jacinta. He said, "[Eat] and drink the Body and Blood of Jesus Christ, horribly outraged by ungrateful men. Repair their crimes and console your God."[113]

We can also console God by making reparation for sins, including our own sins and possibly those of any family members who don't practice the faith. Our world surely needs it.

ACT Find a way to offer reparation to God today.

PRAY Lord Jesus, please accept my humble prayers and works today in reparation for humanity's ingratitude.

Our Father, Hail Mary, and Glory Be.

SAVOR I am blessed with a rich Catholic faith.

July 18

Grandchildren are the crown of the aged,
and the glory of children is their parents.

PROVERBS 17:6

STEEP My friends Lisa and Andy attended their first "Grandparents' Day" at their granddaughter Beth's school. Upon arriving, they spotted Beth and her kindergarten class walking quietly behind the teacher. Lisa shared that Beth, being shy, "didn't even talk to her teacher for the first six months of school."

However, when Beth saw her grandparents, she bolted out of line! Lisa said, "She jumped into my arms, hugging me as though she had completely forgotten about being in line with her class. Her teacher was almost speechless as she had only known Beth to be a quiet, shy, obedient little child." To this day, Lisa reminds Beth about that Grandparents' Day "and what an unexpected but wonderful greeting" she received!

Grandparents help give grandchildren a sense of how special they are. This story beautifully illustrates how people act when they know they are truly loved. Grandmothers have the unique gift of giving that love.

ACT Take turns sharing happy memories or stories with your grandchildren.

PRAY Jesus, Mary, and Joseph, help me show my grandchildren how special and loved they are. Saint Anne, please pray for us.

Our Father, Hail Mary, and Glory Be.

SAVOR God blessed me with the beautiful role of grandmother!

July 19

In the moment when the light of the angel had enveloped Anna in grace, I saw a radiance under her heart and recognized in her the chosen Mother, the illuminated vessel of the grace that was at hand.[114]

Blessed Anne Catherine Emmerich

STEEP I often remind people that even Jesus had a grandmother: Saint Anne! Blessed Anne Catherine Emmerich described a vision she had, in which Saint Anne was greeted by an angel to receive the gift of being the mother of Mary (and the grandmother of Jesus).

Blessed Emmerich said, "What I saw in her I can only describe by saying that I recognized in her the cradle and tabernacle of the holy child she was to conceive and preserve; a mother blessed indeed. I saw that by God's grace Anna was able to bear fruit."

With God's grace and our prayerful example, we will see how our lives have borne fruit in our grandchildren.

ACT Learn more about Saint Anne. Ask her to intercede for your grandchildren.

PRAY Jesus, help me. Saint Anne, guide me.

Our Father, Hail Mary, and Glory Be.

SAVOR Every day as a grandmother is an exquisite gift from God!

July 20

She looks well to the ways of her household,
    and does not eat the bread of idleness.
Her children rise up and call her happy;
    her husband too, and he praises her.

PROVERBS 31:27–28

STEEP Grandmother to seven, Valerie told me, "Don't ever think your grandchildren aren't paying attention." One day, her fifteen-year-old granddaughter confessed she wasn't sure about marriage and said, "I don't know if there is a good man out there like Poppie." She observed how he looks at Valerie, "always helps out, and loves God so much." Valerie reassured her granddaughter that God will send her a good man when the time is right. But Valerie's story can also reassure us that we can set good examples when we don't even realize it. Our grandchildren are keeping an eye on us!

ACT Pray extra for your grandchildren, reach out to them, and let them know how much you appreciate them.

PRAY Jesus, please protect my family. Blessed Mother Mary and Saint Anne, please pray for us.

Our Father, Hail Mary, and Glory Be.

SAVOR God provides endless opportunities to be a shining example.

July 21

Strength and dignity are her clothing,
    and she laughs at the time to come.
She opens her mouth with wisdom,
    and the teaching of kindness is on her tongue.

Proverbs 31:25–26

STEEP My daughter Mary-Catherine texted me to ask for prayers for an important matter while I was at a doctor's appointment. I quickly dictated a message into my cell phone, promising my prayers. The technician at the doctor's office overheard, and I explained that my daughter needed prayers in that moment. Then I paused to quickly pray for her.

This unexpected text conversation with my daughter opened up a long, amazing conversation with the technician. She shared that her mother had died when she was young, and her father had abandoned her. Just eight months prior to our conversation, she reached an extremely dark place in her life and almost didn't make it. We talked a lot about prayer, forgiveness, and God's love.

Through the faithful living out of our vocation and our maternal care for our families, God opens up opportunities to show His love to others, many times to complete strangers.

ACT Be a light to others! Share God's love with someone you meet today.

PRAY Dear Jesus, please shine through me!

Our Father, Hail Mary, and Glory Be.

SAVOR God is love!

July 22

In all our lives, God has placed selfish persons who may be physically close to us, but spiritually are strangers and even enemies . . . unkind, unjust, even cruel people. . . . By loving them, we show something of the kind of love that God expects of His followers.[115]

Servant of God Father John Hardon

STEEP A faithful grandmother sometimes faces misunderstandings or unkind words from family members and others due to her beliefs. Today's quote reminds us of the purpose for challenges and contradictions in our lives. Regarding the people who are unkind to us, Father Hardon suggests, "We can love them, with the help of divine grace, by following the example of Jesus Christ, who died on the Cross out of love for a sin-laden human race."[116] These conflicts provide us an opportunity to show God's love through our example.

ACT Pray for the difficult people and circumstances in your life. Ask for the grace to love them and then move your will to do so.

PRAY Dear Sacred Heart of Jesus, please show me the way.
Our Father, Hail Mary, and Glory Be.

SAVOR The help of divine grace enables us to love everyone.

July 23

Out of the mouths of babes and infants
you have founded a bulwark because of your foes,
to silence the enemy and the avenger.

Psalm 8:2

STEEP The church was very quiet. But Valerie shared that when the bells rang to signal the elevation of the Host, "A tiny, angelic voice said quietly, 'Thank you, Jesus. I love you, Jesus.'" Three times for the Host and three times for the elevation of the chalice—the same angelic voice.

Valerie realized the voice belonged to her three-year-old granddaughter, Mira. Tears filled Valerie's eyes, her heart bursting with love. She later learned that her daughter had whispered those words in Mira's ears when she was an infant, and Mira has been saying them ever since she could talk.

"Now at every Mass, I find myself uttering the same words," Valerie said. "It is so true that the little ones will lead us closer to Jesus!"

ACT Reflect on how the little ones in your life have helped you appreciate Jesus' Divine Presence. Ponder ways to instill a love for Jesus and His Divine Presence in your family.

PRAY Dear Jesus, I love You and I thank You.

Our Father, Hail Mary, and Glory Be.

SAVOR Our children and grandchildren teach us!

July 24

I thank You, Jesus, my Divine Redeemer, for coming upon earth for our sake, and for instituting the adorable Sacrament of the Holy Eucharist in order to remain with us until the end of the world.[117]

FROM CORPUS CHRISTI NOVENA

STEEP We can probably think of many words to describe our grandchildren. Especially when they are little, we might think of them as "adorable." But this word is only truly appropriate when we are describing God, because God is the only One we truly adore.

Babies and children are cute and sweet, and we may devote much of our time and attention to them, but we don't adore them in the sense of worshiping them. We don't even adore the Blessed Mother. We honor her. We only adore God, and we can praise and thank Him for all the good gifts in our lives, including our beloved grandchildren.

ACT Look for ways to adore God today.

PRAY Dear Jesus, I adore You! Mother Mary, help me to adore your Son more perfectly.

Our Father, Hail Mary, and Glory Be.

SAVOR My grandchildren are gifts from the adorable God.

July 25

The figure of Saint Anne reminds us . . . of the paternal home of Mary, the Mother of Christ. . . . There she "learned" from her mother, from Saint Anne, how to be a mother.[118]

SAINT JOHN PAUL II

STEEP Saint Anne is special to my family. Today is my daughter Mary-Catherine's birthday. After a very precarious pregnancy, most of which I spent on complete bed rest, my daughter was born close to the feast of Saint Anne (tomorrow). Because of this, and in thanksgiving for a safe delivery, I gave her the middle name Anne. My mother also suggested the name Anne for my Confirmation name.

Saint Anne was the first to teach Mary. Just as her loving example to Mary helped her to be a wonderful mother to Jesus, she can teach us how to be loving grandmothers.

ACT Get to know the holy women Saint Anne and the Virgin Mary more on a personal level.

PRAY Saint Anne, please pray for me and teach me how to be a holy grandmother.

Our Father, Hail Mary, and Glory Be.

SAVOR I can learn so much from Saint Anne and apply her wisdom to my life.

July 26

It was in the home of Joachim and Anne that the child Jesus came to know his older relatives and experienced the closeness, tender love and wisdom of his grandparents.[119]

Pope Francis

STEEP Due to an ectopic pregnancy, a woman almost died and was told she wouldn't have children. The family stormed Heaven for help. They sought the intercession of the Blessed Mother and Saint Anne.

Despite the odds, she conceived, and her daughter Maria Anne was born. In thanksgiving, Maria Anne's loving grandparents bought a Saint Anne garden statue and a Saint Anne statue for Maria's bedroom. Eighteen months later, Sarah Anne was born, and not long after that, Lisa Anne was born.

No doubt about it—the entire family's loving and fervent prayers, as well as the intercession of Saint Anne and the Blessed Mother, brought about miraculous results!

ACT Even if you have never prayed a family Rosary together, try to arrange one soon. Give thanks for all of the blessings in your life.

PRAY Jesus, help me. Saints Joachim and Anne, pray for me.

Our Father, Hail Mary, and Glory Be.

SAVOR I am blessed with the intercession of the saints!

July 27

Even to your old age I am he,
even when you turn gray I will carry you.
I have made, and I will bear;
I will carry and will save.

Isaiah 46:4

STEEP My ninety-one-year-old friend Mary shared with me that she often spends time with a seminarian friend. They go out to dinner together, they pray together, and they share their hearts and their faith. I have no doubt that Mary's seasoned wisdom greatly benefits her young friend. One day, he asked her if he could call her "Grandma"! Mary was over the moon with delight. She has never married and has no biological children or grandchildren. But now, she's an honorary grandmother! What a blessing for both of them!

Being a grandmother goes beyond the bounds of biological family. No doubt, countless honorary grandmothers fill our world. Perhaps we, too, can be a grandmother influence in someone's life.

ACT Spread Christ's love through your words and actions. Allow the blessings of your grandmotherhood (honorary or other) to shine through to comfort others.

PRAY Jesus, help me to reach out to those in need of grandmotherly love.

Our Father, Hail Mary, and Glory Be.

SAVOR A grandmother's love breaks barriers!

July 28

For this reason I bow my knees before the Father, from whom every family in heaven and on earth takes its name.

EPHESIANS 3:14–15

STEEP When Maria's grandmother was sick, Maria was blessed to spend time with her each week. After Grandma and Aunt Mamie were in bed at night, Maria and her Aunt Fran "laughed and cried at all the pictures and old movies we found." At times, their loud giggles got them into trouble!

Maria was absolutely astounded to discover her grandparents' wedding pictures hanging in the back of a closet, in the same frames they had been in since 1929. She had never seen those pictures. Her grandparents were young teenagers when they came to the United States from Sicily to get married. Maria recalled, "Those times were difficult, but truly a blessing. My grandfather died in April of 1987 and Grandma in July. They always prayed that they should die together."

We, too, can hope that we will someday look back on our family memories of a beautiful life together.

ACT Share old family pictures with your grandchildren. Make new memories by taking or framing family pictures with them.

PRAY Dear Holy Family, please help me reminisce the past but live now in the present.

Our Father, Hail Mary, and Glory Be.

SAVOR Life is an amazing adventure.

July 29

It was not enough for him to die for us, he wanted that we loved one another, that we see him in each other.[120]

SAINT TERESA OF CALCUTTA

STEEP Mother Teresa preached that Jesus tells us clearly that when we die, we will be judged on how we have loved. He will ask us if we have taken care of the poor, the hungry, the naked, the homeless, and so on. She also taught the world that hunger and thirst is not simply about longing for a piece of bread, a dish of rice, or a glass of water. She said the Western world is starving for love. Because of a lack of love, people have been discarded, abandoned, and uncared for and feel miserable and despairing.

Each of us in all our walks of life can make a positive and loving difference in the lives of the suffering. Even a simple smile or kind word can help transform someone's life.

ACT Ponder what you do and do not do to Jesus in others. Talk about it with your grandchildren.

PRAY Jesus, please help me to be merciful and loving.

Our Father, Hail Mary, and Glory Be.

SAVOR We must love one another and see Jesus in others.

July 30

The family . . . must be regarded as the natural, primary cell of human society.[121]

Saint John XXIII

STEEP Valerie's Nani had nine children and thirty-six grandchildren. Valerie recalled, "She taught me how to bake, to make homemade bread and pasta. Everyone loved to be around Nani."

Valerie cared for Nani when she was diagnosed with bone cancer in her eighties. One day, Nani asked Valerie to promise she would continue to bake the Easter bread they had so often made together. "She kept telling me don't forget to put the salt in—it is so important." Valerie wrote down the recipe and promised to carry on the tradition.

The week before she passed away, Nani told Valerie out of the blue, "One day God will give you a baby girl." She didn't know Valerie couldn't have more children. Valerie gave birth to a beautiful baby girl the following year. "I really believe Nani had a word put in for me," Valerie said.

Families are incredible blessings. And grandmothers, from cooking to predictions, make quite an impression on them!

ACT Resurrect an old family recipe and make it!

PRAY Dear Lord God, thank You for my family.

Our Father, Hail Mary, and Glory Be.

SAVOR A grandmother's role in the family is priceless.

July 31

Love begins at home. And love to be true has to hurt.[122]

SAINT TERESA OF CALCUTTA

STEEP Mothers and grandmothers know well about sleepless nights up with tiny babies or worried sick about older children out of the house. Mother Teresa tells us, "Love to be true has to hurt." She doesn't mean we can never feel warm and fuzzy or experience a deep and abiding joy when we love as God asks. She means authentic love is sacrificial in nature. It costs us something—sleepless nights, exhaustion, worry, and concern.

Mother Teresa also preached the need to begin our love at home. We can show our love in many places, even overseas as a missionary, or join worthwhile committees. But we must be sure to first care for those under our own roof. For example, love sometimes requires we sacrifice other things we'd like to do for the sake of putting our families first.

ACT Remember the importance of love if you are called upon to make some sacrifice for your loved ones today.

PRAY Jesus, please increase the virtue of love in my heart.

Our Father, Hail Mary, and Glory Be.

SAVOR Real love requires sacrifice, but it's always worth it!

AUGUST

The Blessed Sacrament

There is a particular need to cultivate a lively awareness of Christ's real presence, both in the celebration of Mass and in the worship of the Eucharist outside Mass. Care should be taken to show that awareness through tone of voice, gestures, posture and bearing. In this regard, liturgical law recalls—and I myself have recently reaffirmed—the importance of moments of silence both in the celebration of Mass and in Eucharistic adoration. The way that the ministers and the faithful treat the Eucharist should be marked by profound respect. The presence of Jesus in the tabernacle must be a kind of magnetic pole attracting an ever greater number of souls enamored of him, ready to wait patiently to hear his voice and, as it were, to sense the beating of his heart. "O taste and see that the Lord is good! (Ps 34:8)"[123]

Saint John Paul II

August 1

> The Eucharist, in a special sense, is our glory and joy and the mystery of our union with Him. There is no greater love than the love of Christ. We can't be holy without Him, so He made Himself the Bread of Life.[124]
>
> SAINT TERESA OF CALCUTTA

STEEP Transubstantiation (the transformation of the bread and wine into the Body and Blood, Soul and Divinity of Christ at the consecration of the Mass) is and should be absolutely central to our Catholic faith. But sadly, at the time of the writing of this book, Pew Research Center surveys reveal that about 70 percent of baptized or self-described Catholics do not believe in the Real Presence of Jesus in the Eucharist.[125]

Members of our own family might fall into that widespread category of disbelief. Though this is indeed a sad thing, we can do our part to radiate Jesus' love to others and seek opportunities to gently teach about Jesus' true Presence in the Eucharist.

ACT Ponder ways to help the skeptical. Perform spiritual works of mercy to counsel the doubtful and instruct the ignorant.

PRAY Dear Jesus, I believe in Your Presence!

Our Father, Hail Mary, and Glory Be.

SAVOR We need Jesus in the Eucharist.

August 2

[Jesus] said to them, "Come away to a deserted place all by yourselves and rest a while." For many were coming and going, and they had no leisure even to eat. . . . Now many saw them going and recognized them, and they hurried there on foot from all the towns and arrived ahead of them.

MARK 6:31, 33

STEEP We might think that to visit Jesus in the Blessed Sacrament, we must stay an hour, or make a "holy hour." But if that were always the case, busy mothers and grandmothers might give up the entire idea of stealing away to be with Jesus in the Blessed Sacrament.

Jesus knows we can't always be in the chapel when we have other obligations. He welcomes any amount of time with Him, as long as we're not stingy with our time.

ACT If possible, bring your grandchildren the next time you go to Adoration.

PRAY Jesus, please send me more opportunities to visit You in the Blessed Sacrament.

Our Father, Hail Mary, and Glory Be.

SAVOR Time with Jesus is precious!

August 3

A life of faith and with peace of soul can be cultivated only by periodical isolation from the cares of the world.[126]

VENERABLE FULTON SHEEN

STEEP Jesus, often absorbed in prayer, retreated to the mountains and desert to pray. Seeking silence, He prayed, fasted, and listened to His Heavenly Father. It's important for us to try to visit the Blessed Sacrament when possible, but we can also be satisfied with whatever the good God provides.

Our lives may be anything but silent or secluded. We may scarcely have opportunities to retreat from the busyness. Even Jesus' prayer was interrupted by the crowds that followed Him! When we can't steal away to His feet, we can certainly still adore Him at home. We can "isolate from the cares of the world" and focus on serving our families when we have made our homes a domestic church and cultivate a spirit of holiness within them.

ACT Schedule a time for silent prayer today, but be prepared for rearrangement if duty calls.

PRAY Jesus, please increase my faith, hope, and love.

Our Father, Hail Mary, and Glory Be.

SAVOR It's essential to carve out time for prayer.

August 4

This is my commandment, that you love one another as I have loved you.

John 15:12

STEEP We might think love is always supposed to be delightful—perhaps especially when we are overcome with love for new grandchildren. We hear people say they "fell out of love," or they "don't feel the love" when things aren't going well. Truthfully, love often hurts. We need to courageously move our wills to choose to love. Sometimes, bravely choosing love will occur at a turning point in our lives and could become a transforming positive milestone.

Our Lord is very clear in today's quote that we are called to choose love. He chose to die on the cross for love of us. Yes, it costs us something to truly love one another, but if we do so, we are following in God's footsteps.

ACT Ponder the loves of your life and those you have trouble loving. Choose to love in a difficult moment today.

PRAY Jesus, help me to love like You.

Our Father, Hail Mary, and Glory Be.

SAVOR Authentic love is profound!

August 5

By contrast, the fruit of the Spirit is love, joy, peace, patience, kindness, generosity, faithfulness, gentleness, and self-control.

GALATIANS 5:22–23

STEEP Debra, her daughter, son-in-law, and two-and-a-half-year-old grandson, Monty, enjoyed a wonderful visit to St. Edmund's Island. She said Monty "chatted with the various saints' statues located around this gorgeous spiritual island." In the chapel, he "went before the monstrance and went down on one knee. He said, 'Hi Jesus,' blew Him a kiss, and then said, 'Back outside!'"

As Debra recalled the sweet encounter between her grandson and Jesus present in the Blessed Sacrament, she smiled and said, "I am certain our Lord smiled upon him with an enormous grin of great love."

When we foster a relationship between our grandchildren and Jesus in the Eucharist, we can trust that our efforts will bear fruit!

ACT Consider how the Lord smiles upon your acts of love. Meditate on His great love for you. Try to visit the Blessed Sacrament soon.

PRAY Jesus, thank You for the great gift of YOU!

Our Father, Hail Mary, and Glory Be.

SAVOR Jesus loves a childlike spirit!

August 6

He said therefore, "What is the kingdom of God like? And to what should I compare it? It is like a mustard seed that someone took and sowed in the garden; it grew and became a tree, and the birds of the air made nests in its branches."

LUKE 13:18–19

STEEP Jesus taught the Parable of the Mustard Seed to His disciples at a time when they had very little understanding of the Kingdom of God. The Jews knew mustard seeds were the smallest of seeds and that black mustard bushes could grow up to fifteen feet tall. The branches were strong enough for the nesting birds.

Another time, Jesus' parable illustrated the strength of faith—how a mustard-seed-sized faith can uproot trees! He said, "If you had faith the size of a mustard seed, you could say to this mulberry tree, 'Be uprooted and planted in the sea,' and it would obey you" (Lk 17:6).

Just as Jesus explained faith through parables His followers would understand, we grandmothers can encourage our grandchildren's faith through storytelling.

ACT Talk about today's parables with your grandchildren.

PRAY Jesus, please increase my faith.

Our Father, Hail Mary, and Glory Be.

SAVOR If I had faith the size of a mustard seed . . .

August 7

Sunday, the "Lord's Day," is the principal day for the celebration of the Eucharist. . . . It is the pre-eminent day of the liturgical assembly, the day of the Christian family, and the day of joy and rest from work.

Catechism of the Catholic Church, 1193

STEEP Holy Mother Church gives wise instructions—to celebrate the Eucharist on Sundays. Our Lord told us to keep His day holy (Ex 20:8–11), and Jesus instituted the Eucharist at the Last Supper to be carried out through the end of the world for our Sunday worship and nourishment.

The Church teaches that we should partake in the Eucharist and also celebrate a day of "joy and rest from work." Sometimes, it's difficult to completely rest. We feel we have much to accomplish. However, pausing to pray, enjoy our family, and rest from work as much as we can will undoubtedly refresh our bodies, minds, and souls.

ACT Keep Sundays holy and special in your family by reaching out to relatives. Do something special this Sunday—a simple phone call can brighten someone's day.

PRAY Jesus, thank You for the gift of Sundays and Yourself in the Eucharist!

Our Father, Hail Mary, and Glory Be.

SAVOR Sunday should be set apart from other days.

August 8

Listen! I am standing at the door, knocking; if you hear my voice and open the door, I will come in to you and eat with you, and you with me.

REVELATION 3:20

STEEP Janine's Meme had fourteen children, sixty-five grandchildren, and seventeen great-grandchildren. Janine would often "hear the soothing sound of the Rosary" prayed in Meme's home. Janine recalled, "It was an everyday occurrence as it later came to be in my own home with my family."

Janine cannot forget Meme's picture of Jesus. "It was Jesus, knocking on a door with no handle. His head was leaning toward the door, listening for someone to come and let Him in. Upon entering the house, you couldn't avoid that image of Christ. You waited with Him, wanting a response. My Meme instilled in me the wonder of God, and eventually I opened that door. I let Him in."

Meme passed at 102 "in peaceful slumber with her prayer beads in hand." Little did she know what a bright beacon of light and hope she was to her family.

ACT Open wide the door of your heart to God today.

PRAY Thank You, God, for praying grandmothers!

Our Father, Hail Mary, and Glory Be.

SAVOR I will be a vibrant example of living faith.

August 9

Let us take the time to kneel before Jesus present in the Eucharist, in order to make reparation by our faith and love for the acts of carelessness and neglect, and even the insults which our Savior must endure in many parts of the world.[127]

Saint John Paul II

STEEP We might forget, or not see or understand, the need to make reparation for sin. Our Lady of Fatima clearly requested penance and prayers for sinners so they won't go to Hell. She even showed a vision of Hell to the three young shepherd children, who dedicated the remainder of their lives to doing all they could to help save souls.

We might also feel saddened when we hear Jesus' Holy Name used in vain. In today's quote, Saint John Paul II offers a solid way in which we can make reparation. Spending more time with Jesus in the Blessed Sacrament can help us both overcome our own sins and make reparation for others' sins.

ACT Remember those in need and pray prayers of reparation to make up for the sins of others.

PRAY Jesus, I am deeply sorry for my sins and for the carelessness, neglect, and insults You receive from others.

Our Father, Hail Mary, and Glory Be.

SAVOR I can offer reparation through loving, faithful prayers.

August 10

There is a particular need to cultivate a lively awareness of Christ's real presence, both in the celebration of Mass and in the worship of the Eucharist outside Mass. Care should be taken to show that awareness through tone of voice, gestures, posture and bearing.[128]

Saint John Paul II

STEEP Our awareness of Christ's Presence should direct our reverence toward the Eucharist both inside and outside of Mass. Gestures such as bowing and genuflecting reveal our deep love of Jesus in the Eucharist. We must be careful not to let these actions become meaningless habits. But even if we are just going through the motions, or even if we do not feel close to God nor feel His love, it matters that we choose to do these actions. Other things such as our tone of voice and posture also matter because they remind us of Jesus' true Presence. These actions are all outward signs of faith that speak volumes and can powerfully move our grandchildren and others by witnessing to what we believe.

ACT Don't shy away from showing your faith. Choose to make an outward act of reverence to God.

PRAY Jesus, I can never thank You enough for Your gift of Yourself!

Our Father, Hail Mary, and Glory Be.

SAVOR Jesus is my All in All—my Everything!

August 11

At all times of our life and with all our being . . . adoration needs to be perpetual because the same God that we adore in the Blessed Sacrament is continually present to us in all places.[129]

Mother Mectilde de Bar

STEEP Mother Mectilde de Bar, who founded the Benedictines of Perpetual Adoration of the Most Holy Sacrament, believed that we can and should adore Jesus perpetually. This doesn't mean we have to be on our knees 24/7 before the Blessed Sacrament. Rather, we should recognize that God "is continually present to us in all places."

Grandmothers can adore Jesus and pray to Him when at the chapel, but also wherever we find ourselves. For example, sometimes illness or health issues confine us to our homes or a nursing home. Through prayer, though, we grandmothers can recognize God's presence in all places in our lives and vocation.

ACT Strive to see God's presence all around you today. Adore Him!

PRAY Jesus, I want to adore You more!

Our Father, Hail Mary, and Glory Be.

SAVOR God is present to me in all places.

August 12

According to St. Margaret Mary, the Sacred Heart is the Holy Eucharist. So it follows that devotion to the Sacred Heart is devotion to the Holy Eucharist. It is infinite Love Incarnate living in our midst in the Blessed Sacrament.[130]

SERVANT OF GOD FATHER JOHN HARDON

STEEP Have we ever recognized this connection between the Sacred Heart of Jesus and the Eucharist? Have we considered the immensity of this gift? When we receive Holy Communion or are in the presence of the Blessed Sacrament, or when we see an image of the Sacred Heart, we can ponder this connection, as well as how it can help us in our lives and vocations.

ACT Encourage your family to spend quiet time in prayer every day. Write it on a "to do" list!

PRAY Dear Jesus, I love You. Thank You for the gift of Your Most Sacred Heart and Your presence!

Our Father, Hail Mary, and Glory Be.

SAVOR I must carve out time with our Lord.

August 13

> Draw deeply from God a reservoir of confidence and ask his pardon for the insult that you have committed in resisting his goodness. He is less offended by a sin than by the defiance of his mercy.[131]
>
> Mother Mectilde de Bar

STEEP According to Mother Mectilde de Bar, our sins are less offensive to God than times when we resist His goodness or "defy" His mercy by refusing to rely on it, preferring our own self-willed ways. Saint Faustina also wrote in her *Diary* that Jesus revealed to her that He is most sad when we do not trust in His great mercy (see *Diary*, 300).

As grandmothers, we certainly want our grandchildren to behave and make good decisions, but perhaps even more than that, we want them to trust in our care and know they are loved. God feels similarly about us!

ACT Endeavor to draw deeply from the treasure of God's great mercy. Ask forgiveness for the times you have not been open to His mercy or have resisted it.

PRAY Jesus, please have mercy upon me. Help me to rely more upon Your mercy.

Our Father, Hail Mary, and Glory Be.

SAVOR God is Love and Mercy and asks me to trust in Him.

August 14

> Then they told what had happened on the road, and how he had been made known to them in the breaking of the bread.
>
> LUKE 24:35

STEEP Many Catholic women lead busy lives—especially grandmothers with multiple generations of family members to keep up with! However, sometimes we stretch ourselves thin if we try to accomplish too much. We can be so busy—or even lonely, thinking God must be far away—that we fail to recognize Jesus so near to us.

We aren't the first to have this problem. After the resurrection, Jesus' own disciples didn't recognize Him at first. But after they eventually recognized their risen Lord during the breaking of the Bread, they excitedly told the others in Jerusalem. When we recognize Jesus—in our daily lives and in the Eucharist—we can endeavor to share the Good News of Jesus with everyone too.

ACT Pause to acknowledge Jesus' presence throughout your day.

PRAY Dear Jesus, please help me to recognize You.

Our Father, Hail Mary, and Glory Be.

SAVOR Jesus is always near, sustaining me with His Love and bringing joy to my heart!

August 15

The Most Blessed Virgin Mary, when the course of her earthly life was completed, was taken up body and soul into the glory of heaven, where she already shares in the glory of her Son's Resurrection, anticipating the resurrection of all members of his Body.

Catechism of the Catholic Church, 974

STEEP Today, we remember the Blessed Virgin Mary, Mother of God, and her Assumption into Heaven, body and soul. Mary, though sinless, was human like us, with a body and a soul which are now in Heaven. On this feast day, we can remember and take comfort in the fact that we, too—and all our loved ones—will someday be reunited with our bodies after we die.

ACT Take time to meditate today on what it means to you that Mary, Most Holy is in Heaven—body and soul.

PRAY Dear Jesus, Mary, and Joseph, please protect my family and lead us to Heaven.

Our Father, Hail Mary, and Glory Be.

SAVOR The Blessed Virgin hears my prayers.

August 16

See yourself always as a little ball of wax in the hand of God, to be shaped according to his good pleasure. A child in the arms of his Father fears nothing: your soul and your whole being are surrounded by God.[132]

Mother Mectilde de Bar

STEEP Our lives are so unpredictable. We might think we have everything planned out. Yet, even in the course of a single day, our so-called perfect plans can change beyond our control. By the time we become grandmothers, surely we've experienced this many times in our lives!

Today's quote suggests that we make ourselves pliable in God's capable hands. He shapes our lives and our plans better than we ever could. Knowing this, we can pray for the graces to be able to fully surrender to Almighty God—to trust Him wholeheartedly as a child trusts his or her own good father.

ACT Surrender your plans for today to God.

PRAY Lord Jesus, I want to trust You much more than ever.

Our Father, Hail Mary, and Glory Be.

SAVOR God knows me through and through and guides me to trust Him with my life.

August 17

May each family rediscover family prayer, which helps to bring about mutual understanding and forgiveness.[133]

Pope Francis

STEEP Janine was fourteen years old when her mother, Germaine, had a massive cerebral hemorrhage and stroke. Janine's family gathered together in earnest prayer for their mother during the eight days she was in a coma. Janine attributes her family's current closeness to this time they spent in prayer together. She said, "I truly believe the reason we are all together today is because we prayed as a family. God kept us relying on Him and each other."

Family prayer can help our families grow closer together and get through countless challenges. As grandmothers, we can be instrumental in initiating family prayer.

ACT Resolve to pray together with your family more often. Consider using video conferencing to join with those at a distance. Be sure to ask for graces for those away from the Church.

PRAY Dear Lord God, thank You for the gift of my family.

Our Father, Hail Mary, and Glory Be.

SAVOR Family prayer is powerful in many ways!

August 18

> You are no longer strangers and aliens, but you are citizens with the saints and also members of the household of God, built upon the foundation of the apostles and prophets, with Christ Jesus himself as the cornerstone. In him the whole structure is joined together and grows into a holy temple in the Lord; in whom you also are built together spiritually into a dwelling place for God.
>
> EPHESIANS 2:19–22

STEEP Cheryl and her toddler daughter walked hand in hand. Suddenly, the girl broke loose, ran toward a homeless man sitting on the curbside, and wrapped her little arms around him. When Cheryl caught up, the man said to her, "She didn't just make my day. She made my life!"

Today's quote tells us how we are all members of God's family. We all belong to a family—no matter what shape or form. We are part of our neighborhood, our community, and our parish. We are an integral part of the Catholic Church. Everyone—from our beloved grandchildren to strangers to those who are lonely—has a place in the human family as a child of God.

ACT Strive to see everyone you meet today as family.

PRAY Dear Jesus, thank You for the gift of the human family. *Our Father, Hail Mary, and Glory Be.*

SAVOR We are one family.

August 19

Those who say, "I love God," and hate their brothers or sisters, are liars; for those who do not love a brother or sister whom they have seen, cannot love God whom they have not seen.

1 John 4:20

STEEP Baby Alaina was old enough to sit up on the bed as my friend Jessica's family sang their nighttime prayers. As they prayed and sang their songs, kneeling around the bed so she wouldn't fall off, Alaina bounced and laughed with delight.

"Hey, Mom," Jessica's son Erik exclaimed, "I think Alaina thinks we're singing to her!"

"Yeah!" Jessica's daughter Emily chimed in. "It's like it's her birthday or something!"

Musing, Erik then said, "It's so wonderful to have Alaina. A baby is just the best thing anyone could ever want."

Witnessing such goodness in sibling relationships warms mothers' and grandmothers' hearts! Family life can be a precious treasure!

ACT As Catholic mothers and grandmothers, we set the atmosphere for prayer in the home, and we arrange times of Eucharistic Adoration too. Ponder ways you can gather the family in prayer—even from afar.

PRAY Dear Jesus, Mary, and Joseph, help our family to be more prayerful.

Our Father, Hail Mary, and Glory Be.

SAVOR Every child and grandchild is a precious, unrepeatable gift.

August 20

As soon as they sprout leaves you can see for yourselves and know that summer is already near.

LUKE 21:30

STEEP Chris from Westerly, Rhode Island, shared how life by the seashore taught her to be attentive. She eloquently elaborated, "Go out too far, and the shrilling whistle of the lifeguards called you back to safety; turn your back to the breaking waves, and you would find yourself knocked down. Ignore the incoming tides, and suddenly your bright red plastic sand shovel, or even more devastating, your sand bucket, would be washed out to sea along with the dream of building the best castle on the beach."

Chris paints a lovely picture of a summer beach day, as well as, perhaps, lessons for life. We need to pay attention to the fierce tides and breaking waves of life (temptations) so we don't get knocked down (by the evil one). Time with Jesus in the Blessed Sacrament provides much grace for us to be attentive.

ACT Make a plan to do something fun today or at least dream about it! Strive to learn spiritual lessons from everyday life.

PRAY Lord, thank You for Your blessings.

Our Father, Hail Mary, and Glory Be.

SAVOR I should strive to be attentive in my spiritual life.

August 21

For by grace you have been saved through faith, and this is not your own doing; it is the gift of God.

EPHESIANS 2:8

STEEP Alzheimer's and dementia attacked Chris' mom, and their treasured beach and carousel outings came to an end. Mom passed and Chris went alone to the lighthouse. She sought solace, peace, and a sign. Tears glistened in her eyes, and the ocean shimmered and wavered in her view. She headed to the village and sat on a bench near the carousel. Eager kids scrambled up on the horses. Chris suddenly became aware of the music playing. The woman next to her said, "I love that hymn, but 'Amazing Grace'? That's kind of an odd choice for a carousel, don't you think?"

Chris stood up, her tears flowing freely. "Not today, not really!" At a time when she desperately missed her mom and their outings together, Chris felt comforted when unexpectedly hearing "Amazing Grace."

Loss of loved ones changes our family's dynamics. However, we hold fast to the warm memories and are comforted by our faith in God.

ACT Treasure your memories and live in this moment. Surrender the future to God.

PRAY Dear Lord, thank You for Your love.

Our Father, Hail Mary, and Glory Be.

SAVOR Life is a beautiful gift!

August 22

The entire body of the faithful pours forth instant supplications to the Mother of God and Mother of men.[134]

Dogmatic Constitution on the Church

STEEP When Jessica was an exhausted young mother, she once earnestly prayed for God to make her inconsolable newborn stop crying. God didn't seem to answer her prayer in that moment, but Jessica is convinced He gave her a better answer.

"God, in His infinite wisdom, knew I needed more than a 'one-time baby stops crying' deal," she said. "Instead, He gifted me a lifelong lesson in how to listen to my baby's heart, her eyes, her mind, her spirit, her soul, her whole being. He taught me to listen to my child with the heart of Mary."

We certainly remember those times as young mothers. But as grandmothers, we also experience moments of exhaustion and frustration throughout our grandchildren's lives. We, too, can strive to have a heart like Mary. We can turn to her for help, knowing that she is also a mother who understands our needs.

ACT Write down the lifelong lessons God has given you.

PRAY Dear Lord, Jesus, thank You for my family. Please help me to have a heart like Your Mother's!

Our Father, Hail Mary, and Glory Be.

SAVOR Mother Mary guides me through life!

August 23

For the likeness [to God] is in this, in the virtue of the soul, when we train our children to be good, to be meek, to be forgiving, (because all these are attributes of God) to be beneficent, to be humane. . . . Let this then be our task, to mold and to direct both ourselves and them according to what is right.[135]

Saint John Chrysostom

STEEP My friend Debbie's three-year-old grandson Bennett often holds her Saint Faustina relic prayer card throughout Mass. One Sunday, while kneeling at Mass, she happened to catch him out of the corner of her eye. He had kissed his fingers and touched his Mimi's prayer card, and then placed the card over his heart.

Debbie was over the moon. She said, "He caught me watching him. As our eyes met we both gave each other a huge smile and then a hug." That experience taught her "that Sunday prayers don't need to be long or drawn out with many words." A child's simplicity is all that is needed to tell Jesus we love Him.

ACT Pay attention to the lessons learned from little ones.

PRAY Dear Lord, thank You for precious children!

Our Father, Hail Mary, and Glory Be.

SAVOR Our lives are full of treasures just waiting to be discovered.

August 24

If we live by the Spirit, let us also be guided by the Spirit.

GALATIANS 5:25

STEEP Our families' tapestries are filled with births and deaths. Yet even when we believe in the promise of Heaven for a life well lived, losing a loved one is extremely difficult. My friend Fran sorely misses her deceased mom. Not a day goes by when Fran does not miss her.

Her six-year-old granddaughter Gabi has helped ease the pain. She makes up songs and sings them to Fran's mom. She reassures Fran that her mom is in Heaven listening to the songs. Fran said, "This not only makes Gabi and me happy, but I know my mom is smiling too!"

When we are facing loss and grief, we too can take comfort in the beautiful tapestry of the connections between generations of our families. The precious expressions, songs, and prayers of the children in our lives can bring a big dose of comfort.

ACT Pray a Divine Mercy Chaplet soon for the dying and deceased.

PRAY Dear Jesus, please pour down Your Divine Mercy upon us. Please help broken and grieving families.

Our Father, Hail Mary, and Glory Be.

SAVOR Life is a precious gift.

August 25

Do everything for the glory of God and the good of His people.[136]

SAINT TERESA OF CALCUTTA

STEEP Every day, opportunities unfold to pause and ponder our purpose and mission. My friend Jessica's son Erik marched in the Memorial Day parades as a Boy Scout. Putting one foot in front of the other, Erik felt very proud to give honor to veterans marching in front of him. He was so full of patriotism and pride that he could hardly swallow, listening to a soldier's speech. He said, "Mom, I've been doing a lot of thinking. I want to do something good that I will be remembered for."

His mother quickly responded, "God has a plan, my son." God surely has a plan for each of us. It continually unfolds each day. As grandmothers, we can help our grandchildren discover their holy purpose and mission in life and encourage them to ask God to help them achieve it.

ACT Talk with your grandchildren about your life, your goals, and the gifts God has given to you.

PRAY Dear Lord God, thank You for my life. Please lead me all the way to Heaven.

Our Father, Hail Mary, and Glory Be.

SAVOR Our lives are filled with countless moments of grace and blessing!

August 26

Be still, and know that I am God!

Psalm 46:10

STEEP Reading today's quote, I can't help but think of Mother Teresa, whose birthday is today. She often spoke about being still and quiet and about searching for silence in which to pray.

Family life is anything but quiet! Even so, we need to somehow search for silence in our busy days. We can carve out specific times to pray at certain times of the day, even if some of these times are brief. Even in the midst of chaotic schedules, we can interiorly offer our hearts to God and pause a while to listen to His whispers to our hearts and souls. Communing with God in these ways will bring tremendous peace, even during strenuous or challenging times. For those whose lives have slowed down, the hidden blessing is more time and space for silent prayer.

ACT Open your heart wider today and listen to God more fervently.

PRAY Jesus, I desire to be as close to You as possible. Help me. *Our Father, Hail Mary, and Glory Be.*

SAVOR I need to be still and recognize God in my life.

August 27

The Eucharist is "the source and summit of the Christian life." [LG 11.] "The other sacraments, and indeed all ecclesiastical ministries and works of the apostolate, are bound up with the Eucharist and are oriented toward it. For in the blessed Eucharist is contained the whole spiritual good of the Church, namely Christ himself, our Pasch." [PO 5.]

Catechism of the Catholic Church, 1324

STEEP As I put my fingers to the keyboard to write this book, many Catholics believe Holy Communion is simply symbolic. What a tragedy! We can certainly pray for a change of hearts for the doubtful and unbelieving.

We can also examine our own attitudes toward the Eucharist and strive to grow in reverence. We can acknowledge Jesus' Presence more fervently and prepare our hearts more carefully before receiving Holy Communion. We can linger longer in our prayers to our dear Jesus after receiving Holy Communion and when visiting Him during Adoration. We can stay with Him in our thoughts and prayers. By living out our own relationship with Jesus in the Eucharist, we inspire others to the same faith.

ACT Stay longer with Jesus in your prayers today.

PRAY Pray the Anima Christi (page 415).

Our Father, Hail Mary, and Glory Be.

SAVOR The Eucharist is Christ Himself. What an incredible mystery and miracle!

August 28

The Eucharist is a mode of being, which passes from Jesus into each Christian, through whose testimony it is meant to spread throughout society and culture.[137]

SAINT JOHN PAUL II

STEEP At the end of the Good Friday liturgy, a gentleman approached Jessie and her family. He said, "I commend you on bringing your children to Mass last night and praying with them afterward. You think people don't notice, but they do." Then he turned to the children and said, "You have honorable parents, kids."

Jessie told me that the man and his wife are now her family's dear friends. She said, "As parents we don't even realize that we are setting examples by what we do. It was a blessing this man pointed it out to us."

Let's strive to be like the man in this story and encourage other parents and families. After all, we grandmothers certainly understand what families with kids experience in church. Sincere compliments will go a long way to encourage them.

ACT Reach out to other families at church and offer assistance to those who might need help.

PRAY Jesus, help me to teach the little ones about You and always set an exemplary example.

Our Father, Hail Mary, and Glory Be.

SAVOR I will be a vibrant example of living faith!

August 29

There is no doubt that the most evident dimension of the Eucharist is that it is a meal. . . . As such, it expresses the fellowship which God wishes to establish with us and which we ourselves must build with one another.[138]

SAINT JOHN PAUL II

STEEP We know that Jesus instituted the Eucharist on Holy Thursday during the Last Supper: a meal with the apostles. Breaking bread in the family is important too. At mealtimes, we can sit together (not separately or in front of the television or computer). We share food and conversation. We can also share our faith.

While at the family table together, we can talk about Jesus and the Eucharist. Just as we are strengthened physically by food and emotionally by time spent with family, we certainly need the spiritual strength from that sacrament of love in the community of the Church to keep headed toward Heaven!

ACT Enjoy a meal with your family. Talk about the faith in ways that you can.

PRAY Jesus, I love You!

Our Father, Hail Mary, and Glory Be.

SAVOR I am strengthened by family meals and the Eucharistic meal.

August 30

> It must not be forgotten that the Eucharistic meal also has a profoundly and primarily sacrificial meaning. In the Eucharist, Christ makes present to us anew the sacrifice offered once for all on Golgotha.[139]
>
> SAINT JOHN PAUL II

STEEP In today's quote, Saint John Paul II speaks about the Eucharistic meal being sacrificial. Jesus gifts us with Himself in the Eucharist, which nourishes our hearts and souls now and propels us on our journey toward Heaven. Christ reassures us that He is always with us, and He will come again at the end of time. What a comfort to our hearts!

A grandmother can never truly compare her vocation to the gift of Jesus in the Eucharist. Yet, her sacrificial life in raising children and grandchildren is somewhat similar. She nourishes the family and makes many a sacrifice to help her family stay on the holy road that leads to Eternal Life. Hopefully, our children and grandchildren will know they can count on us and that we will always be there for them.

ACT Ponder the Eucharist in your life in light of Saint John Paul II's teachings.

PRAY Jesus, please help me to guide my family well.

Our Father, Hail Mary, and Glory Be.

SAVOR What a tremendous gift our Lord has given us in the Eucharist!

August 31

Be still before the LORD, and wait patiently for him.

PSALM 37:7

STEEP Mother Teresa and the saints continually encouraged seeking silence in our lives in order to hear the voice of God speak to our hearts. But many of us these days flee from silence. Perhaps quiet makes us uncomfortable, or we are not content with our own thoughts or the whispers from God tugging at our conscience. Maybe there is some difficulty or pain we are trying to avoid. We might be tempted to escape to senseless chatter and endless activities.

As souls striving for holiness, we must be careful not to get overly busy and miss or avoid God speaking to us. God wants to work in our souls in those vulnerable moments of silence.

ACT Spend some time in silence today, listening for God's voice.

PRAY Dear Jesus, I am listening to You!

Our Father, Hail Mary, and Glory Be.

SAVOR The Holy Spirit works in the silence of my heart.

SEPTEMBER

Our Lady of Sorrows

My afflicted Mother, I will not leave thee alone to weep; no, I will accompany thee with my tears.[140]

Saint Alphonsus de Liguori

September 1

> [W]hile other martyrs suffered by sacrificing their own lives, the Blessed Virgin suffered by sacrificing her Son's life—a life that she loved far more than her own . . . the sight of her Son's torments brought more grief to her heart than if she had endured them all in her own person.[141]
>
> SAINT ANTONIUS

STEEP While moving through each day of September, we can meditate upon Our Lady's life and sorrows. I often encourage people to turn to Mother Mary in all their needs and never fear that she won't understand their plight. She has experienced and endured far more than we can imagine.

Mary's life was extremely sacrificial—ultimately sacrificing her own Divine Son for the salvation of the world. Mary witnessed every bit of His Passion and death on the Cross and suffered deeply in her heart and soul because of Jesus' suffering. She can empathize with our sufferings and sacrifices, including the ones that come through our vocation as grandmothers.

ACT Close your eyes; imagine yourself in Nazareth with the Holy Family—Mary and Saint Joseph praying together, establishing the firm foundation of prayer in their domestic church.

PRAY Dear Holy Family, please pray for me.

Our Father, Hail Mary, and Glory Be.

SAVOR Mary understands my heart.

September 2

[T]hose wounds which were scattered over the body of our Lord were all united in the single heart of Mary.[142]

Saint Bonaventure

STEEP Mary was acutely aware of every pain of her Divine Son, Jesus. She might have counted His holy sighs as He hung from the Cross, after seeing Him wince as the soldiers hammered nails into His sacred hands and feet and raised Him up on the Cross. Earlier, deafening blows from barbed whips mercilessly piercing her Son's flesh echoed in her ears. His blood dripped and smeared across His body. Holy Mary must have wanted to collect all the drops of His precious Blood shed for our salvation. Mary is always united to her Son. As a human mother, she experiences all the pain with Him.

Mary understands how we feel when we see our loved ones suffering greatly and are unable to stop their suffering. Her loving intercession can help us.

ACT Ponder Jesus' holy wounds and say a prayer from your heart. Ask Mary to be with you.

PRAY Lord Jesus, I am sorry for my sins because they caused You great suffering. Dear Mary, please help me.

Our Father, Hail Mary, and Glory Be.

SAVOR As difficult as it is to meditate upon our Lord's Passion and Mary's sufferings, it's so important.

September 3

There is something holy, something divine hidden in the most ordinary situations, and it is up to each one of you to discover it.[143]

Saint Josemaría Escrivá

STEEP Our ordinary lives can truly become extraordinary through ardent prayer and a commitment to live out our state of life with faith, hope, and love. Living our faith to the fullest can be a radiant example to others who are observing without our even knowing it.

Our commitment to faithfully living our "daily duty" is also very pleasing to God. We should always do our very best within our state of life and offer it to God. Faithfully and lovingly responding to the little and big responsibilities that fill our days makes a positive difference in our lives and in the lives of those we serve.

ACT Ponder areas of your life where you do not give your very best. Is there something you can change for the better?

PRAY Thank You, God, for so many opportunities to wholeheartedly serve You.

Our Father, Hail Mary, and Glory Be.

SAVOR Life speeds by. I must seize opportunities to do good.

September 4

Jesus said, "Let the little children come to me, and do not stop them; for it is to such as these that the kingdom of heaven belongs."

Matthew 19:14

STEEP Children's prayers are precious and certainly go directly to the Heart of God. Our Lord must be pleased to hear His children speaking to Him, especially the littlest.

My friend Filomena shared about a day her granddaughter Celeste was visiting during a storm. Little Celeste gripped her grandmother's rosary beads. Filomena said, "All she could say was, 'Jesus be with us and keep us safe,' over and over. And she fervently cried out, 'I love you, Jesus.'" Filomena's heart swelled, touched by her granddaughter's faith-filled and loving prayers. She beamed and said, "That was my beautiful granddaughter, Celeste."

Our grandchildren learn much from us, but we can learn plenty from their tender heartfelt and faith-filled prayers.

ACT Take time to talk about prayer to your grandchildren and all children in your life.

PRAY Dear Jesus, Mary, and Joseph, please keep my family safe.

Our Father, Hail Mary, and Glory Be.

SAVOR Heartfelt prayer is essential for spiritual survival.

September 5

She opens her hand to the poor,
and reaches out her hands to the needy.

PROVERBS 31:20

STEEP Today is Saint Teresa of Calcutta's feast day. I suspect that you might have noticed my love for Mother Teresa because I weave her into the reflections. She was (and still is) a spiritual mother to me, and I can't help but share her wisdom.

The saint of the gutters wholeheartedly believed she was to serve Jesus in each person she met. Whether in deed, word, or prayer, she took seriously Jesus' instructions, "Truly I tell you, just as you did it to one of the least of these who are members of my family, you did it to me" (Mt 25:40). She knew full well what came next. "Truly I tell you, just as you did not do it to one of the least of these, you did not do it to me" (Mt 25:45).

As grandmothers, we can live Mother Teresa's message by serving Jesus in our grandchildren!

ACT Ponder the way you treat Jesus in all you know and meet, especially in your family where love begins.

PRAY Jesus, I want to serve You in others. Mother Teresa, please pray for me.

Our Father, Hail Mary, and Glory Be.

SAVOR Daily opportunities unfold to reach out in love.

September 6

If an earthly mother weeps at the physical death of one of her children, what must have been Mary's grief at the spiritual death of millions of men whose Mother she was called to be by God![144]

VENERABLE FULTON SHEEN

STEEP I observed a beautiful moment between two young children from different families who were at a baptismal party at a parish. Mark and Alyssa had taken it upon themselves to slip into the back of the church. They grabbed a couple rosaries and knelt quietly to pray the Rosary together.

The Rosary is a powerful weapon against evil. Our Blessed Mother asked the Fatima children to pray in order to save sinners. We can all pray, both young and old, for the salvation of souls. Let's be sure to introduce the prayer of the Rosary to the little ones in our lives. With God's grace and our encouragement, a day will come when they pick up the beads themselves to pray the ancient, but ever-new Rosary.

ACT Impress upon your grandchildren the need to pray for others.

PRAY Dear Jesus, Mary, and Joseph, I love you; please save souls.

Our Father, Hail Mary, and Glory Be.

SAVOR Sin is a killer, and prayer is a sure remedy!

September 7

Whoever . . . was present on the Mount of Calvary, might see two altars, on which two great sacrifices were consummated; the one in the body of Jesus, the other in the heart of Mary.[145]

SAINT JOHN CHRYSOSTOM

STEEP We might think Mary's life was easy as the Mother of God, but this month's devotion reminds us that her life was pierced through with tremendous sorrow. Though it might seem paradoxical, Mary still suffers in Heaven because many of her children have turned away from God. Mary asks for our prayers so souls will not go to Hell.

Additionally, because Mary still suffers in Heaven, she can still empathize with our sufferings. This is why we can pray to Our Lady of Sorrows.

ACT Ponder Our Lady of Sorrows' great love for her children and pray for souls.

PRAY Our Lady of Sorrows, thank you for your great love for your children, myself included!

Our Father, Hail Mary, and Glory Be.

SAVOR Compassionate Mary suffered deeply because of her Son's suffering and still suffers for mankind.

September 8

For [Mary] indeed is the flower of the field, from whom sprang the precious lily of the valley.[146]

Saint Augustine

STEEP Today, the Church celebrates the birth of Mary. The Church normally celebrates a person on the day of their death. However, through the privilege of the Immaculate Conception, Mary entered this world sinless, so Mary's birth is certainly a cause for great joy. Her nativity is considered the "dawn of our salvation," according to Saint Paul VI.[147]

Just as we celebrate Mary's birthday, a happy occasion, during the month of Our Lady of Sorrows, we can celebrate happy events in our lives, such as the birth of a grandchild, even during times of sorrow. Our lives are certainly a blending of bliss and pain. God's love sees us through.

ACT With your family, honor Mary with much love today, with bouquets of extra Hail Marys, and maybe even with a song!

PRAY Dear Jesus, Your Mother is my Mother too. I am deeply grateful for that precious gift.

Our Father, Hail Mary, and Glory Be.

SAVOR It's comforting knowing that Mary has been praying since she was a young girl and continues to pray for us from Heaven.

September 9

If you invoke the Blessed Virgin when you are tempted, she will come at once to your help, and Satan will leave you.[148]

SAINT JOHN VIANNEY

STEEP We can each find our own clever and creative ways to evangelize others with the truths of the faith. Years ago, I made business-sized cards containing the above quote from Saint John Vianney. The unflagging confessor knew a thing or two about the Blessed Virgin and gave wise counsel. I wanted to help others to realize how powerful Mary really is, especially when it comes to the devil and temptation.

It is important to know we can invoke Mary, our superhero against evil, at the first sign of temptation. We then prevent the evil one from getting a foothold in our heart. The evil one is very clever, so we should continuously invoke Mary for help and protection.

ACT With your grandchildren, take turns writing something important you want to share about the faith on small cards. Decorate them if desired and distribute them to people!

PRAY Dear Jesus, Mary, and Joseph, help me in times of temptation.

Our Father, Hail Mary, and Glory Be.

SAVOR I will cling to Mary!

September 10

> My daughter, tears shed for My Passion are dear to Me; but as I love My Mother Mary with an immense love, the meditation of the torments which she endured at My death is even more agreeable to Me.[149]
>
> Jesus to Blessed Veronica da Binasco

STEEP Our Blessed Mother is sometimes depicted with a crown of thorns around her Immaculate Heart or with seven swords piercing her heart to represent her seven sorrows, or dolors. Tradition holds that Mary appeared to Saint Bridget requesting devotion to her tears and dolors. She promised seven graces to those who honor her by meditating on her seven sorrows with seven Hail Mary's daily.

Praying with Mary through her seven sorrows gives us empathy for Jesus' and her suffering. Our empathetic hearts can then reach out to our family members, neighbors, and others. Devotion to Our Lady of Sorrows will surely draw us closer to Jesus and Mary and help us in our vocation as grandmothers.

ACT Consider honoring Mary in her seven sorrows by praying this devotion. See the Appendix of Prayers to learn more.

PRAY Mary, I wish to honor you in your seven sorrows. Thank you for your promise of grace and peace to our families.

Our Father, Hail Mary, and Glory Be.

SAVOR Jesus asks for meditation on His Mother's torments.

September 11

> I look around at all who are on earth, to see if by chance there are any who pity me, and meditate upon my sorrows; and I find that there are very few. Therefore, my daughter, though I am forgotten by many, at least do thou not forget me.[150]
>
> Blessed Virgin to Saint Bridget

STEEP Many a grandmother laments the lack of Christian teachings for her dear grandchildren. My friend Dottie had just returned from a family trip and disclosed to me, "I have to admit, I was quite down about how my son and daughter-in-law are raising their children." The following day, Dottie said, "Thankfully, the Lord reminded me that He is in control, and I need to trust Him. I'm feeling much better today."

It's not always easy to navigate our feelings, but we can strive to imitate Mary, who trusted despite sorrowful situations. With God's grace and our prayerful surrender, we too can trust despite our grief.

ACT Strive to imitate Mary during a discouraging situation.

PRAY Our Lady of Sorrows, please help grandmothers who are discouraged or saddened that their grandchildren are not raised in the faith. And please help children everywhere.

Our Father, Hail Mary, and Glory Be.

SAVOR With Mary's help, I will be a radiant example of faith for my family and beyond.

September 12

Love our Lady. And she will obtain abundant grace to help you conquer in your daily struggle.[151]

SAINT JOSEMARÍA ESCRIVÁ

STEEP Carol and Daniel's daughter, Grace, struggled with substance abuse and mental health issues. She called her parents and asked them to care for her two-and-a-half-year-old daughter, Mercy, so she could "figure things out."

"Little did we know that our 'yes' at that point would turn into a five-year journey of caring for our granddaughter," Carol said. The Blessed Mother's example was their guiding light. "We said 'yes' knowing that God was asking us to care for Mercy at the time. Our 'yes' has been made possible only by pressing into God, again and again, for the grace that He provides to us for every moment of every day. God's grace and mercy continue to guide us as the foundation for our lives."

ACT Hand all your difficulties over to God. In addition, do your best to reach out to a struggling family.

PRAY Thank you, dear Lord and Blessed Mother Mary, for help in difficult times. Our Lady of Sorrows, please pray for me.

Our Father, Hail Mary, and Glory Be.

SAVOR God's grace always provides for us, and Mary always takes care of us.

September 13

She loved Him, because He was God; but she loved us, because it was God's will to save us. The first love was her martyrdom; the other her sacrifice.[152]

VENERABLE FULTON SHEEN

STEEP "You better be alive!" the police officer cried out while running like mad through the woods. She was carrying about thirty pounds of police equipment but also the medicine that could potentially reverse the drugs a suicidal young mother had taken.

Thank God, the police officer was able to save the mother's life. God only knows the road ahead for the despairing mother of young children. We can pray for her and all those in her situation, as well as try to be more attentive to the struggles of those around us.

We can also remember that Mary is in the holy business of saving souls. The police officer's fierce love and concern for the suicidal mother mirrors the protective love Mary has for her children—and grandmothers have for our grandchildren.

ACT Love fiercely like Mary today. Pray for those in despair.

PRAY Our Lady of Sorrows, please help us all, especially the sorrowful, despairing, and fearful.

Our Father, Hail Mary, and Glory Be.

SAVOR I will lend my ear and my hands to those who struggle.

September 14

Under her guidance, under her patronage, under her kindness and protection, nothing is to be feared; nothing is hopeless.[153]

BLESSED PIUS IX

STEEP I noticed a small cross tattooed on the wrist of a waitress I met at a family restaurant. I'm not too fond of tattoos, but because it was a cross, I ventured to ask its meaning. The young mother shared her harrowing tale. She had been working double shifts and fell asleep at the wheel going home from work late one night. Her car flipped six times after hitting a stone wall. She was found unconscious on the floor of her car with her grandmother's rosary, which had previously hung from the rearview mirror, wrapped around her hand.

This story can reassure us that we grandmothers, with God's help, can protect our grandchildren, especially with our prayers—even when we aren't physically present to them or don't know they are in danger!

ACT Pray an extra Rosary decade soon for those in danger.

PRAY Our Lady of Sorrows, thank you for your protection.

Our Father, Hail Mary, and Glory Be.

SAVOR My faithful prayers for my grandchildren can be a life preserver.

September 15

> Thus also did Mary suffer all those torments, scourges, thorns, nails, and the cross, which tortured the innocent flesh of Jesus, all entered at the same time into the heart of this Blessed Virgin, to complete her martyrdom.[154]
>
> SAINT ALPHONSUS DE LIGUORI

STEEP Since today is the feast of Our Lady of Sorrows, we can take time to meditate upon Saint Liguori's words above. He tells us Mary suffered torments along with her Son—every one of them.

Can we even imagine Mary's misery when her eyes met her Son's along the Via Dolorosa? She couldn't do a thing to stop what was about to happen to Him. Similarly, Jesus couldn't stop His Mother's tears and sorrow. In our own lives, there will be times when the sufferings of our loved ones will be out of our control. During such times, we can offer the painful sorrow we experience in our hearts to Jesus and Mary and pray that it can become redemptive for the one suffering and perhaps for us as well.

ACT Take time today to meditate on Mother Mary's deep sorrow. Close your eyes and imagine yourself in the scene.

PRAY Our Lady of Sorrows, thank you for your great love.

Our Father, Hail Mary, and Glory Be.

SAVOR Mary suffered along with her Son.

September 16

The Blessed Virgin is like a good Mother who, not content with looking after all her children in general, watches over each one separately.[155]

SAINT JOHN VIANNEY

STEEP I once had a fourth-grade faith formation student, Emily, who aspired to holiness. Certainly, we are all called to seek holiness, but I could see it profoundly in Emily.

In our last class of the year, we discussed vocations. When it was time to bid our farewells at the end of the class, I whispered to Emily while she packed up her books that I thought she might have a vocation to religious life. Her face lit up, and she cried out, "Oh! I am trying so hard to be a nun!" I was amazed to hear a tender young soul express such a sentiment. Six years later, Emily asked me to be her Confirmation sponsor!

We women are blessed with many gifts to use for God's glory. We can use our intuitive attention to others to give prayerful encouragement to anyone around us!

ACT Encourage holiness in someone in your life today.

PRAY Our Lady of Sorrows, please help us.

Our Father, Hail Mary, and Glory Be.

SAVOR I can be attentive, encouraging, and strive to be like Mary, who is very involved with the salvation of her children.

September 17

Is not this the carpenter's son? Is not his mother called Mary?

MATTHEW 13:55

STEEP Just as Jesus took up His foster father Saint Joseph's profession, Ethan James Joseph became interested in carpentry because of his relatives and a special friend. At eight years old, Ethan created a workshop. His mom said, "We swept, cleaned, painted walls, and devised a pegboard in the basement to hang his growing stash of tools." His workshop grew along with him as his family encouraged his endeavor: he received a rolling tool chest from his grandparents, Grandpa's old vise, and a workbench from his uncle.

Amid sawdust, smells of lacquer, wax, and paint, and sounds of drills, saws, and sanders, Ethan spent countless hours designing and creating. Along the way, Ethan grew very fond of Saint Joseph and chose him as his Confirmation saint. His mom said, "Ethan always had a pull toward Saint Joseph, or Saint Joseph always had a pull on him!"

ACT Take an interest in your grandchildren's hobbies. Help them learn about saints who had similar interests to theirs.

PRAY Our Lady of Sorrows, please help my grandchildren discover their passion. Saint Joseph, protect our family.

Our Father, Hail Mary, and Glory Be.

SAVOR Life is an incredible journey of learning and growing in holiness!

September 18

Someone asked [Jesus], "Lord, will only a few be saved?" He said to them, "Strive to enter through the narrow door; for many, I tell you, will try to enter and will not be able."

LUKE 13:23–24

STEEP My friend Cathy found a one-hundred-dollar bill on her front lawn. She desperately tried to find the owner, but to no avail. At the time, I was a struggling single mother. Cathy selflessly split her newly found treasure and sent half to me. May God richly reward her!

When we hear that we must enter through the narrow door, we might be tempted to focus on our own salvation alone. But Jesus shows us how loving God and others is actually the very way to enter Heaven. Cathy's kind deed certainly helped her walk the narrow way, along with helping me in my hour of need!

ACT Ponder your love for others. Are you helping them get to Heaven and relieving their struggles?

PRAY Dear Jesus, Mary, and Joseph, please help me.

Our Father, Hail Mary, and Glory Be.

SAVOR I need to strive to enter by the narrow door and help others to do so as well.

September 19

Pray for us, O Holy Mother of God, that we may be made worthy of the promises of Christ!

FROM THE ANGELUS PRAYER

STEEP Mary teaches us how to serve, love, and pray. Raised with great love and taught the truths of her Jewish faith by Saints Anne and Joachim, Mary was offered at just three years old to the service of the Temple as her parents had promised God.

Later, at the Annunciation, Mary offered her selfless "yes" to God. She went quickly over hill country to assist her elderly cousin Saint Elizabeth. Rather than worry about herself and the gargantuan vocation gifted to her, and even any pregnancy discomforts, Mary chose to help another. Mary was selflessly present to Elizabeth for a joyful occasion, but she was also selflessly present to Jesus at the most sorrowful time of their lives.

There are times in our own lives when we put aside our needs to be present to our family members. We can look to Mary, whose loving, faithful life gives an exemplary example to follow.

ACT Spend time with Mary in prayer. Ask her to pray for you.

PRAY Lord God, thank You for the gift of Mary.

Our Father, Hail Mary, and Glory Be.

SAVOR The Blessed Virgin Mary will teach me!

September 20

> It cost Jesus His Mother to make her our mother; it cost Mary her Divine Son to make us her sons. It was a poor exchange, but she believes it worth it.[156]
>
> Venerable Fulton Sheen

STEEP We naturally mourn the loss of loved ones. There is also another type of loss of loved ones: abandonment. Mary was familiar with this deep pain. After all, she watched as her Son Jesus' friends and followers abandoned Him.

I befriended an elderly woman, Carol, who lived alone in a secluded spot. After a few visits and servings of chicken soup, she revealed she was lonely because her two adult daughters never visited.

Bitter and depressed, Carol didn't believe in God. She asked me complicated questions about the faith, which I answered as best as I could without preaching at her. I simply loved her and prayed earnestly for her. One day, Carol thanked me for my prayers and asked for more. An atheist acknowledged prayer and began to believe.

ACT Turn to Mary in your sorrows and difficulties.

PRAY Dear Sorrowful Mother, help me to help others.

Our Father, Hail Mary, and Glory Be.

SAVOR Mary will grant graces to me for the asking.

September 21

> A virtue is an habitual and firm disposition to do the good. It allows the person not only to perform good acts, but to give the best of himself. The virtuous person tends toward the good with all his sensory and spiritual powers; he pursues the good and chooses it in concrete actions.
>
> *Catechism of the Catholic Church*, 1803

STEEP A single word scratched on my teen son Joseph's to-do list made my heart soar. "Pray!" Looking back, I think it is absolutely brilliant. We should all pen that word on our to-do lists to be reminded what is most important.

How do we acquire virtue? We pray! We move our wills to pray and perform good acts, giving the best of ourselves, tending always to the good, choosing always what is good. Influencing our children and grandchildren to be prayerful helps them resist the negative aspects of the culture and choose virtue instead. The young ones can do the same for us—like my son did for me!

ACT Carve out time to pray and to instill that need in the young people in your life.

PRAY Dear Jesus, Mary, and Joseph, please teach me to pray!

Our Father, Hail Mary, and Glory Be.

SAVOR I can pray for graces to resist the culture's allurements and to do good.

September 22

As for me and my household, we will serve the LORD.

JOSHUA 24:15

STEEP When browsing in a store, I came across pretty autumn-themed dishes. A woman nearby remarked, "We should have a set of dishes for every season!"

This reminds me of my mother's vow to use her good china upon returning from the hospital. And not just for special occasions—for any time! She said it was time to take the dishes out of the china cabinet and use them. My dear mother didn't make it home from the hospital, and I never forgot her desires.

Time together in the family should be celebrated! We can find things to celebrate and appreciate in both good times and difficult times. Even without a set of fancy dishes for every season, we can be festive any day (perhaps especially on Sundays) with a tablecloth, cloth napkins, flowers, or candles. And smiles—every day!

ACT Decorate to suit the occasions in your family's life. Bring a big dose of joy to the family table.

PRAY Dear Holy Family, teach me to celebrate family life. Our Lady of Sorrows, watch over us.

Our Father, Hail Mary, and Glory Be.

SAVOR Family celebrations are appropriate every single day!

September 23

I can say with certainty that Jesus has never forgotten me, even when I was far from Him. He follows me everywhere with His love.[157]

SAINT PADRE PIO

STEEP Even Padre Pio admitted he was capable of abandoning the Lord. Perhaps it was his deep humility that helped him to realize this. Whatever the case, he desired to have Jesus close so that he didn't forget Him.

Occupied and preoccupied, we busy women can forget Jesus too. That's why it is very important to carve out specific times for prayer in addition to the spontaneous prayer rising from our heart. Holy reminders, such as statues, pictures, and icons, draw our hearts heavenward. Sacramentals like rosaries are perfect tangible remedies. Even Catholic jewelry can remind us to pray. When it is blessed it, too, becomes a sacramental.

ACT Choose three ways to be more cognizant of Jesus' presence in your life.

PRAY Jesus, stay with me, please. Our Lady of Sorrows, teach me to stay with Jesus.

Our Father, Hail Mary, and Glory Be.

SAVOR I will try to stay longer with Jesus in prayer.

September 24

> It is Mary who will teach us how to be silent, how to listen for the voice of God in the midst of a busy and noisy world. It is Mary who will help us to find time for prayer.[158]
>
> Saint John Paul II

STEEP Tradition holds that the Blessed Mother appeared to Richeldis de Faverches, a pious noblewoman, in 1061 in the village of Walsingham in Norfolk, England. It is said that within a religious ecstasy, the Blessed Mother took Richeldis' soul and carried it to Nazareth to the Holy Family's house. Richeldis was instructed to make a replica of this house in Walsingham. Known as the "Holy House," it became a shrine where tens of thousands have pilgrimaged every year.

We can try to make our homes spiritual replicas of the Holy House. After all, Catholic families are encouraged to create a domestic church to mirror the "big" Church. Fostering a prayerful atmosphere and inviting holiness to the dinner table is a very good start!

ACT Find ways to create more of a Holy House atmosphere in your home.

PRAY Our Lady of Sorrows, please watch over and protect my family. Holy Family, help us make our home like yours.

Our Father, Hail Mary, and Glory Be.

SAVOR Mary teaches us to live in God's presence.

September 25

A great number of the people followed him, and among them were women who were beating their breasts and wailing for him.

LUKE 23:27

STEEP Saint Alphonsus de Liguori discussed Our Lady's sorrows in his book, *The Glories of Mary*. He said: "If her body was not wounded by the hand of the executioner, her blessed heart was transfixed by a sword of grief at the passion of her Son; grief which was sufficient to have caused her death, not once, but a thousand times." Can we even imagine this? He went further to say that "her whole life may be said to have been a prolonged death."[159]

As Mother of the Savior, Mary suffered a long martyrdom that lasted her whole life. We might not normally ponder these facts when thinking of Mary. However, Mary's sorrowful life can give great hope to those of us whose experience as grandmothers involves suffering long martyrdoms. Certainly, Mary's powerful intercession can be a consolation to us all.

ACT Take time with Mary. Close your eyes and be with her in your prayers. Ask her to guide you.

PRAY Our Lady of Sorrows, I am moved by your martyrdom. Keep me close to you and lead me to your Son.

Our Father, Hail Mary, and Glory Be.

SAVOR Our Lady of Sorrows will help me in my grandmothering.

September 26

Under the mantle of Mary even sinners obtain salvation.[160]

SAINT ALPHONSUS DE LIGUORI

STEEP It would be difficult to imagine any mother (or grandmother!) who would not want the absolute best for her children. Sure, there are some who have failed to love in this way. Yet, for the most part, a mother's heart is for her children. She desires for them to be well, to succeed, to be happy, and so on.

Ultimately, a Catholic mother wants very much for her children to reach Heaven. She trains them in the virtues and, along the way, learns a few herself! Mothering is not for the faint of heart! Without a doubt, God supplies the graces for the asking.

Our Holy Mother longs for all of her children to be in Heaven with her one day. She will not stop working until she can safely escort us to Heaven.

ACT Jot down three ways you can help others turn to Mary, who will in turn lead them to her Son. Put these ideas into practice soon.

PRAY Dear Mary, please help me to help my family reach Heaven.

Our Father, Hail Mary, and Glory Be.

SAVOR There is great safety under Mary's mantle.

September 27

The heart of Mary became, as it were, a mirror of the Passion of the Son, in which might be seen, faithfully reflected, the spitting, the blows and wounds, and all that Jesus suffered.[161]

SAINT LAWRENCE JUSTINIAN

STEEP It's difficult to discuss or ponder the deep sufferings of Jesus and His dear Mother Mary. We love them and don't like to be reminded of their pain. Perhaps we would rather focus on happier things. We might distract ourselves with various pleasures and keep so busy that we don't have time to meditate on those sufferings or unite ourselves in prayer with them.

Jesus told Saint Faustina He was pleased most when she meditated upon His Passion and that much light would fall upon her soul (see *Diary*, 1337, 267). When we meditate upon Jesus' Passion and death on the Cross, we console Jesus and Mary by our attentive prayers. We can also grow in gratitude for Jesus' sacrifice and in our resolve to live holier lives.

ACT Do your best to meditate upon Jesus' and Holy Mary's sufferings. Pray for graces and the conversion of sinners.

PRAY Jesus, I love You! Dear Mary, help me. Saint Faustina, please pray for me.

Our Father, Hail Mary, and Glory Be.

SAVOR Mary's Sorrowful and Immaculate Heart is my refuge.

September 28

> If our Lord withdraws Himself from the sight of a soul which loves Him, He does not, therefore, depart from the heart; He often conceals Himself from a soul, that she may seek Him with a more ardent desire and greater love.[162]
>
> SAINT ALPHONSUS DE LIGUORI

STEEP During a dark night in the spiritual life, we might feel like God is absent, when in fact, He is there all along. He allows us to long more deeply for Him and, in the process, to become shaped and refined like a brilliant multifaceted diamond. A raw diamond found in a mine is not capable of reflection. It must be cut perfectly so that its facets act as mirrors to show off its brilliance.

At times when we feel that God is far away from us, we must seek Him with greater love and gusto. Spending time in meditation during Adoration will be beneficial to our souls.

ACT Seek Mary when in darkness, pain, or uncertainty. She will always help us to find Jesus! Also, make great efforts to be in touch with grandchildren who are far away.

PRAY Our Lady of Sorrows, please grant the graces to me that I need most.

Our Father, Hail Mary, and Glory Be.

SAVOR I will always seek Jesus, especially when I feel His absence.

September 29

The grief which filled Mary's heart, as a torrent flowed into and embittered the heart of Jesus. So much so that Jesus on the cross suffered more from compassion for His Mother than from His own torments.[163]

Saint Bernard

STEEP Jesus loved His Mother so much. We hear in today's quote that He suffered more from her suffering than His own! Jesus wants us to love His Mother too, and to depend upon her. As Scripture teaches, from the Cross, Jesus lovingly gave us the most precious gift of His own Mother (see Jn 19:26–27). We are indeed blessed to have such a Mother!

As a little child is persistent in asking her mother—or grandmother!—to spend time with her, play with her, feed her, and care for her needs, we should become as little children and earnestly run to the Sorrowful and Immaculate Heart of Mary, trusting in her loving protection and intercession. Each and every day we can beseech Mary for our needs. We ask her help for the salvation of every soul. She will always lead us to her Divine Son Jesus.

ACT Run to Mary.

PRAY Jesus, I love You. Dear Sorrowful Mother, I wish to console you.

Our Father, Hail Mary, and Glory Be.

SAVOR Jesus and Mary show me how to love.

September 30

I can truly say that at the burial of my Son one tomb contained as it were two hearts.[164]

BLESSED MOTHER TO SAINT BRIDGET

STEEP As we finish out the month of September, we are again reminded of Mary's deep sorrows. Sorrowful Mary grieved after her Son's body was sealed away in the tomb. It is said that all who saw her tears cried out of sorrow for her, perhaps even more so than for her Son. They could feel her grief.

After Jesus' resurrection, Mary was privileged to see and spend glorious time with her Son. Consoled as she was after having felt buried away in the tomb with Him, she relished this great joy for a time. Knowing that Mary experienced joy after her suffering gives grandmothers great hope in our own vocations.

ACT Ponder how meditating upon Mary's sorrows has transformed the way you understand the role of suffering in your life.

PRAY Our Lady of Sorrows, please pray for my family.

Our Father, Hail Mary, and Glory Be.

SAVOR The Blessed Mother is a light to my life.

OCTOBER

The Rosary

Why should we not have recourse to the Rosary, with the same faith as those who have gone before us? The Rosary retains all its power and continues to be a valuable pastoral resource for every good evangelizer.[165]

SAINT JOHN PAUL II

October 1

I beg you, O my Divine Bridegroom, to be the Restorer of my soul. . . . Tomorrow, with the help of your grace, I will begin a new life in which each moment will be an act of love and renunciation.[166]

Saint Thérèse of Lisieux

STEEP Beloved modern-day saint and Doctor of the Church Thérèse of Lisieux, known for her "Little Way" of remaining childlike in her faith, kicks off our month of October. Thérèse loved our Lady but often had trouble focusing when praying the Rosary. However, she overcame this difficulty. As she said, "I think that the Queen of heaven, since she is *my MOTHER*, must see my good will and she is satisfied with it."[167] From then on, she trusted Mary! This gives us great hope that we, too, can become saints, even if we struggle with praying the Rosary. Just as Saint Thérèse trusted the Blessed Virgin Mary was pleased with her efforts, we can too!

ACT Turn to Saint Thérèse today. Ask for her help and strive to make each prayer of the Rosary an act of love and renunciation.

PRAY Dear Saint Thérèse, please teach me your "Little Way" of love.

Our Father, Hail Mary, and Glory Be.

SAVOR Even saints struggled with praying the Rosary. With God's grace, I can persevere.

October 2

So many times the Devil has said: "We cannot do anything to you, because you are too protected." I have my guardian angel. . . . I have so much help from above.[168]

FATHER GABRIELE AMORTH

STEEP Since our guardian angels are invisible, we might not think to ask their help often. Yet, Scripture and many saints tell us our guardian angel is our very real companion and powerful protector. If we could remember Father Gabriele Amorth's wise advice above, we would breeze through temptations with greater ease because we have invoked the help of our angel! The evil one flees when we do so. That should be music to our ears—as should the fact that our dear grandchildren have guardian angels too! They are protecting them even when we can't be there to do so.

ACT Get into the habit of invoking your guardian angel at least every morning and night. Invoke your grandchildren's guardian angels too.

PRAY Angel of God, my guardian dear,
To whom his love commits me here,
Ever this day be at my side,
To light and guard, to rule and guide. Amen.

Our Father, Hail Mary, and Glory Be.

SAVOR God has gifted me with a guardian angel who will work hard to get me to Heaven!

October 3

The greatest method of praying is to pray the Rosary.[169]

SAINT FRANCIS DE SALES

STEEP The holy Rosary, when prayed with devotion, is a beautiful way to journey closer to the Heart of Jesus through the Immaculate Heart of Mary. Private revelation suggests that Mary gave the prayer of the Rosary to Saint Dominic, along with fifteen promises to those who faithfully pray the Rosary.

The first promise of the Blessed Mother is: "Those who faithfully serve me by the recitation of the Rosary shall receive signal graces."[170] Signal graces are extraordinary graces that move the soul through the intellect and the will. They are like fortifications in our faith journey—like hugs from Heaven! They can be simple signs that answer our questions in prayer or an interior knowledge of the right decision to make. Signal graces have been the cause of great conversions!

ACT Strive to pray the holy Rosary with more faith, attention, and fervor. Ask Mary for the graces to do so and for the blessing of signal graces.

PRAY Our Lady of the Rosary, teach me to pray the Rosary more faithfully.

Our Father, Hail Mary, and Glory Be.

SAVOR The Rosary can transform my day and my very life!

October 4

> I promise my special protection and the greatest graces to all those who shall recite the Rosary.[171]
>
> Blessed Virgin Mary (second promise)

STEEP As women and as grandmothers, we are often busy. Some of our busyness can't be avoided, but some of it might be our own doing. If we don't make time for daily prayer, it might not happen as it should. Because the Rosary can seem like a mammoth undertaking, we might be tempted to skip it. Perhaps we have health issues and lack the energy to pray it all at once.

Truthfully, to pray five decades of the Rosary requires only about fifteen minutes. When we are pressed for time or don't feel well, we can pray the Rosary a decade at a time throughout the day. Our Lord and our Lady surely know of our demands and issues.

Our Lady of the Rosary promises her "special protection and the greatest graces" when we recite the Rosary. What are we waiting for?

ACT Do your best to please our Lady with your fervent, loving Rosaries, even one decade at a time.

PRAY Our Lady of the Rosary, thank you for your amazing promises.

Our Father, Hail Mary, and Glory Be.

SAVOR Mary will protect me and grant special graces for my faithfulness to praying the Rosary.

October 5

The Rosary shall be a powerful armor against hell. It will destroy vice, decrease sin, and defeat heresies.[172]

BLESSED VIRGIN MARY (THIRD PROMISE)

STEEP Our Lady's promises above give us great reasons to take up the beads often!

Saint Louis de Montfort told the following story in his book, *The Secret of the Rosary*, about a Franciscan friar who prayed the Rosary each day before dinner. One day, he sought his superior's permission to be late for dinner since he had not yet prayed it. Permission was granted, and he prayed in his cell.

After a long while, a friar was sent to fetch him and found him facing our Lady and two angels. Bathed in heavenly light, beautiful roses issued from his mouth upon praying each Hail Mary and were carried by angels and woven in a crown on Mary's head. Smiling Mary did not leave until the Rosary was completed.

Incidentally, the word Rosary means "crown of roses."

ACT Pray the Rosary and ponder the life of Jesus and Mary.

PRAY Queen of the Most Holy Rosary, pray for me.

Our Father, Hail Mary, and Glory Be.

SAVOR I can strive to crown Mary with my fervent prayers.

October 6

> The recitation of the Rosary will cause virtue and good works to flourish. It will obtain for souls the abundant mercy of God. It will withdraw the hearts of men from the love of the world and its vanities, and will lift them to the desire of eternal things. Oh, that souls would sanctify themselves by this means.[173]
>
> BLESSED VIRGIN MARY (FOURTH PROMISE)

STEEP A mother of two young daughters was going through a divorce and struggling with sadness and anxiety. Her entire world was crumbling. She began to sink into desperation.

Though she was not Catholic, I ventured to give her a rosary. I passed the blue wooden beads over to her open hand. "Just hold these beads and pray," I told her. "Call on Mother Mary for help. She will surely help you." And she did!

Later, my friend told me she didn't know what she "would do without those beads," for they brought her great comfort. Helping my friend was a way of being a spiritual mother to her and a spiritual grandmother to her children.

ACT Is there someone you can help by gifting them a rosary?

PRAY Queen of the Holy Rosary, please help me to help others.

Our Father, Hail Mary, and Glory Be.

SAVOR The Rosary obtains for souls the abundant mercy of God.

October 7

It was because Our Lady wanted to help us in the great task of working out our salvation that she ordered St. Dominic to teach the faithful to meditate upon the sacred mysteries of the life of Jesus Christ.[174]

SAINT LOUIS DE MONTFORT

STEEP After the Crusades, in October 1571, Saint Pius V requested all of Europe to pray the Rosary. Catholics were at a huge disadvantage against Muslim forces. Rosaries were prayed by young and old, rich and poor. The Christian fleet defeated the Muslim Turks in the Battle of Lepanto on October 7, 1571.

Special artifacts from this event are venerated today. The image of Our Lady of Guadalupe that the commander of Catholic forces Admiral Andrea Doria carried into battle is now in the Church of San Stefano in Aveto, Italy. Don Juan of Austria's ship's crucifix, shot by the Turks' cannon, is at the Cathedral of San Eulalia in Barcelona, Spain. Jesus' corpus had miraculously swerved to the right when struck. It remains in that position today.

ACT Entrust a "battle" in your life to Mary today.

PRAY Mary, help me in my battles now and at the hour of my death.

Our Father, Hail Mary, and Glory Be.

SAVOR Praying the Rosary can help not just in spiritual battles but in physical ones too.

October 8

Just as you did it to one of the least of these who are members of my family, you did it to me.

MATTHEW 25:40

STEEP In the twelfth century, Saint John de Matha established the Trinitarian Order to free thousands of Christians who had been captured by Muslims and sold into slavery. He and his Order, under the patronage of the Blessed Mother, raised funds to then "buy" (ransom) the Christian slaves and set them free.

The Trinitarians became known for their devotion to Mary under the title of "Remedy," or "Good Remedy." Altars and images were set up and confraternities established to honor Mary under this title. Mary manifested her pleasure by granting signal graces.

Families may turn to their mother or grandmother to remedy difficult situations they face. As mothers and grandmothers, we can imitate Mary through our loving role in the family and seek good remedies for our loved ones too.

ACT Ask Mary, as a good mother, to obtain a good remedy for a situation you or your family are facing.

PRAY Our Lady of Good Remedy, source of unfailing help, grant that all may draw from your treasury of graces in time of most need.

Our Father, Hail Mary, and Glory Be.

SAVOR Mary knows a remedy for every affliction and misery we encounter.

October 9

The soul which recommends itself to me by the recitation of the Rosary shall not perish.[175]

Blessed Virgin Mary (fifth promise)

STEEP Countless grandmothers have prayed multitudes of Rosaries. My Grandma Alexandra instilled a special love for the Rosary in my heart. She didn't sit me down and teach me every step. As a young girl, I watched and learned by the sparkle in her eyes and her gentle smile as the beads made their way through her aged fingers.

We might not realize that our examples affect future generations of potential prayer warriors! Hopefully, we have had the opportunity to impress upon their hearts the powerful and loving prayer of the holy Rosary. But even if we have not had that opportunity, and even if we do not see the fruits of our prayers or examples, our prayers will aid our growing grandchildren, no matter their age.

ACT Pray a decade of the Rosary daily for a special intention for your grandchildren.

PRAY Dear Mary, I love you!

Our Father, Hail Mary, and Glory Be.

SAVOR It's never too late to pick up the beads for or with my grandchildren.

October 10

> Those who recite my Rosary devoutly, applying themselves to the consideration of its sacred mysteries, shall never be conquered by misfortune. In his justice, God will not chastise them; nor shall they perish by an unprovided death, i.e., be unprepared for heaven. Sinners shall convert. The just shall persevere in grace and become worthy of eternal life.[176]
>
> BLESSED VIRGIN MARY (SIXTH PROMISE)

STEEP While tending their flocks in the fields, the three young shepherd children at Fatima prayed the Rosary daily. But, in a hurry to eat lunch and play, they rushed through their Rosaries. After meeting Our Lady of Fatima, they sincerely prayed with much fervor and devotion, desiring to please our Lady and to help save souls.

Young grandchildren might not have learned the patience required to pray slowly and are easily distracted. Perhaps they would rather play instead. This is when our steady patience comes into play, lovingly directing and guiding them, always setting a prayerful example. With time and practice, we and our grandchildren will be praying more devoutly.

ACT Whether you have much or little time to pray today, strive to pray devoutly.

PRAY Our Lady of Fatima, dear Saint Francisco, Saint Jacinta, and Venerable Lucia, please pray for me.

Our Father, Hail Mary, and Glory Be.

SAVOR Our Lady desires my earnest prayers.

October 11

Those who have a true devotion to the Rosary shall not die without the sacraments of the Church.[177]

BLESSED VIRGIN MARY (SEVENTH PROMISE)

STEEP Our Lady of the Rosary has given us fifteen promises for those who are devoted to her beautiful Psalter (for centuries the Rosary was known as "Our Lady's Psalter" because it involved the recitation of 150 Hail Mary's—one for each Psalm). The modest daily investment of prayer time is a very tiny price to pay for such unfathomable, yet true promises.

That said, we certainly shouldn't pray the Rosary simply to be given something in return, like a grandchild who does something good to earn a piece of candy, a cookie, or some other reward. Or, perhaps like grandchildren doing chores, we also shouldn't do it just because we think we're supposed to, but without a deeper love behind it. Our aim should be to possess a sincere and loving desire to please our Lady and help Heaven's plans to save souls.

ACT Ponder your life, your desires, your daily schedule. Is Mary a big part of it? Why or why not?

PRAY Dear Mary, please lead me closer to your Son.

Our Father, Hail Mary, and Glory Be.

SAVOR The Rosary will please Mother Mary and enliven my heart and soul!

October 12

Those who faithfully recite the Rosary shall have, during their life and at their death, the light of God and the plenitude of his graces. At the moment of death, they shall participate in the merits of the saints in paradise.[178]

Blessed Virgin Mary (eighth promise)

STEEP My friend Lisa began a family Rosary tradition. She invited her adult children and their families to come over on Sunday afternoons for dinner and the Rosary.

Rosary beads were aplenty for the grandchildren. A blessed candle flickered as Lisa and her husband, Andy, led the prayers of the Rosary. With busy schedules and lots of little ones, Lisa was joyfully surprised at how it came together—no doubt with Mother Mary's help. There might have been some chaotic times as well, but those times can remind us that families are a work in progress, and we work out our salvation together in the heart of the home.

ACT Endeavor to include your family in the Rosary. Consider starting a family Rosary.

PRAY Our Lady of the Rosary, please help us and especially families who are far away from God.

Our Father, Hail Mary, and Glory Be.

SAVOR Families are called to grow in holiness together.

October 13

> It must be admitted that [the Miracle of the Sun] was not an afternoon of celestial fireworks enjoyed by simple and unlettered people predisposed to accept any flash of lightening as the Lord's own signal. The 70,000 witnesses included believers and nonbelievers, pious old ladies and scoffing young men.[179]
>
> John de Marchi

STEEP While writing my book *Our Lady of Fatima: 100 Years of Stories, Prayers, and Devotions* (Servant Books, 2017), approaching the hundredth anniversary of the Fatima apparitions, I met Maria Vida, who shared an intriguing claim to fame. Maria's older relatives were actual eyewitnesses of the Great Miracle of the Sun in Fatima! I was soon in touch with her cousin Mary, who filled me in further about her grandparents, Erminia and Antonia. What an amazing true story these grandparents passed down to their family. Every grandparent can pass down their rich experiences to their grandchildren. We should be sure to do so to keep meaningful memories alive.

God is not to be outdone in His generosity! I included Erminia and Antonia's story in my book.

ACT Tell your grandchildren a meaningful story from your life.

PRAY Lord Jesus, thank You for Your blessings in my life!

Our Father, Hail Mary, and Glory Be.

SAVOR Family life is a rich tapestry of experiences meant to be shared.

October 14

I shall deliver from purgatory those who have been devoted to the Rosary.[180]

Blessed Virgin Mary (ninth promise)

STEEP Our Lady mentioned Purgatory in her promises. Saint Faustina had an experience of Purgatory early in her religious life when asking Jesus for whom she should pray. Her guardian angel took her to Purgatory. Saint Faustina described Purgatory as a "great crowd of suffering souls" undergoing purification. The souls are "praying fervently, but to no avail, for themselves; only we can come to their aid" (*Diary*, 20).

Though the idea of Purgatory might seem a bit scary, it doesn't have to be. The existence of Purgatory, and God's great mercy in allowing souls to be purified before entering Heaven, is a beautiful gift! We can share this perspective with our grandchildren or with anyone who struggles with believing the Church's teaching about Purgatory, and of course, we can remember to pray for the holy souls in Purgatory to reach Heaven.

ACT Pray for your departed loved ones each day.

PRAY Our Lady, please pray for us and the souls in Purgatory. *Our Father, Hail Mary, and Glory Be.*

SAVOR The holy souls depend upon my prayers.

October 15

The faithful children of the Rosary shall merit a high degree of glory in heaven.[181]

Blessed Virgin Mary (tenth promise)

STEEP Tomorrow is Saint Gerard Majella's feast day. He is a good saint to get to know when one's children and grandchildren are having children. He was born in Muro Lucano, Italy, on April 6, 1726. At fourteen, he applied to enter the Capuchin Friary, but poor health prevented entrance. In 1749, he became a Redemptorist lay brother. Gerard was blessed with the gift of prophecy and the ability to read hearts and perform miracles. He died at Materdomini on October 16, 1755, and was canonized by Saint Pius X on December 11, 1904. He is invoked as patron of expectant mothers.

One time, Saint Gerard forgot his handkerchief at his friend's home. The young teen daughter ran to give it to him. He providentially said, "Keep it. It may be useful to you someday."[182] Years later, when almost dying in childbirth, she remembered the handkerchief and called for it. The danger miraculously passed, and her baby was delivered safely.

ACT Seek the intercession of the saints and pray the Rosary with fervor.

PRAY Dear Mary, thank you for your promises.

Our Father, Hail Mary, and Glory Be.

SAVOR Our Catholic faith is a treasure!

October 16

Who but God can give you peace? Has the world ever yet satisfied the heart?[183]

SAINT GERARD MAJELLA

STEEP Today is the feast of Saint Gerard Majella, known as a patron saint for mothers and pregnancies. Full of charity, he earned the title of "Father of the Poor."

My friend Lisa faithfully prayed a novena to Saint Gerard for her niece, who was expecting a baby. She prayed for the birth to be free of danger and excessive pains, and for the baby to be healthy. When Lisa told our mutual friend Debbie about her novena, Debbie quickly pointed out how amazing it was that the baby was born on October 16—Saint Gerard's feast day!

Lisa said, "I felt as though God was letting me know in some small way to keep on praying!" Since then, Lisa has prayed that same novena for many other expectant mothers—including for all the childbirths of her own twelve grandchildren!

ACT Be generous with your prayers for others and open to opportunities to help an expectant mother.

PRAY Dear Lord, thank You for Your many blessings. Saint Gerard, please pray for my family.

Our Father, Hail Mary, and Glory Be.

SAVOR Life is a gift! I need to relish it.

October 17

By the recitation of the Rosary you shall obtain all that you ask of me.[184]

Blessed Virgin Mary (eleventh promise)

STEEP I often meet people who lament to me that they don't believe in God because He doesn't answer their prayers. They give up on God, but they don't consider that God might not have answered their prayer because it was not in line with His holy will for them.

If our grandchildren received everything that they asked for, they would become spoiled, and sometimes they would receive the wrong things—things that would harm them. It would be the same for us if we received every single thing that we ask from God. A good parent or grandparent protects their children and wants them to get to Heaven. It's even more so with God. When we are unhappy in this life because we don't receive what we want in prayer, it's important to remember that He has created us to be happy with Him forever in Heaven.

ACT Today, with help from Mary, try praying only for God's holy will to be done.

PRAY Dear God, help me to want only Your will for my life. Jesus, Mary, and Joseph, please pray for us.

Our Father, Hail Mary, and Glory Be.

SAVOR God listens and answers every prayer.

October 18

Those who propagate the holy Rosary shall be aided by me in their necessities.[185]

Blessed Virgin Mary (twelfth promise)

STEEP Bartolo Longo, born in 1841, studied law during a time when Paganism and Satanism abounded. Longo followed in the footsteps of professors who hated the Church. Confused and unhappy, he consulted with occult mediums, gave his soul to a demon, and became a satanist priest.

His family enlisted help from a Catholic professor who was able to get Longo's attention, warning him he could die in an asylum or worse, suffer eternal damnation. Longo renounced the evil and re-converted to Christianity but fell into despair, fearing the devil still had hold of him. Then he recalled Mary's twelfth promise (see today's quote). He fell to his knees and vowed to propagate the Rosary the remainder of his life. Saint John Paul II beatified Longo in 1980.

If we feel burdened by past sins or concerned that our grandchildren or other loved ones are "too far gone" to come back to the Church, the story of Bartolo Longo can reassure us that every person is redeemable.

ACT Ponder the blessings of saints and holy people in your life.

PRAY Dear Blessed Bartolo Longo, please pray for me.

Our Father, Hail Mary, and Glory Be.

SAVOR Every person is redeemable.

October 19

I have obtained from my Divine Son that all the advocates of the Rosary shall have for intercessors the entire celestial court during their life and at the hour of their death.[186]

Blessed Virgin Mary (thirteenth promise)

STEEP Catholic Austria was terrorized under the tyrannical rule of Soviet Russia after World War II. Located strategically and possessing rich resources, Austria was valuable to the Russians. A Franciscan priest, Father Petrus, inspired by the miracle at the Battle of Lepanto, rallied an army of seventy thousand prayer warriors who promised to pray the Rosary daily for the intention of Austria being let loose from Russian rule.

Miraculously, on May 15, 1955, the atheistic Russian regime uncharacteristically signed the agreement to leave Austria. Not one bullet was ever fired, and no one killed. Even today, military strategists are scratching their heads.

Those seventy thousand prayer warriors and other Rosary devotees know full well why it happened! The Rosary is a powerful weapon. Grandmothers also know the power of the Rosary!

ACT Ponder your prayer life. Give great thanks to God for all of the blessings in your life (and those to come).

PRAY Dear God, thank You for my life.

Our Father, Hail Mary, and Glory Be.

SAVOR Through her Rosary, Mary miraculously provides.

October 20

All who recite the Rosary are my beloved children and the brothers and sisters of my only Son, Jesus Christ.[187]

Blessed Virgin Mary (fourteenth promise)

STEEP Eight German Jesuit missionaries faithfully prayed the Rosary daily at their home in Hiroshima, Japan. Germany and Japan were allies at that time, and these men were permitted to minister to the Japanese people during World War II. Their home was attached to a church that was destroyed on August 6, 1945, when an atomic bomb was dropped on the town and killed or injured as many as 140,000 people.

In addition to surviving the atomic bomb with only minor injuries, all eight men lived long after that fateful day with absolutely no radiation illness, any effect to their hearing, or any other sicknesses. Hundreds of times, the men were physically examined by health care workers and interviewed. Their survival was unprecedented, being only one kilometer from where the atomic bomb went off. Survivor Father Schiffer remarked that the missionaries believed they were spared because they were living out the Fatima message in praying the Rosary daily for the salvation of sinners.

ACT Give great thanks to Jesus and Mary today.

PRAY Jesus and Mary, please help my family.

Our Father, Hail Mary, and Glory Be.

SAVOR We are Mary's beloved children.

October 21

Devotion for my Rosary is a great sign of predestination.[188]

BLESSED VIRGIN MARY (FIFTEENTH PROMISE)

STEEP Some people scoff at the Rosary, assuming it is a bunch of rote prayers, or it is worshipping Mary, or even that it is boring. Sadly, perhaps even our own grandchildren or other family members may think this way. However, all of the above complaints or objections can be overcome. First of all, we are in good company praying the Rosary, knowing that many popes and saints have highly promoted this form of prayer. It's anything but boring—pondering the lives of Jesus and Mary! Additionally, Mary herself has promised that devotion to her Rosary is a sign the devotee is on the right track to Heaven (predestination). We should certainly give it a try, beginning slowly and working up to five decades a day. One decade at a time is perfectly fine. Much growth in holiness will come through devotion to the holy Rosary.

ACT Ask your grandchildren what they think about the Rosary. Let it start a conversation!

PRAY Dear Jesus and Mary, please help me to pray the Rosary with reverence and attention and help others appreciate its value. *Our Father, Hail Mary, and Glory Be.*

SAVOR Our Lady works tirelessly to help us work out our salvation!

October 22

With the Rosary, the Christian people sits at the school of Mary and is led to contemplate the beauty on the face of Christ and to experience the depths of his love. Through the Rosary the faithful receive abundant grace, as though from the very hands of the Mother of the Redeemer.[189]

Saint John Paul II

STEEP During his pontificate, Saint John Paul II drew from Blessed Bartolo Longo and added the Luminous Mysteries to the Rosary. In his Apostolic Letter *Rosarium Virginis Mariae*, the pontiff wrote, "As a true apostle of the Rosary, Blessed Bartolo Longo had a special charism. His path to holiness rested on an inspiration heard in the depths of his heart: 'Whoever spreads the Rosary is saved!'"[190]

Catholic grandmothers can be true apostles of the Rosary too! My own grandmother's shining example of devotion to that ancient but ever-new prayer etched an impression on my heart as a little girl. Now, I endeavor to spread devotion to the holy Rosary as well. Every faithful grandmother can do the same through her teachings and example.

ACT Reflect upon the miracle stories in the life of your family.

PRAY Pray Saint John Paul II's Prayer (page 419).

Our Father, Hail Mary, and Glory Be.

SAVOR I can be an apostle of the Rosary in my own way today!

October 23

The rosary is heavenly medicine, an antidote that draws the poison of sin and vice out of our hearts.[191]

Father Donald Calloway

STEEP In the 1100s and 1200s in France, many Catholics were corrupted by Albigensian heretics who believed that the material world and the body were evil. In the early 1200s, the Blessed Mother gave the holy Rosary to Saint Dominic to defeat the heresy. In addition, Saint Dominic continuously encouraged all to honor Jesus and Mary through the Rosary.

Saint Louis de Montfort wrote of Saint Dominic's devotion, "As a reward he received countless graces from her. . . . The greatest honor of all was that she helped him crush the Albigensian heresy and made him the founder . . . of a great religious order."[192]

As Catholic grandmothers, we certainly will not encounter Albigensians in the twenty-first century. Yet, by faithfully praying the holy Rosary, setting examples, and speaking and teaching about the Rosary, we can help dispel false teachings and misconceptions about the faith that often bombard our families in today's culture.

ACT If you haven't already, speak to your grandchildren about the Rosary and establish a Rosary prayer habit with them.

PRAY Mary, please teach me your ways.

Our Father, Hail Mary, and Glory Be.

SAVOR The Rosary is a heavenly medicine.

October 24

It is really pathetic to see how most people say the holy rosary —they say it astonishingly fast and mumble so that the words are not properly pronounced at all.[193]

Saint Louis de Montfort

STEEP In today's quote, Saint Louis de Montfort bemoans the way we can fall into thoughtlessly racing through the Rosary. Although his phrasing may seem harsh, let's not let his words offend us, but instead, learn from them.

When we look at the essence of what he's saying, he is absolutely correct! The things we do for our grandchildren and families are more meaningful when it's clear that we have put time and thought into them rather than doing something halfheartedly or rushing through it. The same applies to how we pray the Rosary. We can set a beautiful example of loving prayer to our young ones by slowing down and offering our prayers with great love and devotion. Let's keep this in mind.

ACT Take time to pray and act slowly and meaningfully today.

PRAY Lord Jesus and Blessed Mother Mary, I am sorry for not giving you my full loving attention.

Our Father, Hail Mary, and Glory Be.

SAVOR I should take my time in the company of Jesus, Mary, and the saints.

October 25

When we say the rosary—we are saying to God, the Trinity, to the Incarnate Savior, to the Blessed Mother: "I love you, I love you, I love you."[194]

VENERABLE FULTON SHEEN

STEEP The medieval king Alphonsus wore a large rosary on his belt, but he didn't pray it. On the brink of death, he had a vision of himself about to be sentenced to Hell. The Blessed Mother called for a pair of scales. Alphonsus' sins were placed on one side and his rosary, together with all Rosaries prayed because of his example, on the other. The Rosaries outweighed his sins, so our Lady obtained graces to spare his life. She asked him to live wisely and do penance. He spread devotion to the holy Rosary the remainder of his life, praying it daily.[195]

One person's influence can bring many others closer to God. Isn't it interesting that King Alphonsus inspired others to pray even when he didn't pray himself? Even through our imperfections, our Lord and our Lady work.

ACT Pray the Rosary with great devotion and keep a Rosary visible to others.

PRAY Dear Blessed Trinity and sweet Mother Mary, I love you, I love you, I love you!

Our Father, Hail Mary, and Glory Be.

SAVOR Being a holy example transforms hearts and souls!

October 26

I know of no other way of establishing the kingdom of God than to unite vocal and mental prayer by saying the rosary.[196]

Saint Louis de Montfort

STEEP In 1980, when asked about the Third Secret of Fatima, Saint John Paul II held up his Rosary and said, "Here is the remedy against evil. Pray, pray and ask for nothing else. Put everything in the hands of the Mother of God. . . . We must be attentive to the prayer of the Rosary."[197]

We are blessed with such passionate words from the saints that encourage us to stay true to our devotion to the holy Rosary—reminders that the Rosary is a sure remedy against evil. So often, we mothers and grandmothers lament that our children and grandchildren have left the Church. We can feel helpless. However, by turning our grave concerns into passionate prayers, with God's grace and Mary's help, we can help to steer our offspring back to holy Mother Church.

ACT Make time for the Rosary. Don't give up on its powerful life-transforming prayers. Tell your grandchildren about your love for the Rosary.

PRAY Lord God, thank You for my life. Queen of the Most Holy Rosary, please pray for me.

Our Father, Hail Mary, and Glory Be.

SAVOR My family and I can help establish the Kingdom of God by praying the Rosary.

October 27

The Rosary has accompanied me in moments of joy and in moments of difficulty. To it I have entrusted any number of concerns; in it I have always found comfort.[198]

SAINT JOHN PAUL II

STEEP During a precarious era in my life, a rosary showed up at a time of captivity. Holding that rosary gave me exceptional comfort. Certainly, the holy beads can bring comfort, but also connection. I once sat nearby an elderly woman on a transcontinental flight. She looked down, her lips moving silently, her hands together, concealing something. Thinking she was praying the Rosary, I looked at her and raised my rosary beads. You should have seen her face! She ecstatically held up her beads, smiled, and affectionately slapped my arm, while saying something in Italian. And we hugged.

Some grandmothers feel lonely because we are the only ones in our families who pray the Rosary. Others of us may be in nursing homes or unable to see family regularly. If we cannot pray with our family, we may find both comfort and connection by finding (or starting!) a group to pray with.

ACT Consider starting a Rosary group for grandmothers.

PRAY Dear Queen of the Holy Rosary, pray for us.

Our Father, Hail Mary, and Glory Be.

SAVOR I will entrust all my concerns to Mary through the Rosary.

October 28

To recite the Rosary is nothing other than to contemplate with Mary the face of Christ.[199]

Saint John Paul II

STEEP Saint John Paul II, the great Rosary Pope, was deeply in love with Mary and her Psalter. He spoke much about the Blessed Virgin, and he encouraged others to pray the Rosary and grow to love her too. At one point, he questioned his great love of Mary, fearing that it could take away from the praise he owed to Jesus Christ. The great Marian saint Louis de Montfort allayed his fears because he stressed the fact the Mary always leads us to Jesus. She grants graces, strengthens, and protects her devotees.

In particular, Saint John Paul II encourages us to contemplate the face of Christ with Mary. When we pause to remember loved ones who have passed away or those we can't see in person, looking at something that reminds us of them helps bring their face to mind. The Rosary can do something similar for us with Christ, with Mary as our guide.

ACT Slow down and take time with Mary. Invite her to help you to meditate deeply.

PRAY Jesus, help me to contemplate Your Face. Mary, please pray for me.

Our Father, Hail Mary, and Glory Be.

SAVOR The holy Rosary is a great gift.

October 29

One cannot recite the Rosary without feeling caught up in a clear commitment to advancing peace.[200]

Saint John Paul II

STEEP In 1985, one million people in the Philippines committed to the World Apostolate of Fatima's "Blue Army Pledge" to pray the Rosary daily. On February 23, 1986, during the People Power Revolution, a Blue Army spokesperson stood by the National Pilgrim Virgin of Fatima statue and delivered a message by loudspeaker to several thousand people kneeling on the roads. Hundreds of combat-ready marines from the Marcos regime, threatening tanks, and armored cars faced the people, ready to strike. The people continued to kneel and pray the Rosary.

The troops stopped, and the tanks were halted. The immediate change was not because they saw the praying crowds. Soldiers had told his Eminence, Cardinal Sin, "A very beautiful lady appeared. The vision said, 'Stop! Don't attack my people. I am the Queen of this land.'"[201]

The World Apostolate of Fatima reported, "This was indisputably a 'Rosary miracle' of a bloodless transition from dictatorship to democracy."[202]

ACT Expect miracles. Pray the Rosary.

PRAY Our Lady of Fatima, thank you for your love.

Our Father, Hail Mary, and Glory Be.

SAVOR Fervent prayer changes things.

October 30

> Perseverance in praying the rosary has proven to be a tremendous means of helping a person avoid sin and remain in a state of grace.[203]
>
> Father Donald Calloway

STEEP Many of us grandmothers have learned the art of perseverance through our life experiences—getting through tough situations, big and small. We can use that sage wisdom to strive to stay faithful to our devotion to the Rosary. We might sometimes give up or forget the beads, or feel we don't have time for them. We need to reexamine those thoughts and do our best to persevere—even if it is simply to pray one decade at a time. We can all pray for graces to persevere in our Rosaries. In addition, we can ask our guardian angel to give us a daily nudge. No doubt, Jesus and Mother Mary will be pleased with our efforts.

ACT Write down reasons you may give up on praying the Rosary, and resolutions to help you persevere.

PRAY Jesus, Mary, and Joseph, help me to persevere in praying the Rosary.

Our Father, Hail Mary, and Glory Be.

SAVOR The Rosary is a wonderful help in my spiritual life.

October 31

As a prayer for peace, the Rosary is also, and always has been, a prayer of and for the family. . . . We need to return to the practice of family prayer and prayer for families, continuing to use the Rosary.[204]

Saint John Paul II

STEEP In his Apostolic Letter *Rosarium Virginis Mariae*, Saint John Paul II spoke about the family, "menaced by forces of disintegration on both the ideological and practical planes," as well as the need for "the revival of the Rosary in Christian families" to be "an effective aid in countering" evil.[205] He notes that we might fear the future, but we can have hope that our beautiful Mother Mary will assist today's families.

Mothers and grandmothers have an integral role in introducing the powerful prayer of the Rosary to our families through loving teachings, example, and time carved out specifically to pray the Rosary. Even if we are the only ones faithful to the Rosary at this time, we need to hang in there and pray for our families and the world.

ACT Continue on with the Rosary each day, including as many family members as possible.

PRAY Dear Mary, thank you for the gift of the Rosary!

Our Father, Hail Mary, and Glory Be.

SAVOR The Mother of Christ wants her children to pray the contemplative prayer of the Rosary.

NOVEMBER

All Saints and All Souls

History shows that all forms of holiness, even if it follows different paths: the path of the priesthood, the path of the consecrated life, contemplative life, the married or widowed life—it always passes through the way of the Cross. It always goes through this way of self-denial. This is the common thread.[206]

FATHER MIGUEL MARIE SOEHERMAN

November 1

St. John the Beloved . . . saw a vision of "a great multitude which no one could count from every nation, race, people and town." Most likely there are many more uncanonized saints in heaven than there are canonized. That's why we have today's great Feast of All Saints—to honor not only the canonized but also and especially the uncanonized saints today.[207]

Father Miguel Marie Soeherman

STEEP Father Miguel Marie Soeherman, MFVA, gave a powerful homily on All Saints Day. He said the special quality of saints is "their ability to be joyful and peaceful in the midst of trials and difficulties of their lives." He said, "This is a very typical pattern we find in the life of every saint."

Every saint was a "work in progress" just like you and me. They fell, but they got up again, dusted themselves off with Confession, and kept moving forward with God's grace. We are all called to be saints! We can strive to imitate the saints' virtues while we work at becoming a saint through our vocation.

ACT Keep going—have faith! Pray for the graces!

PRAY Dear holy saints, please pray for me.

Our Father, Hail Mary, and Glory Be.

SAVOR Heaven is populated with a multitude of saints. I pray I can one day be there too!

November 2

One of the doctrines that people often dismiss as unimportant or even nonexistent is the teaching on Purgatory.[208]

FATHER ANDREW APOSTOLI

STEEP Father Andrew Apostoli, CFR, preached extensively on Our Lady of Fatima's message. Part of Mary's message is that Heaven, Hell, and Purgatory exist. Father Andrew stated, "The existence of Purgatory is an official teaching of the Catholic Church and therefore should not be denied."

Today, All Souls Day, we should pray for the souls in Purgatory. We can remember deceased loved ones on this day—both in our prayers and in reminiscing about their lives. We can make a point to share stories with our grandchildren about our loved ones who have died and encourage them to pray for their souls. In addition to their own informal prayers, we can also teach the children the short Requiem Aeternam prayer: "Eternal rest grant unto him/her, O Lord, and let perpetual light shine upon him/her. May he/she rest in peace. Amen."

ACT Visit a cemetery with your grandchildren, if possible. Honor your deceased loved ones by putting up pictures of them and praying for them.

PRAY Jesus, Mary, and Joseph, please help my deceased family rest in peace.

Our Father, Hail Mary, and Glory Be.

SAVOR The holy souls need my prayers.

November 3

If a person dies with mortal sin they will be sent to hell. But if they die with venial sins on their soul, they need a place of purification before entering into the presence of the absolute holiness of God Himself. This is why Purgatory exists.[209]

FATHER ANDREW APOSTOLI

STEEP No one knows the day nor the hour when we will leave this planet. We have to be ready, leading holy lives and remaining in a state of grace. When we have something to confess, we should pray an Act of Contrition immediately, followed up by Confession as soon as we can. And of course, we should not receive Holy Communion if we have not gone to Confession for a mortal sin.

As Catholic grandmothers, we can explain Purgatory to our grandchildren by comparing it to the scenario of a child in trouble for breaking a valuable item. He or she has confessed, but he or she might have to do something, such as a chore, to be back in good graces with their parents.

ACT Have an age-appropriate conversation with your grandchildren about Purgatory today or soon.

PRAY Lord God, thank You for Your mercy and love.

Our Father, Hail Mary, and Glory Be.

SAVOR Life is an incredible journey in which we work out our salvation.

November 4

St. Catherine of Genoa says that the joy of the souls in Purgatory is exceeded only by the joy of the saints in Heaven. Purgatory has been given a bad name.[210]

FATHER BENEDICT GROESCHEL

STEEP No doubt, Saint Catherine of Genoa was emphasizing the fact that souls in Purgatory anticipate their eternal reward in Heaven at the proper time. In today's quote, Father Benedict, in typical "Father Benedict style," makes a straight from the shoulder, yet brilliant point! We learn that Purgatory is not simply a place of purification or suffering. It is a place of waiting with joyful anticipation. Father Benedict often said he hoped to make it to Purgatory. He knew Purgatory was a good place. As Catholic grandmothers, we can emphasize this joy to our grandchildren when we tell them that we have a very merciful and loving God, Who wants us with Him in complete happiness in Heaven one day.

ACT Pray for the souls in Purgatory and get to know more about the saints this month.

PRAY Dear Lord God, thank You for my life and for the hope of Eternal Life ahead.

Our Father, Hail Mary, and Glory Be.

SAVOR I need to lead my life earnestly striving for holiness.

November 5

Rejoice in hope, be patient in suffering, persevere in prayer.

ROMANS 12:12

STEEP Grandmothers' role in earnestly praying for their grandchildren to make it to Heaven one day begins when their grandchild is hidden in utero, tucked beneath their mama's heart. A grandmother's prayer and example continue all throughout her grandchild's life and even beyond, when we consider that she also prays for her grandchildren when she is in Heaven. She is always prayerfully involved, even from afar—even if the parents of her grandchild are away from the Church and do not practice the faith. Grandmothers' prayers are never wasted. They are invaluable! Our important prayers can help mold our grandchildren's consciences and help them get to Heaven.

ACT Consider adding a special novena to Saint Anne, a Chaplet of prayer, or an extra decade of the Rosary each day, specifically for your grandchildren.

PRAY Jesus, Mary, and Joseph, please pray for my family. Dear Saint Anne, help me to be the grandmother God calls me to be.

Our Father, Hail Mary, and Glory Be.

SAVOR Heaven needs my grandmotherly prayers.

November 6

> My mortifications consisted in breaking my will, always so ready to impose itself on others, in holding back a reply, in rendering little services without any recognition, in not leaning my back against a support when seated . . .[211]
>
> Saint Thérèse of Lisieux

STEEP The humble nun Saint Thérèse confessed that she "felt no attraction" to penances that she knew she should perform in order to grow in holiness. She felt it came from her own "cowardice." She stated she could have "found a thousand little ways" to take on small penances in order to break her own will and become more united to God's holy will.

Saint Thérèse lets us in on a secret to her holiness. "It was through the practice of these *nothings* that I prepared myself to become the fiancée of Jesus."[212] Saint Thérèse's wisdom can aid us grandmothers too. Every Christian is called to a life of holiness and can offer penances to God for the sanctification of their own souls and others.'

ACT Offer today's little penances and mortifications to God for yourself and your family.

PRAY Dear Saint Thérèse, please pray for me.

Our Father, Hail Mary, and Glory Be.

SAVOR "Little nothings" can amount to big "somethings!"

November 7

I consider that the sufferings of this present time are not worth comparing with the glory about to be revealed to us.

ROMANS 8:18

STEEP On All Saints Day, my friend Father Miguel Soeherman, MFVA, spoke of the martyrdom that every saint endures. He said, "Great distress doesn't always mean red martyrdom; it could be white martyrdom where there is no blood shed for the faith but just dealing with unjust treatment—all those types are what Archbishop Sheen would call white martyrdom."

He said, "This is what our Lord means when he said that those who are poor, mourning, persecuted—they are blessed." In enduring a white martyrdom in our vocation as grandmothers, when we feel shunned, lonely, misunderstood, or experience any number of deep struggles, we could feel that the sufferings are absolutely endless.

"The saints tell us," Father Miguel said, "that this is nothing... no matter if it's the most horrible tragedy any of us experience here, it is nothing compared to the glory that the Lord is preparing for us—nothing."[213]

ACT Ponder your life and struggles. Prayerfully offer everything to God.

PRAY Jesus and Mary, please help me. Holy saints, please pray for me.

Our Father, Hail Mary, and Glory Be.

SAVOR Our Lord is preparing us for great glory!

November 8

Persevere in overcoming yourself in the little everyday frustrations that bother you; let your best efforts be directed there.[214]

Saint Francis de Sales

STEEP Saint Francis de Sales points out that laboring for our salvation is essential. Beholding the face of God doesn't happen overnight nor effortlessly. We cannot aim to just slide into Heaven under the wire. It would be taking a huge risk not to prayerfully labor during our pilgrimage through life or to expect to get there effortlessly. Additionally, caring only about getting ourselves to Heaven with little effort means that we will not have worked to help others get there too.

Working out our salvation means that we will be a radiant example of living faith to others, inspiring them to lead prayerful lives as well. We can do none of this on our own merits—only by the wonderful and merciful grace of God!

ACT Work earnestly and prayerfully at getting to Heaven, lighting the way for every person you meet along the way.

PRAY Jesus, Mary, and Joseph, help me to help others. Saint Francis de Sales, please pray for me.

Our Father, Hail Mary, and Glory Be.

SAVOR Hard work and prayer win the race!

November 9

If we are able to speak to our Lord, let us do so; let us praise Him, pray to Him, listen to Him. If we are unable to speak because our voice fails us, let us, nevertheless, stay in the hall of the King.[215]

SAINT FRANCIS DE SALES

STEEP We all love the warm and fuzzy feelings. Snuggling with our grandchildren, being with loved ones, and beaming with loving pride when our children and grandchildren excel are times when our hearts swell with love and thanksgiving.

Spending time in prayer with Jesus can make our hearts swell too. When we feel Him near, we know He loves us and cares deeply about our salvation. But when He seems absent or "afflicts" us with something to endure, do we reject Him?

If we are open and prayerful, we begin to understand that we must always push our wills to pray, whether we feel God's presence or feel all alone in our prayer. At times, we might not feel like praying at all, or feel that our prayers are insignificant. Yet, we must not rely upon our feelings, but instead, trust God to know what we need to grow in holiness.

ACT Consider your response in prayer in good times and in bad.

PRAY Jesus, please grant me graces to trust You more.

Our Father, Hail Mary, and Glory Be.

SAVOR My relationship with Jesus needs to be based on "true love."

November 10

You must strive to free yourselves even from venial sins and seek what is the most perfect.[216]

Saint Teresa of Avila

STEEP It's easy to get lazy in our spiritual lives. We are distracted in countless ways each day. Mothers and grandmothers often have their hands full with responsibilities. At times, all the stuff we are doing (or think we have to do) can get in the way of our prayer life and efforts to grow in holiness. But we can—and should—work out our salvation in the midst of the busyness.

Saint Teresa of Avila gives us succinct reminders today. Heeding her wise advice, we can try to be mindful, keep our eyes on Heaven, and not let our guards down or become complacent in our spiritual lives.

ACT List three distractions that might cause you to neglect your spiritual life and three ways you can keep on track.

PRAY Jesus, forgive me for my sins and spiritual complacency. *Our Father, Hail Mary, and Glory Be.*

SAVOR I need to be attentive and strive for holiness.

November 11

There is a true sense of Christian love which is also capable of forgiveness when, before dying, [Maria Goretti] speaks of the one who stabbed her, exclaiming: "Through love of Jesus, I forgive him with all my heart."[217]

Cardinal Angelo Sodano

STEEP Saint Maria Goretti forgave Alessandro Serenelli when she was on her deathbed. She had resisted his attempts to rape her, telling him his actions were sinful. Alessandro then stabbed her fourteen times. The next day, young Maria died in the hospital.

While Alessandro was in prison, he had a vision of Maria smiling at him and offering him a bouquet of lilies. The lilies transformed into white flames when he accepted them from the girl he had murdered. Alessandro converted and testified in Maria's cause for canonization. Maria was canonized in 1950, and her mother—who had also forgiven Alessandro—was present at the ceremony.

Forgiveness is powerful and essential. Alessandro's acceptance of Maria's forgiveness played a huge role in his conversion and change of heart. Sometimes, we might feel like we don't deserve forgiveness, but by God's amazing grace, accepting others' forgiveness can totally transform our lives.

ACT Learn from the virtuous lives of saints.

PRAY Jesus, help me to forgive. Dear Saint Maria Goretti, please pray for me.

Our Father, Hail Mary, and Glory Be.

SAVOR I need to forgive and to accept forgiveness.

November 12

Saint Augustine says quite emphatically that there is no spiritual exercise more fruitful or more useful to our salvation than continually turning our thoughts to the sufferings of Our Savior.[218]

SAINT LOUIS DE MONTFORT

STEEP Some might find it difficult to meditate on Jesus' suffering because it seems morbid. They might be accustomed to focusing on the "finer things in life," concentrating on comfort and searching for happiness.

It is understandable that people want to feel joyful and might hide from suffering. However, prayerfully meditating upon the great love of our Savior in giving His life for our salvation is indispensable for a serious Christian.

Saint Louis de Montfort pointed out that "Blessed Albert the Great, who had Saint Thomas Aquinas as his disciple, learned in a revelation that by simply thinking of or meditating on the passion of Our Lord Jesus Christ, a Christian gains more merit than if he had fasted on bread and water every Friday for a whole year."[219]

ACT Endeavor to spend time meditating on our Crucified Lord. Teach your grandchildren about Jesus' great sacrifice for our salvation.

PRAY Jesus, I am sorry for my sins.

Our Father, Hail Mary, and Glory Be.

SAVOR I desire to comfort Jesus in His pain.

November 13

I ask only this of you, that you remember me at the altar of the Lord, wherever you may be.[220]

Saint Monica to Saint Augustine

STEEP As holy as Saint Monica was, before closing her eyes on this world, she begged her son to pray for her. Those were her final words. She anticipated Eternal Life and wholeheartedly knew the power of prayer.

After all, Monica had prayed long and hard through floods of tears for her son Augustine to repent of his sinful life and turn to God. She was blessed to witness the miraculous transformation of his soul before she died.

The care of the soul is often neglected, but it is indispensable to our eternal life. Mothers and grandmothers help form their offspring's consciences, which influences their very souls. We can see how Saint Monica's care about Augustine's soul bore fruit in her life and his, and we can all hope and pray to witness our loved ones' conversions in our lifetimes like she did.

ACT Ponder your influence on your children and grandchildren. Consider adding a special novena of prayer for them to your prayer repertoire.

PRAY Saint Monica and Saint Augustine, please pray for my family.

Our Father, Hail Mary, and Glory Be.

SAVOR My soul is a tremendous gift that requires tending.

November 14

My child, if your heart is wise,
my heart too will be glad.

Proverbs 23:15

STEEP My grandsons keep me on my toes. They have great imaginations and are completely honest about their observations. If you ever want an honest opinion, ask a child!

One summer day, during a video call, Shepherd shared, "There's only one problem with my mom [my daughter, who was out of the room at the time]." My interest piqued.

"Oh? What is it?" I ventured to ask.

"She never goes in the sprinkler with us. She is always busy." I held in my laughter. My daughter came back into the room, and I asked Shepherd if we could tell her about the "one problem." He did. We all laughed out loud. I heard that shortly thereafter, she went in the sprinkler with the boys! Our grandchildren's funny and honest comments can help us reflect on how they see us and can inspire us to change.

ACT Have fun and create special memories with your family.

PRAY Dear Holy Family, please guide us and protect us.
Our Father, Hail Mary, and Glory Be.

SAVOR There is nothing that can compare to the blessing of being a grandmother!

November 15

Praise and glory be to you, most loving Jesus Christ, for the most sacred wound in your side, and by your infinite mercy which you made known in the opening of your breast to the soldier Longinus, and so to us all.[221]

Saint Clare of Assisi

STEEP Saint Clare's words above about God's mercy are powerful. Jesus taught Saint Faustina to pray these words for the conversion of souls: "O Blood and Water, which gushed forth from the Heart of Jesus as a fount of mercy for us, I trust in You" (*Diary*, 84).

Regarding the image of Divine Mercy, Jesus told Saint Faustina, **"These two rays issued forth from the very depths of My tender mercy when My agonized Heart was opened by a lance on the Cross"** (*Diary*, 299). Grandmothers can meditate upon Jesus' Divine Mercy for souls when praying for our loved ones to stay on the road to Heaven, as well as for those who have strayed to come back to the flock.

ACT Ponder God's great mercy. Be merciful.

PRAY O Blood and Water, which gushed forth from the Heart of Jesus as a fount of mercy for us, I trust in You!

Our Father, Hail Mary, and Glory Be.

SAVOR I will praise and thank God for His great mercy.

November 16

> [I] beheld our Lord descending into purgatory with a golden rod in His Hand, . . . He appeared to draw [the souls] into a place of repose. [I] understood by this, that whenever anyone prays generally, from a motive of charity, for the souls in purgatory, the greater part of those who, during their lives, have exercised themselves in works of charity, are released.[222]
>
> SAINT GERTRUDE

STEEP Pious tradition holds that Saint Gertrude the Great, a German Benedictine nun, mystic, and early devotee of the Sacred Heart, was visited by Jesus, Who told her how powerful our prayers for the souls in Purgatory can be. He taught her a beautiful prayer, worthy of praying for the holy souls.

Today is Saint Gertrude's feast day. It's a good day to talk to your grandchildren about Eternal Life, especially if they have a loved one who has died. Knowing about eternity helps ease sorrows and brings peace.

ACT Throughout this month of holy saints and souls, join the many saints who have earnestly prayed for the souls in Purgatory.

PRAY Jesus, please release souls from Purgatory.

Our Father, Hail Mary, and Glory Be.

SAVOR My prayers can help the holy souls.

November 17

What years of Purgatory will there be for those Christians who have no difficulty at all in deferring their prayers to another time on the excuse of having to do some pressing work! If we really desired the happiness of possessing God, we should avoid the little faults as well as the big ones, since separation from God is so frightful a torment to all these poor souls![223]

SAINT JOHN VIANNEY

STEEP We've heard the old adage that the road to Hell is paved with good intentions. Similarly, today's quote warns of putting our prayers off. We can't neglect our family's care to drop to our knees to pray, but we must be souls of prayer in order to manage our familial duties. Prayer is necessary for our whole family's spiritual survival.

Let's carve out necessary times for prayer, being flexible for arising needs of the family. We can always lift our hearts in prayer as we go about our duties. When our formal prayer gets rearranged by life, we can later pick up where we left off.

ACT Write down the ways you put prayer off and ways you might avoid doing so.

PRAY Jesus, I am sorry for neglecting times with You.

Our Father, Hail Mary, and Glory Be.

SAVOR Prayer is essential for spiritual survival.

November 18

No suffering . . . will go unrewarded in eternal life. Trust and hope in the merits of Jesus and in this way even poor clay will become finest gold which will shine in the palace of the king of heaven.[224]

SAINT PADRE PIO

STEEP My dear friend Father Bill introduced me to Saint Padre Pio. His relic is tucked behind my Miraculous Medal in a locket I wear daily. One year, on Padre Pio's feast day, my husband, Dave, was rushed to the hospital with excruciating pain and vomiting. Tests determined that Dave's gallbladder was extremely infected and had to come out immediately. He was wheeled into surgery exactly at 3:00 PM, the Hour of Great Mercy. Later, the surgeon told me that the surgery was miraculous—if he'd operated even five minutes later, it would have been a completely different story!

Dave and I have no doubt that our beloved Saint Padre Pio was interceding for us. Saint Pio's many illnesses in youth, and experiences with and love for the sick and suffering, prodded him to establish a hospital. His holy compassion can be a comfort to us all.

ACT Don't hesitate to pray to the saints!

PRAY Saint Padre Pio, pray for me, please.

Our Father, Hail Mary, and Glory Be.

SAVOR God often works miracles through His saints!

November 19

A medal must be struck on this model, and those who carry one . . . will enjoy the special protection of the Mother of God.[225]

Our Lady to Saint Catherine Labouré

STEEP I met JoAn in the waiting room the day my husband was wheeled into emergency surgery. Her husband, John, was in surgery recovery. We chatted, and after pausing to pray for both husbands, I gave two blessed Miraculous Medals to JoAn. She was delighted and felt comforted in speaking with me. Though JoAn and John weren't Catholic, they put the medals on and felt a tingling on their skin. John had had nightmares for many years since his open-heart surgery, but that night and thereafter, John slept like a baby for the first time in years.

Our Lord is continually pushing us forth to impart His love and mercy to others. Even in the midst of family challenges, Catholic women can reach out to be a comfort and light to others.

ACT Reach out with God's love to a stranger soon.

PRAY Jesus, thank You! Saint Catherine Labouré, please pray for me.

Our Father, Hail Mary, and Glory Be.

SAVOR Every day is a holy mystery ready to unfold. I should open my heart to God's grace.

November 20

Bear one another's burdens, and in this way you will fulfill the law of Christ.

Galatians 6:2

STEEP My dear friends lost their adult son to a fatal brain aneurysm. Their family was always tight knit; their Catholic faith was central to their lives. Sundays were spent attending Holy Mass and having dinner together at night. What a joy it was for Julie and Alan to have their son, daughter-in-law, and grandchildren over every Sunday.

That all changed after their son died. Everyone in the family grieved, but sadly, Sunday family get-togethers ended. The family just stopped visiting. Julie and Alan were brokenhearted enough to lose their son so abruptly, but they grieved the loss of their family time too.

Family tragedies might threaten to separate family members or disrupt family traditions, but even in the midst of grief, grandmothers can encourage their families to bear one another's burdens and be there for each other in difficult times.

ACT Create family memories and keep your valuable family traditions alive!

PRAY Dear Holy Family, please help my family and especially disconnected families.

Our Father, Hail Mary, and Glory Be.

SAVOR We can bear one another's burdens together and preserve our family times.

November 21

Blessed rather are those who hear the word of God and obey it!

LUKE 11:28

STEEP Today, we remember the Blessed Virgin's presentation in the Temple at just three years old by her parents, Saints Anne and Joachim. When her holy parents were barren, they promised God that they would dedicate their child to God's service. That little girl was destined by God to become the great Mother of God.

Jesus' grandparents, Saints Anne and Joachim, only had their child for three years before giving her to the Temple. Some grandmothers might also feel like their time with their grandchildren is short, or it's hard to live far away from them. We can ponder the feast of the Presentation of Mary today and pray for the graces to be a happy grandmother, trust that our grandchildren are destined for great things, and introduce them to the Blessed Virgin Mary!

ACT Stay close to Mary and help the little ones in your life get to know her.

PRAY Dear Mary, help me to teach about you.

Our Father, Hail Mary, and Glory Be.

SAVOR I am blessed to hear God's Word, and I must obey it.

November 22

As my friend Frank Sheed said about purgatory, "The very thought of appearing before the Divine Majesty in my present unseemly state fills me with horror."[226]

FATHER BENEDICT GROESCHEL

STEEP Our merciful Lord provides Purgatory so we don't have to feel the "horror" mentioned above. Nevertheless, we should still pray for souls in Purgatory to be consoled.

Saint Gemma Galgani, an Italian mystic, once prayed for Passionist Sister Maria Teresa of the Infant Jesus, who was on her deathbed. Shortly after her death, Sister Maria Teresa appeared to Saint Gemma, sorrowfully begging for prayers to be released from Purgatory. Saint Gemma petitioned the Lord with many tearful prayers and penances. Later, the Blessed Mother appeared to Saint Gemma, along with Jesus, Sister Maria Teresa, and her guardian angel. Sister Maria Teresa told her that she was truly happy and on her way to Heaven.

While we might never experience something as extraordinary as a soul begging prayers of us, we can certainly pray for the souls in Purgatory and offer a little penance for them.

ACT Prepare your heart for God. Pray for others.

PRAY Dear Jesus, have mercy on us.

Our Father, Hail Mary, and Glory Be.

SAVOR Purgatory is a gift, but we should also pray for souls to get to Heaven.

November 23

The Lord said to me, "**The loss of each soul plunges Me into mortal sadness. You always console Me when you pray for sinners. The prayer most pleasing to Me is prayer for the conversion of sinners. Know, My daughter, that this prayer is always heard and answered.**"

SAINT FAUSTINA, *DIARY*, 1397

STEEP My friend Janeane's Grandma Fern was a daughter of a rural Baptist pastor and married a Baptist missionary pastor. Janeane said, "She spent the majority of her waking hours praying for missionaries and ministering to others."

Janeane converted to Catholicism and deeply desired to share her newfound faith with her Grandma Fern. But Fern was ninety-nine years old and had dementia. Since Fern, as a Protestant, wouldn't receive last rites, Janeane prayed "that God would allow me to, at the very least, pray the Chaplet of Divine Mercy for her, specifically during her last hours, with the intention of asking God for His mercy and salvation."

We can be assured that even if our loved ones die without the sacraments, God in His infinite mercy still works powerfully through our prayers.

ACT Pray for those who will die today without the sacraments.

PRAY Dear Jesus, please have mercy on dying souls.

Our Father, Hail Mary, and Glory Be.

SAVOR I must be generous with my prayers.

November 24

I realize more and more how much every soul needs God's mercy throughout life and particularly at the hour of death.

SAINT FAUSTINA, *DIARY*, 1036

STEEP Janeane's Grandma Fern, at one hundred years old, took a turn for the worse. Janeane began to call her daily, reading Catholic prayers to her. "She had faithfully prayed for me every day; it was the very least that I could do in return."

Hospice care began. Janeane knew her beloved Grandma Fern could pass anytime, so she prayed for a peaceful and speedy passage of her soul into Heaven. She knew Fern was a godly woman, but she also knew about the reality of Purgatory.

While Fern grew weaker, Janeane and her children got a bad stomach virus. Janeane felt bad she couldn't complete the Divine Mercy Chaplets and Rosaries she had vowed to pray, being constantly interrupted. But God knew her heart and all she had going on.

God knows our hearts when illness or challenges interrupt our prayers. When we are unable to take care of our loved ones, God is still taking care of them and of us!

ACT Entrust your loved ones to God's loving mercy.

PRAY Dear Jesus, help me.

Our Father, Hail Mary, and Glory Be.

SAVOR Life is precious and Eternal Life is our goal.

November 25

And now faith, hope, and love abide, these three; and the greatest of these is love.

1 Corinthians 13:13

STEEP From afar, Janeane prayed earnestly for her one-hundred-year-old Grandma Fern, who was in her last hours, but with everything going on at home, she struggled to get through the prayers. She shared, "The sleep loss from both my newborn and older children awakening at night, as well as the sadness and grief from my grandmother's imminent passing, was so draining that I only managed one or two decades per day." Janeane intentionally prayed each decade very slowly and fervently, so that she could focus clearly and pray sincerely in the midst of her household chaos.

Finally, days after starting a Divine Mercy Chaplet, Janeane finished the prayer and collapsed in exhaustion at 10:30 PM. Her father's phone call roused her in the morning, sharing the sorrowful news of Grandma Fern's passing. Janeane asked him when she had passed.

"I could hardly believe my ears! She had died at exactly 10:30 PM!"

ACT Make time for a special family activity. Tell stories about beloved family members who have passed away.

PRAY Dear Jesus, I love You!

Our Father, Hail Mary, and Glory Be.

SAVOR God is love, and He provides all we need.

November 26

> Temptation is necessary to us to make us realize that we are nothing in ourselves. St. Augustine tells us that we should thank God as much for the sins from which He has preserved us as for those which He has had the charity to forgive us.[227]
>
> SAINT JOHN VIANNEY

STEEP Only the humble will enter Heaven. Saint John Vianney reminds us that God helps us to stay humble by providing temptations and challenges in life. How will we respond to them? Do we think we can do it on our own? Or will we depend upon our Creator?

Jesus said, "Let the little children come to me; do not stop them; for it is to such as these that the kingdom of God belongs" (Mk 10:14). Grandmothers can encourage the humility of our grandchildren's beautiful, innocent hearts by telling them stories of the saints and guiding them to aspire to humility through everyday life.

ACT Observe how babies and small children depend upon adults in their lives to provide for them, teach them, and guide them. Be that way with God.

PRAY Lord God, thank You for my life. I trust in You.

Our Father, Hail Mary, and Glory Be.

SAVOR Jesus, I trust in You!

November 27

Come to the foot of the altar. Graces will be shed on all, great and little, especially upon those who ask for them.[228]

BLESSED MOTHER TO SAINT CATHERINE LABOURÉ

STEEP In 1830, the Blessed Virgin appeared to Saint Catherine Labouré and promised a shower of graces through the Miraculous Medal, which is one of the most famous sacramentals of our Church.

Earlier this month, I mentioned I gave two blessed Miraculous Medals to JoAn and her husband at the hospital. Though Protestant, they wore them faithfully. A year later, JoAn told me she felt a tender relationship with Mary and prays to her often.

We can give the blessed medal to our grandchildren, other loved ones, or complete strangers. I have witnessed many transformations all around the world in the people I have gifted the Miraculous Medal to, particularly in those who need a mother figure in their lives. This blessed sacramental could be just the holy "medicine" a person needs.

ACT Don't hesitate to share your Catholic faith.

PRAY Jesus, please help me. Mary, please grant graces to my family. Saint Catherine Labouré, please pray for us.

Our Father, Hail Mary, and Glory Be.

SAVOR Mary promises to grant graces for the asking, and she keeps her promises!

November 28

O Mary, conceived without sin, pray for us who have recourse to thee.[229]

PRAYER ON THE MIRACULOUS MEDAL

STEEP I was on the edge of my seat at a retreat when my former spiritual director, Servant of God Father John Hardon, SJ, told us about "one of the most memorable experiences" he ever had. A visiting Vincentian priest had recommended that all the priests enroll in the Confraternity of the Miraculous Medal. Though not very impressed, Father Hardon enrolled anyway. He tucked the leaflet into his Divine Office prayer book and forgot about it.

Months later, Father Hardon was assigned as a chaplain at a busy children's hospital. One day his job was to console parents of a comatose nine-year-old boy with a fractured skull. Father suddenly remembered the Vincentian's words, "The Miraculous Medal works!" He decided to put it to the test. Father Hardon called for a Miraculous Medal, but at first, not one could be found.

This story can remind us that the spur-of-the-moment decisions we make as grandmothers, no matter the outcome, can bring holy wisdom into our own grandchildren's lives.

ACT Pray for an increase in faith.

PRAY O Mary, conceived without sin, pray for us who have recourse to thee.

Our Father, Hail Mary, and Glory Be.

SAVOR Our Catholic Church is rich in graces.

November 29

The wonders the Blessed Mother performs, provided we believe, are extraordinary.[230]

SERVANT OF GOD FATHER JOHN HARDON

STEEP Yesterday's reflection left Father Hardon in the young comatose boy's hospital room. Eventually, a Miraculous Medal was found. Father began to doubt himself. Nonetheless, he blessed the medal while the boy's father held the investiture prayer. "No sooner did I finish the prayer," Father stated, "than he opened his eyes for the first time in almost two weeks. He saw his mother and said, 'Ma, I want some ice cream.'"

The doctor came immediately, and a battery of tests were performed. The boy was completely cured of all brain damage! Father Hardon shared, "This experience so changed my life that I have not been the same since. My faith in God, faith in His power to work miracles, was strengthened beyond description."[231]

Whether or not we witness or experience a miraculous healing, we Catholic grandmothers can increase our families' faith by sharing stories like this one and by using blessed sacramentals such as the Miraculous Medal.

ACT Ponder God's love. Sit with Him in thankful prayer.

PRAY Our Lady of the Miraculous Medal, please pray for me.

Our Father, Hail Mary, and Glory Be.

SAVOR God calls me to believe in His miracles.

November 30

In entrusting [the holy souls] to the Lord, we recognize our solidarity with them and share in their salvation in this wondrous mystery of the communion of saints. . . . I therefore encourage Catholics to pray fervently for the dead, for their family members, and for all our brothers and sisters who have died.[232]

Saint John Paul II

STEEP How blessed we are to know our Church teaches, "All who die in God's grace and friendship, but still imperfectly purified, are indeed assured of their eternal salvation; but after death they undergo purification, so as to achieve the holiness necessary to enter the joy of heaven" (*CCC* 1030). Our Lord is loving and merciful.

As you finish this month, before stepping into December, find time to ponder the Church's teachings on Eternal Life. Today is a good day to make a resolution to pray daily for the souls in Purgatory and for the dying who also need our prayers. In addition, you can strive to find opportunities to teach your grandchildren about the importance of praying for others.

ACT Pray heartily for the souls in Purgatory and impress upon your family the need to lead holy lives.

PRAY Dear Jesus, Mary, and Joseph, I love you. Please save souls.

Our Father, Hail Mary, and Glory Be.

SAVOR The holy souls in Purgatory need my prayers and will reward me for my generosity.

DECEMBER

The Birth and the Coming of Christ

Keep awake therefore, for you do not know on what day your Lord is coming. . . . Therefore you also must be ready, for the Son of Man is coming at an unexpected hour.

MATTHEW 24:42, 44

December 1

Your lives must be like Mine: quiet and hidden, in unceasing union with God, pleading for humanity and preparing the world for the second coming of God.

Blessed Mother to Saint Faustina, *Diary*, 625

STEEP We begin our December journey mindful of two things: the need to prepare our hearts for the coming of the Christ Child at Christmas and also to prepare for the Second Coming of Christ. Often, these important focuses are forgotten or pushed aside due to the bombardment of advertisements for Christmas presents for our grandchildren or the focus on preparing for the holidays with our families. Our good intentions might fall to the wayside amid myriad distractions.

"Stay awake" should be our December motto! Being extra busy this month might tire us out, but this is a time to stay vigilant in our spiritual lives and dig deeper into our faith. In addition to preparing our hearts through prayer, spiritual reading, the sacraments, and even penance, we must be careful not to allow ourselves to get caught up in a whirlwind of busyness.

ACT Plan times for daily prayer and spiritual reading during Advent.

PRAY Jesus, Mary, and Joseph, please help me to prepare my heart.

Our Father, Hail Mary, and Glory Be.

SAVOR Seeking quiet times for prayer will nourish my faith.

December 2

Therefore, keep awake—for you do not know when the master of the house will come, in the evening, or at midnight, or at cockcrow, or at dawn, or else he may find you asleep when he comes suddenly. And what I say to you I say to all: Keep awake.

MARK 13:35–37

STEEP My friend Father Andrew Apostoli, CFR, offered a moving example of how to put today's quote into practice. Father Andrew intently listened to our Lord and our Lady and stayed awake—so much so that he actually wore down the floorboards of the friary chapel from his walking back and forth, praying his Rosaries and Chaplets. He didn't want to fall asleep! He was such a busy soul-tender that, due to fatigue, he sometimes needed to get up and walk while he prayed.

Even if we may not literally "wear out the floorboards"—due to limited mobility or health conditions that require rest—we can bring this level of dedication to tending the souls of our grandchildren and others (including our own souls!) through our dedicated prayers.

ACT Ponder your prayer life. Do you "wear out the floorboards" praying?

PRAY Jesus and Mary, help me pray.

Our Father, Hail Mary, and Glory Be.

SAVOR I need to stay awake and pay attention to God.

December 3

I thought of *Little* Jesus whom I loved so much, and I said: "Oh! how happy I would be if they called me Thérèse of the Child Jesus!"[233]

SAINT THÉRÈSE OF LISIEUX

STEEP Saint Thérèse of the Child Jesus was a beautiful soul who honored and praised the Infant Jesus, taking this devotion as part of her religious name. She could not understand how anyone should be afraid of God, because He came to us as a little baby. She approached God as a child approached her parents: with humility and trust. She was aware of her own littleness, while knowing that God raises the lowly and humble hearted. She prayed that God would manifest His great love through all the little things she did with great love and attention.

During Advent, we can present "little things" to God, offering them for our dear grandchildren. We will find that our "little" prayers and offerings are not so little after all, for they make a huge difference in everyone's life!

ACT Strive to imitate Saint Thérèse's innocent, pure love for God.

PRAY Lord God, thank You for Your great love! Saint Thérèse, please pray for me.

Our Father, Hail Mary, and Glory Be.

SAVOR God's great love emits "sparks of grace"!

December 4

Love your enemies, do good to those who hate you, bless those who curse you, pray for those who abuse you.

LUKE 6:27–28

STEEP We sometimes get irritated—frustrated with the way our day unfolds or upset because we or others are treated poorly. It's okay to feel put out or even angry, if the shoe fits. However, what is most essential is how we respond to the challenges we face. Do we lash out? Do we become passive-aggressive? Or do we turn to God and ask for His grace?

Today's verse doesn't mean that we don't correct wrongs or that we become a "doormat" for persecution. We don't have to invite the person who offends us to lunch; however, we do need to love that person with God's love—that means with prayer. A grandmother's example of love and patience during times of frustration can teach our grandchildren how to manage their own emotions better during difficult times.

ACT Jot down ways you can better handle negative situations. Prayerfully put them into practice the next time you face frustration.

PRAY Dear Jesus, I want to be like You! Help me to grow in holiness and be a good example.

Our Father, Hail Mary, and Glory Be.

SAVOR God helps me love everyone with His tender love.

December 5

> Help me, O Lord, that my hands may be merciful and filled with good deeds, so that I may do only good to my neighbors and take upon myself the more difficult and toilsome tasks.
>
> SAINT FAUSTINA, *DIARY*, 163

STEEP It is easy to allow God's love through us when everything is calm. But it's not easy when stuff hits the proverbial fan. Nevertheless, God would like us to be steady and dependable in our prayer lives and works of mercy so He can work through us.

Saint Teresa of Calcutta wrote to her Missionaries of Charity Sisters at the beginning of one Advent, reminding them to keep everything about them pure, especially their hearts, so that Christ could work through them. Many saints have preached the idea of Jesus working through us—for example, Saint Teresa of Avila's famous "Christ has no body on earth now but yours" prayer, or Saint Faustina's "Prayer to be Merciful" from her *Diary*. We can live this teaching through our vocation by being the hands and feet of Christ to our beloved grandchildren.

ACT Ponder how you can put the saints' beautiful teachings into practice.

PRAY Dear Jesus, please work through me. Dear Mary, please accompany me through Advent.

Our Father, Hail Mary, and Glory Be.

SAVOR The saints show me how to become holy.

December 6

> [We] should give ourselves to Him with complete determination, and we should empty the soul in such a way that He can store things there or take them away as though it were His own property . . . He doesn't give Himself completely until we give ourselves completely.[234]
>
> Saint Teresa of Avila

STEEP Saint Teresa of Avila, from practical experience and deep prayer, wrote *The Way of Perfection* to help her sisters attain spiritual perfection. She teaches a deep and lasting love of prayer through a treatment of the three essentials of the prayer-filled life: fraternal love, detachment from created things, and true humility.

Today, we learn that our Lord wants our wholehearted surrender, in a sense, our empty soul. Within our deepest being, He gives Himself and heals us. Advent is the perfect time to go deeper into our faith, to strive to wholeheartedly trust our Lord with our lives and be open to His healing for us. Doing so will surely help us be a better grandmother and Catholic woman of faith!

ACT "Empty" your soul by going to Confession soon and experiencing the great mercy of God!

PRAY Dear Jesus, I wish to surrender my heart fully to You.

Our Father, Hail Mary, and Glory Be.

SAVOR Our Lord wants to dwell in my heart.

December 7

We love because he first loved us.

1 John 4:19

STEEP A special Grandma I know shared about her grandson Dillon, whose parents divorced when he was young. Bertha said, "Watching him pack his little bag for his visit to the parent who had custody that week always left me with a heavy heart." The only positive outcome was that he constantly kept in touch with Bertha by phone.

After his high school graduation, at eighteen years old, "His mother actually threw him out," Bertha said. She questioned this method of tough love, but added, "Fortunately, he went to live with his father, and they developed a strong bond. On a daily basis, he started to call me to chat."

One day, Dillon told his grandma he was not attending Mass. He happened to be parked in a Catholic church parking lot, so Bertha suggested he go inside and find a priest or deacon to talk to. Bertha said, "It was an amazing outcome."

Less-than-ideal situations can lead to good outcomes through prayer. Grandmothers' prayers are powerful!

ACT Through prayer or otherwise, reach out to estranged family members.

PRAY Dear Jesus, Mary, and Joseph, help my grandchildren.
Our Father, Hail Mary, and Glory Be.

SAVOR God answers our prayers!

December 8

> In Mary, the New Eve, Mother of the New Adam, the Father's original, wondrous plan of love was re-established in an even more wondrous way.[235]
>
> SAINT JOHN PAUL II

STEEP Today, we celebrate the Blessed Virgin Mary's Immaculate Conception. Though she lived a joyful life, she also lived under the shadow of the Cross of her Son and experienced much sorrow. Still, Mary reached out to help others.

I came across a news story about a brave Scottish grandmother of three, Mavis Paterson, who will celebrate her eighty fifth birthday on her bicycle to honor her three deceased children she lost in the span of four years. In 2019, she became the oldest woman to cycle 960 miles. Mavis stated that her cycling is a form of therapy when she can sing and enjoy the ride. She has cycled across several countries to support charities and to relieve the grief of losing her children. While not every grandmother can do the same, we can be inspired and find ways to prayerfully deal with grief in our own lives, as well as reach out to help others.

ACT Consider how you can put your interests toward a good cause.

PRAY Dear Virgin Mary, please help me.

Our Father, Hail Mary, and Glory Be.

SAVOR God invites me to imitate Mary.

December 9

Into his garden the divine bridegroom comes, when he visits a devoted soul. . . . In that garden his own hands have planted the gratifying love we have for his goodness, the love on which we feed.[236]

Saint Francis de Sales

STEEP It's almost winter, but let's think of something summery! Early one summer, I lamented I had forgotten to plant one of my favorite flowers. Sunflowers make my heart sing—but if you don't plant the seeds, you won't have the flowers! Shortly after, I was delighted to see sunflowers. My fine feathered friends must have dropped a few seeds into my flower garden!

Today's quote and story remind us of the idiom "Bloom where you are planted." Some of us might wonder how we can do this—for example, if adverse family situations make our role as grandmothers difficult. Perhaps health issues or living at a distance prevent us from being as active in our grandchildren's lives as we'd like to. Whatever our situations, pondering ways to stay connected and praying for peace are so important.

ACT Pick one thing to do to help you bloom where God has planted you.

PRAY Jesus, thank You for Your holy will.

Our Father, Hail Mary, and Glory Be.

SAVOR God invites me to bloom.

December 10

Have a holy daring; for God helps the strong and He shows no partiality.[237]

SAINT TERESA OF AVILA

STEEP After five years trying to conceive and lab reports pointing to infertility, Susan felt hopeless. Seeing parishioners with bustling families caused further anguish. She wanted to "stop pestering God," but "could not accept not having any more children."

Susan headed to the monastery for a much-needed retreat. The priest entered to prepare the altar. Susan boldly handed him her wedding band. "Father, would you please pray for God's will for my husband and me?" Father slid the ring under the corporal on the altar "with a big smile," Susan recalled.

At the Consecration, he bent over the host, his hands on the corporal. Susan recalled, "The power of those words of Consecration—burgeoning Divine Life shooting through everything . . . !" Susan and her husband conceived their second daughter that week and named her for the abbess of the monastery: Marguerite Christine—"Little Pearl of Christ."

God never tires of our "pestering." He calls us to trust in His Divine Providence.

ACT Thank God for all of your blessings and trust His Providence.

PRAY Jesus, please have mercy on me.
Our Father, Hail Mary, and Glory Be.

SAVOR God's will is most perfect.

December 11

God's love was revealed among us in this way: God sent his only Son into the world so that we might live through him.

1 JOHN 4:9

STEEP Janeane grew up deeply affected by her Grandma Lois singing "Jesus Loves Me" when rocking her before bedtime. Later, she realized just how crucial her grandmother's love was to her mental and spiritual stability.

Janeane became depressed at college and began to doubt her faith because the curriculum contradicted her beliefs. She called her Grandma, crying and pouring out her heart. Her grandmother admitted she didn't know what to say to help, but then she started singing "Jesus Loves Me."

Janeane said, "I realized there were many things I did not know, but I could feel confident that this was indeed the truth: Jesus loves me." Janeane also realized she couldn't live without Jesus' love. She "decided to continue being committed to following Jesus."

A grandmother's love is powerful and transforming—providing love and comfort no matter how old our grandchildren are!

ACT Sing to your grandchildren! Share the faith through other forms of media they enjoy.

PRAY Dear Jesus, thank You for loving me. Saint Anne, please pray for me.

Our Father, Hail Mary, and Glory Be.

SAVOR A grandmother's love and prayers are powerful!

December 12

> Listen, put it into your heart, my youngest and dearest one, that the thing that frightened you, the thing that afflicted you, is nothing. Do not let it disturb you. . . . Am I not here, I, who am your mother? Are you not under my shadow and protection? . . . Are you not in the hollow of my mantle?[238]
>
> Our Lady to Saint Juan Diego

STEEP Our Lady of Guadalupe's words to Saint Juan Diego remind me of my friend Father Andrew's blessings. Whether the blessing was in person or over the phone, Father Andrew would ask the Blessed Mother to place her mantle upon me and to protect me. I sincerely could sense Mother Mary's mantle being placed upon me through Father Andrew's powerful blessing.

Our Lady is our dear Mother who is continuously working hard for our salvation. That said, she needs our cooperation with God's graces. We must confess our sins, resist temptation, and follow her Son. During this holy season, we can feel comfort in Mary's protection and intercession.

ACT Turn to the Blessed Mother as often as possible and let her lead you to Jesus.

PRAY Dear Jesus, thank You for Your Mother. Our Lady of Guadalupe, please pray for us.

Our Father, Hail Mary, and Glory Be.

SAVOR Mary tells us not to let anything disturb us. She is with us and will help us.

December 13

I am the light of the world. Whoever follows me will never walk in darkness but will have the light of life.

John 8:12

STEEP Ten years after helping Janeane through her college crisis, Grandma Lois fell and broke several bones. Janeane lived far away and felt helpless, but resigned herself to prayer and video chats. The roles were reversed, and this time she was the one on the phone, not knowing how to comfort her grandmother.

Janeane thought, "Maybe I could try to soothe her in the same way that she had managed to calm me." Janeane and her toddler daughter sang "Jesus Loves Me" to Grandma Lois, over and over.

"Her face seemed to change from a twisted grimace into a peaceful sleep as she smiled and said thank you." They wouldn't see one another again. Janeane is so grateful for this final, precious memory of her grandmother and how God used a lullaby to comfort them both.

In God's wonderful plan, sometimes the roles are reversed, and grandchildren help their dear grandmothers. A grandmother's love and care shown to them over the years will beautifully prepare their hearts.

ACT Love with all your might!

PRAY Dear Jesus, I love You!

Our Father, Hail Mary, and Glory Be.

SAVOR When roles reverse, God loves through us.

December 14

O Lord, how true that all harm comes to us from not keeping our eyes fixed on You; if we were to look at nothing else but the way, we would soon arrive. But we meet with a thousand falls and obstacles and lose the way because we don't keep our eyes . . . on the true way.[239]

SAINT TERESA OF AVILA

STEEP It's easy to get lost in the busyness of life. There's so much to do and not enough hours in the day. Additionally, women of all ages are regularly bombarded with demands for perfectionism from a lopsided culture beckoning us to act in certain ways—even to abandon our own unique feminine God-given gifts. It can get confusing. It's essential to keep our eyes on the "true way" and help others to do the same, especially the most vulnerable young girls. We can avoid much trouble if we focus on Jesus and what really matters: to get to Heaven and bring others with us!

ACT Ponder whether your eyes are on the true way. If not, practice ways to get back on track.

PRAY Jesus, please don't let me wander off the path. Keep my eyes on You!

Our Father, Hail Mary, and Glory Be.

SAVOR I need to stay on the true way.

December 15

Pay close attention to yourself and to your teaching; continue in these things, for in doing this you will save both yourself and your hearers.

1 Timothy 4:16

STEEP Jennifer's grandmother, Alice, was a reading specialist and a lector at church. She had a very close relationship with Jesus. Jennifer shared, "She was not afraid to speak His Name." Jennifer's grandmother always asked for prayers and assured Jennifer of her prayers. "Perhaps the best way she taught me my Catholic faith was by her witness of continual acts of charity," Jennifer said.

A model of faithfulness, Alice lived ninety-eight years and spent most of her last days praying without ceasing. "She taught me that even when she could no longer accomplish God's will with action, she could move mountains with prayer." Jennifer reflected, "The greatest gift my grandmother gave to me was my Roman Catholic faith."

A grandmother's faith is shown in a variety of ways—many times without her knowledge. Grandmothers can be wonderful witnesses of faith to their grandchildren whether through actions, prayers, or a combination of both.

ACT Pray for families all over the world. Your prayers will surely benefit them.

PRAY Dear Jesus, please help us.

Our Father, Hail Mary, and Glory Be.

SAVOR Grandmothers are wonderful givers of the faith!

December 16

True humility consists very much in great readiness to be content with whatever the Lord may want to do with them and in always finding oneself unworthy to be called His servant.[240]

SAINT TERESA OF AVILA

STEEP Saint Teresa of Avila reminded her sisters that Saint Martha was so blessed to have "merited so often to have Christ our Lord in her home, give Him food, serve Him, and eat at table with Him [and even from His plate]? If she had been enraptured like the Magdalene, there wouldn't have been anyone to give food to the divine Guest."[241] She wanted her community to realize that everyone is called to different tasks and prayer lives.

Grandmothers are both active and contemplative in our prayer lives. Each is called to a different balance and can prayerfully discern how we are called to live out our vocation. With God's grace, we find the proper balance.

ACT Write down the special gifts or skills God has given you that help you in your vocation as grandmother. Strive to consciously put those into practice today.

PRAY Jesus, help me. Saint Teresa of Avila, pray for me.

Our Father, Hail Mary, and Glory Be.

SAVOR God gives me specific gifts to use for His glory.

December 17

Consider [yourselves] lucky to serve with Martha.[242]

Saint Teresa of Avila

STEEP We are given special gifts to glorify God. In *The Way of Perfection*, Saint Teresa of Avila instructed that those called to the active life "shouldn't complain about those who are very much absorbed in contemplation, for these active ones know that the Lord will defend the contemplatives, even though these latter are silent since for the most part contemplation makes one forgetful of self and of all things." She reminded her sisters, "Recall that it is necessary for someone to prepare His meal."[243]

Busy grandmothers may be tempted to envy people whose lives are quieter or who have more time for prayer—but God gives each of us the specific prayer life and the ways of serving that He knows we most need! If we are feeling busy, unappreciated, or even unhappy about serving during the holiday season, the example of serving like Martha could be especially encouraging.

ACT Whatever your schedule looks like, offer your heart to God all throughout the day.

PRAY Jesus, help me to pray as I should. Saint Teresa of Avila, please pray for me.

Our Father, Hail Mary, and Glory Be.

SAVOR Prayer and activity are both important.

December 18

Be assured that the grace of eternal salvation for certain souls in their final moment depends on your prayer.

Jesus to Saint Faustina, *Diary*, 1777

STEEP Susan rushed to the nursing home with an image of The Divine Mercy. Her friend Father James was very ill and failing. Susan placed the image near Father James' bed. She silently began to pray the Chaplet, when suddenly Father James awoke with a gasp. He asked Susan if she had brought the Blessed Sacrament. She told him that another priest, Father Bill, was coming to bring the Eucharist and anoint him. Father James insisted, "I felt that Jesus was here."

Susan explained that Jesus told Saint Faustina that the rays of His mercy emanate from the Divine Mercy image. "I think that is the presence that you are experiencing."

Father nodded and fell asleep. Father Bill arrived and administered the sacraments. Susan said, "I believe I witnessed a Divine Mercy miracle that day."

God's love and mercy are powerful. God gives us Catholic women many opportunities to share it with others, sometimes through tangible signs.

ACT Find ways to bring Jesus to the people you encounter today.

PRAY Dear Jesus, please have mercy on us, especially the dying. *Our Father, Hail Mary, and Glory Be.*

SAVOR Jesus, we trust in You!

December 19

To gather round the Bethlehem grotto contemplating there the Holy Family, enables us to appreciate the gift of family intimacy in a special way, and spurs us to offer human warmth and concrete solidarity in those unfortunately numerous situations which, for various reasons, lack peace, harmony, in a word, lack "family."[244]

Saint John Paul II

STEEP We are blessed to be part of the human family. We are given the gift of life in order to work out our salvation in this world and enjoy eternal happiness with God in the next. However, as Saint John Paul II points out in today's quote, not everyone lives in harmony, peace, or a loving family situation. Some families do not experience peace at Christmas time, which is so often seen as a family-oriented holiday. As Christmas approaches and as we focus on preparing our hearts for the Christ Child, let us be extra mindful of praying for our brothers and sisters who are unfortunate for any number of reasons. They certainly need our loving prayers, visits, and phone calls.

ACT If possible, reach out to a person or family in need of comfort and love.

PRAY Dear Holy Family, show us the way.

Our Father, Hail Mary, and Glory Be.

SAVOR God has created me to be a part of the human family.

December 20

So we, who are many, are one body in Christ, and individually we are members one of another.

ROMANS 12:5

STEEP Grace's great-grandmother Alice purchased tickets for herself and her nine children to journey to New York aboard the *Titanic*. Alice's husband, Gustav, had traveled ahead to the United States. He planned to meet Alice and the children upon their arrival. However, two of the children came down with diphtheria, so they had to cancel their trip. The quarantined family later made it safely to Ellis Island aboard another ship.

Grace's grandmother Dorothy was one of the nine children. She attributed their absence from the ship to God's will. If they had been on the *Titanic*, the family likely would've been lost, and Grace would never have existed. She wouldn't be here to tell the story to me so that I can tell you! It's amazing to consider that if even one event in our family history had happened differently, our lives would be entirely changed. So would the lives of our grandchildren and all future generations. God truly works in the events that have led to the lives and families we have now!

ACT Count your blessings! Praise God!

PRAY Jesus, please have mercy on us.

Our Father, Hail Mary, and Glory Be.

SAVOR Life is a fascinating adventure.

December 21

> What our Lady spoke of to the three little children of Fatima was a message that emphasizes that heaven is real. It also makes it clear that our supreme responsibility is to live in such a way that we may be found worthy to enter the kingdom of heaven.[245]
>
> FATHER ANDREW APOSTOLI

STEEP When lived well, Advent can help us meditate on Eternal Life—our supreme goal—and pray that others too may enjoy eternal happiness in Heaven. During a season that can seem chaotic because of the hustle and bustle, we can commit to a specific prayer routine to help us to be more focused and try to find a balance. In Advent, we prepare for Heaven through our sincere prayers, our penances, and our works of mercy for others. Grandmothers have a unique role in helping to shape our grandchildren's consciences. Though our grandchildren may want to excitedly rush into Christmas, we can teach them the importance of preparing and waiting during Advent.

ACT Choose three ways to help your grandchildren appreciate and learn about the season of Advent.

PRAY Jesus, Mary, and Joseph, help us. Saint Francisco, Saint Jacinta, and Venerable Lucia, pray for me.

Our Father, Hail Mary, and Glory Be.

SAVOR This life is meant to work out my salvation.

December 22

> Our prayer each day should be, "Let the joy of the Lord be my strength." Cheerfulness and joy were Our Lady's strength. This made her a willing handmaid of God.[246]
>
> SAINT TERESA OF CALCUTTA

STEEP Christmas is fast approaching. Mother Teresa reminds us to allow the joy of the Lord to be our strength. But for some, joy seems to be absent at this time of year. For example, we might be struggling due to loss of a loved one or some other sorrow.

During Advent, we ponder Mary and Joseph's great joy with their newborn Son. We must remember, though, the holy couple went through a lot of hardship before they could savor those holy moments in the stable in Bethlehem. However, our Lord gives us great joy despite our sufferings.

Mother Teresa taught her sisters to turn to Mary in every need. She said they should cling to Mary like little children. Let us, too, cling to Mary and learn from her example of finding strength in joy.

ACT Be mindful of the Blessed Mother's joy and her willingness to be a handmaid for the Lord.

PRAY "O most pure heart of Mary, allow me to enter your heart, to share your interior life."[247]

Our Father, Hail Mary, and Glory Be.

SAVOR The joy of the Lord needs to be my strength.

December 23

Therefore a man leaves his father and his mother and clings to his wife, and they become one flesh.

GENESIS 2:24

STEEP Susan's husband called from the car. "I'll be back. I have to pick up one of your gifts." It was Christmas Eve, and his destination was an hour away. Susan kept busy in the kitchen preparing for their annual Christmas gathering. Amid the mess of brown sugar and bacon chicken wraps and mixing the German stuffing, Susan's mind shot back to a few years earlier when her daughter had shared her plan—with her master's under her belt, she would launch out to South Korea to teach! Susan felt immediate pain in the pit of her stomach—"wrenching pain that mothers understand." She prayed constantly.

Meanwhile, her husband was stuck in traffic. *My poor husband*, she thought. *How can he do this to himself on Christmas Eve*?

Sometimes, we struggle with the pain of separation from family during the holidays, whether they are a short or long distance away from us. At such times, prayer can soothe our troubled hearts.

ACT Cling to Jesus and Mary in your prayers. Entrust all your loved ones to them.

PRAY Holy Family, please pray for my family.

Our Father, Hail Mary, and Glory Be.

SAVOR The blessing of family is too beautiful to describe.

December 24

There are two births of Christ, one unto the world in Bethlehem; the other in the soul, when it is spiritually reborn.[248]

Venerable Fulton Sheen

STEEP Susan's husband finally returned. He smiled and headed down the hallway. Confused, she followed him. The doorbell rang. "Is there anyone home?" a voice called out.

Susan turned and, "There, as tall and beautiful as a long-stemmed rose, stood my daughter." The two embraced and Susan "wept away the anguish, worry, and pain until the joy surfaced like a fresh spring." A few years later, Susan would meet "a beautiful, handsome Catholic Air Force captain who became my son-in-law. Trusting in God through the cross brings with it an unfailing resurrection of joy. It was the merriest Christmas!"

If we are suffering right now, we can be assured that God is working in our suffering and will eventually bring us an abundance of joy and blessings. We need to hang in there with prayerful trust in God.

ACT Pray much and expect miracles!

PRAY Dear Lord God, thank You for Your Son and for my family.

Our Father, Hail Mary, and Glory Be.

SAVOR Blessings abound!

December 25

But the angel said to them, "Do not be afraid; for see—I am bringing you good news of great joy for all the people: to you is born this day in the city of David a Savior, who is the Messiah, the Lord."

LUKE 2:10–11

STEEP When I was a single mother, my teenaged daughter Chaldea gave a precious, unexpected gift to me. Shortly before Christmas, we celebrated my birthday quietly with homemade cake and handmade birthday cards. I tucked everyone into bed and discovered a white envelope on my dresser inscribed with the word, "Mom." Inside was roughly one hundred dollars and a simple note. "Maybe you can use this to buy Christmas presents." She selflessly gave all of her babysitting money to me.

When I read her note, I had to sit down because I began to shed some tears and my knees started to buckle under me. Someday, my daughter will realize just how much her selfless gift pierced my heart. Maybe now that she is a mother, she will better understand why it meant so much to me.

ACT Drink in the many graces and blessings of Christmas!

PRAY Dear Holy Family, thank you!

Our Father, Hail Mary, and Glory Be.

SAVOR Family is love. We need to nurture it.

December 26

Glory to God in the highest heaven,
and on earth peace among those whom he favors!

LUKE 2:14

STEEP By today, the Christmas gift wrappings might have been tossed into the trash, and maybe the house is tidied a bit after the festivities of Christmas Day (or maybe not!). However, we can still ponder the wondrous event of Jesus' birth in Bethlehem. It's still Christmas, after all! We are in the Christmas season—the time that spans between the birth of Christ and the coming of the Magi. No doubt, you might be tired from all the preparations for Christmas. Perhaps you have more time than you did before Christmas to spend resting and prayerfully enjoying the rest of the season. Or, if things continue to be busy with visiting family and events, you can be the one who reminds your family to keep these busy days prayerful!

ACT Try to slow down today and breathe in the many graces.

PRAY Dear God, I praise You for Your Son, Jesus. Holy Family, please touch my heart.

Our Father, Hail Mary, and Glory Be.

SAVOR It is a very joyous time, but also a time to reflect and to pray for graces.

December 27

For a child has been born for us,
 a son given to us;
authority rests upon his shoulders;
 and he is named
Wonderful Counselor, Mighty God,
 Everlasting Father, Prince of Peace.

Isaiah 9:6

STEEP Saint Augustine said, "Rejoice, you who are just. It is the birthday of Him who justifies. Rejoice, you who are weak and sick. It is the birthday of Him who makes well. Rejoice, you who are in captivity. It is the birthday of the Redeemer. . . . Rejoice, you Christians all. It is Christ's birthday."[249]

The birth of our Lord Jesus Christ has certainly changed our world forever. This is a very special and holy time of the liturgical year—a time to be quiet, to drink in all of the graces, and a time to reach out and connect to family and friends. We can also consider how each of our grandchildren, family members, and friends have changed our world forever.

ACT Take time to deeply ponder Christ's birth and enjoy your family. Share your gratitude for the positive ways your loved ones have changed your life!

PRAY Dear Holy Family, watch over us.

Our Father, Hail Mary, and Glory Be.

SAVOR I will strive to observe the blessings of these holy days, giving thanks for my Redeemer.

December 28

Therefore the LORD waits to be gracious to you;
therefore he will rise up to show mercy to you.

ISAIAH 30:18

STEEP Countless mothers and grandmothers wait for their children and grandchildren to call them. Similarly, today's verse reminds us that our Lord is waiting lovingly for us to strike up a conversation. He wants our love, our sharing with Him. Some folks fear establishing a prayer life, thinking it is daunting or too complicated, or they don't know where to start. Maybe they can't remember traditional prayers or are in too much of a rush to connect with their Creator.

Prayer is very simple. Our humble and contrite prayers touch the Heart of God! Hopefully, throughout this year, you may have formed some prayer commitments. Continue with the prayer commitments you've established even after you've finished this book, keeping the line of communication open with God.

ACT Do all you can to encourage good communication between family members, as well as to keep open the lines of communication with our Lord.

PRAY Lord Jesus, thank You for being near, awaiting my conversations with You.

Our Father, Hail Mary, and Glory Be.

SAVOR God is always waiting. He loves me more than I can comprehend this side of Heaven.

December 29

Look at St. Francis de Sales, who tells us that if he had only one good work to do, he would choose to do it for someone who had done him some wrong rather than for someone who had done him some good service.[250]

SAINT JOHN VIANNEY

STEEP I enjoyed a blessed conversation with Abdul, a twenty-year-old Muslim lad from Afghanistan who had sought refuge in the United States. Abdul speaks with his family daily. They hope to come to the United States someday. Abdul told me a terrorist group had ransacked his parents' home. They were looking for guns and had terrorized the family in the process.

"I am praying for them. We are to pray for our enemies," he told me. A beautiful conversation unfolded. I admire that young man who chose to bless rather than curse.

It's especially hard to pray for people who harm our families, but, like Abdul, we can seek the grace to do so. God calls us to it.

ACT Choose to do something kind for someone who has wronged you or your family, or someone you don't get along with well.

PRAY Dear Jesus, help me love my contrary neighbor.

Our Father, Hail Mary, and Glory Be.

SAVOR God commands me to love and grants graces to do so.

December 30

By wisdom a house is built,
and by understanding it is established.

PROVERBS 24:3

STEEP Valerie and John's fiftieth wedding anniversary approached. They told their adult children they only wanted a special Mass and time with family. So, their grandsons took John shopping for a shirt and tie while the granddaughters shopped for the perfect dress with Valerie. On their anniversary morning, a limousine whisked them off to Mass. Their priest son concelebrated Mass, and their grandchildren sang their hearts out, did the readings, and brought up the gifts.

Valerie shared, "Our jaws hurt from smiling so much!" Tears of joy flowed as their seven beautiful grandchildren, ages three to sixteen, "were so reverent and loving." Friends and family crafted a video, featuring the grandchildren expressing their love and "how they looked up to us as models of what love is supposed to be, how they were so grateful to God for our lives," Valerie said. "Does it get better than this?"

ACT Plan or help to plan a special event for someone in your family, perhaps in the coming year.

PRAY Dear Lord God, thank You for the gift of life!

Our Father, Hail Mary, and Glory Be.

SAVOR A Catholic family is a treasure to behold!

December 31

Live your life in a manner worthy of the gospel of Christ, so that . . . you are standing firm in one spirit, striving side by side with one mind for the faith of the gospel.

Philippians 1:27

STEEP My friend Mariola told me about her grandchildren's different developmental stages and personalities. Jonathan, age eight, is the "bookworm, junior adult, quasi parent to his younger siblings, and Monopoly master!" Stanley, age six, is an "aspiring Evil Knievel daredevil!" Lucy, age four, is "the little princess, femme fatale!" And baby Ella, at one and a half, is a "future track star!"

She pondered, "How did these kids become so gentle, loving, and caring with each other at such young ages?" She knows without a doubt that children need lots of love and guidance. She prays to be a loving and faith-filled example to them as they blossom and mature. Whatever our grandchildren's ages, personalities, or family situations, may we all strive to do the same as we live out our grandmotherly vocation of love.

ACT Reflect on what you have learned in the past year from this book. Ponder how you can go forward continuing to live your vocation well.

PRAY Dear Holy Family, help us and all families.

Our Father, Hail Mary, and Glory Be.

SAVOR We are so very blessed! All glory to God forever!

Source Acknowledgments

Excerpts from *The Dialogue* and *Letters of Spiritual Direction* are used with permission of Paulist Press, paulistpress.com

"A Prayer of Thanks," and "The Death of St. Monica" from *The Confessions of Saint Augustine* by St. Augustine, translated by John K. Ryan, translation copyright © 1960 by Penguin Random House LLC, copyright renewed 1988 by Winona National and Savings Bank. Used by permission of Doubleday, an imprint of the Knopf Doubleday Publishing Group, a division of Penguin Random House LLC. All rights reserved.

Every effort has been made to trace copyright holders and to obtain their permission for the use of copyright material. The publisher apologizes for any errors or omissions in the above list and would be grateful if notified of any corrections that should be incorporated in future reprints or editions of this book.

Appendix of Prayers

"If you knew the gift of God!" (Jn 4:10) The wonder of prayer is revealed beside the well where we come seeking water: there, Christ comes to meet every human being. It is he who first seeks us and asks us for a drink. Jesus thirsts; his asking arises from the depths of God's desire for us. Whether we realize it or not, prayer is the encounter of God's thirst with ours. God thirsts that we may thirst for him.

Catechism of the Catholic Church, 2560

Litany of the Holy Name of Jesus

Lord, have mercy on us. *Christ, have mercy on us.*
Lord, have mercy on us. Jesus, hear us. *Jesus, graciously hear us.*
God the Father of Heaven, *have mercy on us.*
God the Son, Redeemer of the world, *have mercy on us.*
God the Holy Spirit, *have mercy on us.*
Holy Trinity, one God, *have mercy on us.*
Jesus, Son of the living God, *have mercy on us.*
Jesus, splendor of the Father, R.
Jesus, brightness of eternal light, R.
Jesus, King of glory, R.
Jesus, sun of justice, R.
Jesus, Son of the Virgin Mary, R.
Jesus, most amiable, R.

Jesus, most admirable, R.
Jesus, the mighty God, R.
Jesus, Father of the world to come, R.
Jesus, angel of great counsel, R.
Jesus, most powerful, R.
Jesus, most patient, R.
Jesus, most obedient, R.
Jesus, meek and humble of heart, R.
Jesus, lover of chastity, R.
Jesus, lover of us, R.
Jesus, God of peace, R.
Jesus, author of life, R.
Jesus, example of virtues, R.
Jesus, zealous lover of souls, R.
Jesus, our God, R.
Jesus, our refuge, R.
Jesus, father of the poor, R.
Jesus, treasure of the faithful, R.
Jesus, good Shepherd, R.
Jesus, true light, R.
Jesus, eternal wisdom, R.
Jesus, infinite goodness, R.
Jesus, our way and our life, R.
Jesus, joy of Angels, R.
Jesus, King of the Patriarchs, R.
Jesus, Master of the Apostles, R.
Jesus, teacher of the Evangelists, R.
Jesus, strength of Martyrs, R.
Jesus, light of Confessors, R.
Jesus, purity of Virgins, R.

Jesus, crown of Saints, R.
Be merciful, *spare us, O Jesus.*
Be merciful, *graciously hear us, O Jesus.*
From all evil, *deliver us, O Jesus.*
From all sin, R.
From Your wrath, R.
From the snares of the devil, R.
From the spirit of fornication, R.
From everlasting death, R.
From the neglect of Your inspirations, R.
By the mystery of Your holy Incarnation, R.
By Your Nativity, R.
By Your Infancy, R.
By Your most divine Life, R.
By Your labors, R.
By Your agony and passion, R.
By Your cross and dereliction, R.
By Your sufferings, R.
By Your death and burial, R.
By Your Resurrection, R.
By Your Ascension, R.
By Your institution of the most Holy Eucharist, R.
By Your joys, R.
By Your glory, R.

Lamb of God, who takest away the sins of the world,
spare us, O Jesus.
Lamb of God, who takest away the sins of the world,
graciously hear us, O Jesus.
Lamb of God, who takest away the sins of the world,
have mercy on us, O Jesus.

Jesus, hear us, *Jesus, graciously hear us.*

Let us pray.

O Lord Jesus Christ, You have said, "Ask and you shall receive, seek, and you shall find, knock, and it shall be opened to you." Grant, we beg of You, to us who ask it, the gift of Your most divine love, that we may ever love You with our whole heart, in word and deed, and never cease praising You.

Give us, O Lord, as much a lasting fear as a lasting love of Your Holy Name, for You, who live and are King for ever and ever, never fail to govern those whom You have solidly established in Your love. Amen.

Spiritual Communion

My Jesus, I believe that You are present in the Most Holy Sacrament. I love You above all things, and I desire to receive You into my soul. Since I cannot at this moment receive You sacramentally, come at least spiritually into my heart. I embrace You as if You were already there and unite myself wholly to You. Never permit me to be separated from You. Amen.

Memorare

Remember, O most gracious Virgin Mary,
that never was it known that anyone who fled
 to your protection,
implored your help or sought your intercession,
 was left unaided.
Inspired by this confidence, I fly unto you,
 O Virgin of virgins, my Mother.
To you do I come, before you I stand, sinful and sorrowful.

O Mother of the Word Incarnate, despise not my petitions,
but in your mercy hear and answer me. Amen.

Memorare to Saint Joseph

Remember, O most pure spouse of Mary,
and my dearly beloved guardian, Saint Joseph,
that never was it known that anyone who invoked your care
and requested your help was left without consolation.
Inspired with this confidence, I come to you
and with all the ardor of my spirit I commend myself to you.
Do not reject my prayer, O Foster Father of the Savior,
but graciously receive and answer it. Amen.

Act of Consecration by Pope Leo XIII

(May 25, 1899)

Most sweet Jesus, Redeemer of the human race, look down upon us, humbly prostrate before your altar. We are yours and yours we wish to be; but to be more surely united with you, behold each one of us freely consecrates himself today to your most Sacred Heart. Many, indeed, have never known you, many too, despising your precepts, have rejected you. Have mercy on them all, most merciful Jesus, and draw them to your Sacred Heart. Be you king, O Lord, not only of the faithful who have never forsaken you, but also of the prodigal children who have abandoned you; grant that they may quickly return to their father's house, lest they die of wretchedness and hunger. Be you king of those who are deceived by erroneous opinions, or whom discord keeps aloof, and call them back to the harbor of truth and unity of faith, so that soon there may be but one flock and one shepherd. Be you king also of all those who sit in the ancient superstition of the Gentiles, and refuse not you to deliver them out of darkness into the light and kingdom of God. Grant, O Lord, to your Church, assurance of freedom and immunity from harm; give peace and order to all nations, and make the earth resound from pole to pole with one cry: Praise to the divine heart that wrought our salvation; to it be glory and honor forever. Amen.

Angel of Peace Prayer

(From third apparition of Angel of Peace at Fatima, fall 1916)

Most Holy Trinity, Father, Son and Holy Spirit, I adore You profoundly, and I offer You the most precious Body, Blood, Soul and Divinity of Jesus Christ, present in all the tabernacles of the world, in reparation for the outrages, sacrileges and indifference with which He Himself is offended. And, through the infinite merits of His most Sacred Heart and the Immaculate Heart of Mary, I beg of You the conversion of poor sinners.[251]

Sacrifice Prayer

O my Jesus! This is for love of You,
for the conversion of sinners, . . .
and in reparation for the sins committed against
the Immaculate Heart of Mary![252]

The Blessed Virgin Mary gave the Fatima shepherd children this prayer on June 13, 1917. It can be recited when you offer up any suffering to God.

Prayer in Honor of Saint Joachim and Saint Anne

O Lord, God of our Fathers,
who bestowed on Saints Joachim and Anne this grace,
that of them should be born the Mother of your
  incarnate Son,
grant, through the prayers of both,

that we may attain the salvation
you have promised to your people.
Through our Lord Jesus Christ, your Son,
who lives and reigns with you in the unity of the Holy Spirit,
God, for ever and ever.[253]

Anima Christi Prayer

(Attributed to Saint Ignatius of Loyola)

Traditionally prayed after receiving Holy Communion

Soul of Christ, sanctify me.
Body of Christ, save me.
Blood of Christ, inebriate me.
Water from the side of Christ, wash me.
Passion of Christ, strengthen me.
O good Jesus, hear me.
Within Thy wounds hide me.
Separated from Thee let me never be.
From the malignant enemy, defend me.
At the hour of death, call me.
And close to Thee bid me.
That with Thy saints I may be Praising Thee,
forever and ever. Amen.

Litany of the Most Precious Blood

Lord, have mercy. *Lord, have mercy.*
Christ, have mercy. *Christ, have mercy.*
Lord, have mercy. *Lord, have mercy.*
God our Father in heaven, *have mercy on us.*
God the Son, Redeemer of the world, *have mercy on us.*
God the Holy Spirit, *have mercy on us.*
Holy Trinity, one God, *have mercy on us.*

Blood of Christ, only-begotten Son
of the eternal Father, *save us.*
Blood of Christ, incarnate Word of God, R.
Blood of Christ, of the new and eternal covenant, R.
Blood of Christ, spilled upon the earth in agony, R.
Blood of Christ, shed freely in the scourging, R.
Blood of Christ, streaming forth from
the crown of thorns, R.
Blood of Christ, poured out on the cross, R.
Blood of Christ, price of our redemption, R.
Blood of Christ, offering forgiveness and pardon for sin, R.
Blood of Christ, Eucharistic refreshment of souls, R.
Blood of Christ, river of mercy, R.
Blood of Christ, victor over evil, R.
Blood of Christ, strength of martyrs, R.
Blood of Christ, fortitude of the saints, R.
Blood of Christ, sustenance of virgins, R.
Blood of Christ, help of those in peril, R.
Blood of Christ, relief of the burdened, R.
Blood of Christ, solace in sorrow, R.
Blood of Christ, hope of the repentant, R.
Blood of Christ, consolation of the dying, R.
Blood of Christ, peace and comfort for hearts, R.
Blood of Christ, pledge of eternal life, R.
Blood of Christ, hope of glory, R.
Blood of Christ, most worthy of all honor, R.
Lamb of God, you take away the sins of the world,
have mercy on us.
Lamb of God, you take away the sins of the world,
have mercy on us.
Lamb of God, you take away the sins of the world,
have mercy on us.

You redeemed us by your blood, O Lord.
And made us a kingdom to serve our God.

Let us pray.

Almighty and eternal God, you gave your Son to us to be our Redeemer. Grant that his saving Blood be a safeguard against every evil, so that we may rejoice in its fruits forever in heaven. Through the same Christ our Lord. Amen.

Litany of the Most Sacred Heart of Jesus

Lord, have mercy. *Lord, have mercy.*
Christ, have mercy. *Christ, have mercy.*
Lord, have mercy. *Lord, have mercy.*
Christ, hear us. *Christ, hear us.*
Christ, graciously hear us. *Christ, graciously hear us.*
God the Father of Heaven, *have mercy on us.*
God the Son, Redeemer of the world, *have mercy on us.*
God the Holy Spirit, *have mercy on us.*
Holy Trinity, One God, *have mercy on us.*
Heart of Jesus, Son of the Eternal Father, *have mercy on us.*
Heart of Jesus, formed by the Holy Spirit in the womb of the Virgin Mary, R.
Heart of Jesus, substantially united to the word of God, R.
Heart of Jesus, of infinite majesty, R.
Heart of Jesus, sacred temple of God, R.
Heart of Jesus, tabernacle of the Most High, R.
Heart of Jesus, house of God and gate of Heaven, R.
Heart of Jesus, burning furnace of charity, R.
Heart of Jesus, abode of justice and love, R.
Heart of Jesus, full of goodness and love, R.
Heart of Jesus, wellspring of all virtues, R.
Heart of Jesus, most worthy of all praise, R.
Heart of Jesus, King and center of all hearts, R.

Heart of Jesus, in whom are all the treasures of wisdom and knowledge, R.
Heart of Jesus, in whom dwells the fullness of Divinity, R.
Heart of Jesus, in whom the Father was well pleased, R.
Heart of Jesus, of whose fullness we have all received, R.
Heart of Jesus, desire of the everlasting hills, R.
Heart of Jesus, patient and most merciful, R.
Heart of Jesus, enriching all who invoke you, R.
Heart of Jesus, fountain of life and holiness, R.
Heart of Jesus, atonement for our sins, R.
Heart of Jesus, overwhelmed with insults, R.
Heart of Jesus, bruised for our offenses, R.
Heart of Jesus, obedient unto death, R.
Heart of Jesus, pierced with a lance, R.
Heart of Jesus, source of all consolation, R.
Heart of Jesus, our life and resurrection, R.
Heart of Jesus, our peace and reconciliation, R.
Heart of Jesus, victim for sins, R.
Heart of Jesus, salvation of those who trust in you, R.
Heart of Jesus, hope of those who die in you, R.
Heart of Jesus, delight of all Saints, R.

Lamb of God, who takes away the sins of the world, *spare us, O Lord.*
Lamb of God, who takes away the sins of the world, *graciously hear us, O Lord.*
Lamb of God, who takes away the sins of the world, *have mercy on us.*
Jesus, meek and humble of Heart, *make our hearts like unto Thine.*

Let us pray.

Almighty and Eternal God, look upon the Heart of your dearly beloved Son and upon the praise and satisfaction He offers you in the Name of sinners and for those who seek your mercy; be appeased, and grant us pardon in the name of the same Jesus Christ, your Son, who lives and reigns with you forever and ever. Amen.

Prayer of Saint John Paul II

O Blessed Rosary of Mary, sweet chain which unites us to God, bond of love which unites us to the angels, tower of salvation against the assaults of Hell, safe port in our universal shipwreck, we will never abandon you. You will be our comfort in the hour of death: yours our final kiss as life ebbs away. And the last word from our lips will be your sweet name, O Queen of the Rosary of Pompei, O dearest Mother, O Refuge of Sinners, O Sovereign Consoler of the Afflicted. May you be everywhere blessed, today and always, on earth and in heaven.[254]

Prayer to God Invoking Our Lady of Guadalupe

O God, Father of mercies,
who placed your people under the singular protection
of your Son's most holy Mother,
grant that all who invoke the Blessed Virgin of Guadalupe,
may seek with ever more lively faith
the progress of peoples in the ways of justice and of peace.
Through our Lord Jesus Christ, your Son,
who lives and reigns with you in the unity of the Holy Spirit,
God, for ever and ever.[255]

Saint Michael Prayer

Saint Michael the Archangel, defend us in battle.
Be our protection against the wickedness and
snares of the devil;

May God rebuke him, we humbly pray;
And do thou, O Prince of the Heavenly Host,
by the power of God, thrust into hell Satan
and all evil spirits who wander through the world
for the ruin of souls. Amen.

The Seven Sorrows of Mary Devotion

Tradition holds that in the fourteenth century, the Blessed Virgin Mary appeared to Saint Bridget of Sweden (1303–1373), requesting devotion to her tears and dolors. She promised seven graces to those who honor her by mediating upon her seven sorrows daily.

Consider spending a few minutes a day to honor Mary in her seven sorrows by praying seven Hail Marys daily (or seven for each sorrow daily) while meditating upon each sorrow. The reflections and prayers included here are by Donna-Marie Cooper O'Boyle.

First Sorrow: The Prophecy of Simeon

> Then Simeon blessed them and said to his mother Mary, "This child is destined for the falling and the rising of many in Israel, and to be a sign that will be opposed so that the inner thoughts of many will be revealed—and a sword will pierce your own soul too" (Lk 2:34–35).

First Promise of Grace: Peace to their families.

Consider that what should have been a happy occasion for parents presenting their beloved Baby in the Temple did not turn out that way. Normally, parents would experience great joy and thanksgiving in fulfilling the law and basking in the goodness of God, Who had gifted their child to them. However, in the case of the Holy Family, the experience was very different. A sword of sorrow had pierced Mother Mary's heart upon hearing the holy prophecy of Simeon.

Meditate upon the sorrow in Mary's heart as she heard the prophecy about her Son.

Pray: Mary, I wish to honor you in your seven sorrows. Thank you for your promise of grace and peace to our families. *Now, pray one Our Father and seven Hail Marys.*

Second Sorrow: The Flight into Egypt

> Now after they had left, an angel of the Lord appeared to Joseph in a dream and said, "Get up, take the child and his mother, and flee to Egypt, and remain there until I tell you; for Herod is about to search for the child, to destroy him." Then Joseph got up, took the child and his mother by night, and went to Egypt, and remained there until the death of Herod. This was to fulfill what had been spoken by the Lord through the prophet, "Out of Egypt I have called my son" (Mt 2:13–15).

Second Promise of Grace: They will be enlightened about divine mysteries.

Consider the Holy Family's flight into Egypt. How hard this was for their little family. Consider Mary grabbing hold of her sweet Baby Jesus and wrapping Him quickly to set out on a perilous journey to safety. Though a woman of deep faith, she was also intensely concerned for the life of her holy Child.

Meditate upon Mary's heavy Immaculate Heart in her rush to Egypt and pray wholeheartedly.

Pray: Our Lady of Sorrows, please help me. Thank you for the promise of grace to enlighten devotees about divine mysteries. *Now, pray one Our Father and seven Hail Marys.*

Third Sorrow: The Loss of the Child Jesus in the Temple

> When the festival was ended and they started to return, the boy Jesus stayed behind in Jerusalem, but his parents did not know

> it. Assuming that he was in the group of travelers, they went a day's journey. Then they started to look for him among their relatives and friends. When they did not find him, they returned to Jerusalem to search for him (Lk 2:43–45).

Third Promise of Grace: I will console them in their pains and I will accompany them in their work.

Consider this third sorrow of Mary. Her precious Child Jesus was lost for three entire days and her motherly heart was in turmoil. She prayed and searched with Saint Joseph. Can we imagine the torment we would feel in not knowing how to find our beautiful child at a time without our modern technology? The holy couple traipsed all over to finally find the Boy Jesus. He told them that He was doing His Father's business.

Ponder Mary's sorrows, especially in losing her Son.

Pray: Dear Our Lady of Sorrows, thank you for the promise of grace that you will console us in our pains and accompany us in our work. *Now, pray one Our Father and seven Hail Marys.*

Fourth Sorrow: The Meeting of Jesus and Mary on the Way of the Cross

> A great number of the people followed him, and among them were women who were beating their breasts and wailing for him. But Jesus turned to them and said, "Daughters of Jerusalem, do not weep for me, but weep for yourselves and for your children. For the days are surely coming when they will say, 'Blessed are the barren, and the wombs that never bore, and the breasts that never nursed'" (Lk 23:27–29).

Fourth Promise of Grace: I will give them as much as they ask for as long as it does not oppose the adorable will of my divine Son or the sanctification of their souls.

Consider this fourth sorrow of Mary. Can we imagine seeing our own son carrying a cross on the way to his death? When their eyes met, Mary's heart was breaking, though she knew what had to happen for the salvation of souls. She was (and is still) totally connected to her Son's work. Her holy tears ran down her sorrowful face as she fervently prayed.

Take time to ponder Mary's tears and sorrow.

Pray: Dear Our Lady of Sorrows, please help me. Thank you for your promise of the grace of giving us as much as we ask for as long as it is within God's holy will. *Now, pray one Our Father and seven Hail Marys.*

Fifth Sorrow: The Crucifixion

> Meanwhile, standing near the cross of Jesus were his mother, and his mother's sister, Mary the wife of Clopas, and Mary Magdalene. When Jesus saw his mother and the disciple whom he loved standing beside her, he said to his mother, "Woman, here is your son." Then he said to the disciple, "Here is your mother." And from that hour the disciple took her into his own home (Jn 19:25–27).

Fifth Promise of Grace: I will defend them in their spiritual battles with the infernal enemy and I will protect them at every instant of their lives.

Consider Mary, after having followed behind as her divine Son carried the Cross to His death, with grave sorrow, witnessing huge nails being pounded into His Sacred hands and feet. Then, when He was raised up on the wooden Cross, Mary watched her Son's Precious Blood drip down His body. It was impossible for her to put a stop to her Son's agonizing death. Helplessly, she watched as her Son forgave others, promised Eternal Life to the good thief hanging beside Him, and gave the eminent gift of His own Blessed Mother to John and all mankind.

Meditate upon Mary's sorrow and the gift of Mother Mary in your life.

Pray: Dear Our Lady of Sorrows, thank you for your promise of the grace of defending me in spiritual battles and for such great protection. *Now, pray one Our Father and seven Hail Marys.*

Sixth Sorrow: The Taking Down of the Body of Jesus from the Cross

> Then the soldiers came and broke the legs of the first and of the other who had been crucified with him. But when they came to Jesus and saw that he was already dead, they did not break his legs. Instead, one of the soldiers pierced his side with a spear, and at once blood and water came out (Jn 19:32–34).

SIXTH PROMISE OF GRACE: I will visibly help them at the moment of their death; they will see the face of their Mother.

Consider the excruciating pain and heartache of Mother Mary as she watched the soldier thrust a sword into her dear Son's Sacred Heart. Yet, that very Blood and Water which gushed forth was in reality the beginning of the Church and a sure sign of Divine Mercy for the world. After a while, when the time was right, Jesus' dead Body was lowered from the cruel Cross, and the Divine Son was placed on Mother Mary's lap, against her breast, to be lovingly cradled in her aching arms.

Can we even imagine her sorrow?

Meditate on Mother Mary's deep sorrow. Close your eyes, take your time, pray, and imagine yourself in the scene.

Pray: Dear Our Lady of Sorrows, thank you for your great promise to visibly help me at the hour of my death. *Now, pray one Our Father and seven Hail Marys.*

Seventh Sorrow: The Burial of Jesus

> After these things, Joseph of Arimathea, who was a disciple of Jesus, though a secret one because of his fear of the Jews, asked Pilate to let him take away the body of Jesus. Pilate gave him permission; so he came and removed his body. Nicodemus, who had at first come to Jesus by night, also came, bringing a mixture of myrrh and aloes, weighing about a hundred pounds. They took the body of Jesus and wrapped it with the spices in linen cloths, according to the burial custom of the Jews. Now there was a garden in the place where he was crucified, and in the garden there was a new tomb in which no one had ever been laid. And so, because it was the Jewish day of Preparation, and the tomb was nearby, they laid Jesus there (Jn 19:38–42).

Seventh Promise of Grace: I have obtained (this Grace) from my divine Son, that those who propagate this devotion to my tears and dolors, will be taken directly from this earthly life to eternal happiness since all their sins will be forgiven, and my Son and I will be their eternal consolation and joy.

Consider, when Jesus was buried in the tomb, how Mother Mary's Immaculate Heart was aching beyond anything we can imagine. Yet, as a faith-filled and prayerful Jewish woman, she prayed earnestly as she tenderly helped with the burial of her own Son. Her holy tears must have mingled with the spices and sweet-smelling herbs. Can we imagine her loving and sorrowful gaze as she observed her Son's battered dead Body?

Meditate upon Mary's deep and grievous sorrow. Place yourself in the scene with her in prayer.

Pray: Dear Our Lady of Sorrows, please help me. I am sorry you suffered excruciatingly to have to bury your own beloved Son. Thank you for the great graces that you promise to devotees of your sorrows. *Now, pray one Our Father and seven Hail Marys.*

Notes

1. Paul VI, *Marialis Cultus* (The Holy See, February 2, 1974), 5, www.vatican.va.

2. Augustine, *The Confessions of St. Augustine*, trans. John K. Ryan (New York: Doubleday, 1960), 22.

3. Maria Faustina Kowalska, *Diary of Saint Maria Faustina Kowalska: Divine Mercy in My Soul* (Stockbridge, MA: Marian Press, 2012), 1184. We will follow the style of the *Diary*, indicating the words of Christ in boldface and the words of the Blessed Virgin Mary in italics.

4. Paul O'Sullivan, OP (EDM), *The Wonders of the Holy Name* (Rockford, IL: TAN Books, 1993), 3.

5. O'Sullivan, *Holy Name*, 4.

6. Michalenko, Seraphim, MIC, "So Why Is Divine Mercy So Important? Here's Why," April 2014, Bolivia, https://www.marian.org/videos/So-Why-Is-Divine-Mercy-So-Important-Heres-Why-5849.

7. Fulton J. Sheen, *Way to Happiness* (Staten Island: Alba House, 1998), 86.

8. O'Sullivan, *Holy Name*, 4.

9. Sheen, *Way to Happiness*, 89.

10. O'Sullivan, *Holy Name*, 4.

11. Michalenko, "So Why Is Divine Mercy So Important? Here's Why."

12. Sheen, *Way to Happiness*, 90.

13 *Catechism of the Catholic Church*, 2nd ed. (Huntington, IN: Our Sunday Visitor, 1994), 1655. Also referred to as *CCC*.

14. Sheen, *Way to Happiness*, 90.

15. Benedict XVI, Angelus, Castel Gandolfo, August 27, 2006, The Holy See, www.vatican.va.

16. Francis de Sales, *Introduction to the Devout Life* (New York: Cosimo, Inc, 2007), 45.

17. Francoise Bouchard, *Bernadette: Her Story* (Paris: Salvatore, 2007), 17.

18. John Bosco, "The Companion of Youth," in *The Spiritual Writings of Saint John Bosco* (New Rochelle, NY: Don Bosco Publications, 1984), 77.

19. Personal letter from Mother Teresa to the author, September 1989.

20. John Paul II, *Gratissimam Sane* (*Letter to Families*), (The Holy See, February 2, 1994), 23, www.vatican.va.

21. John Paul II, Angelus, December 30, 2001, The Holy See, 2, www.vatican.va.

22. John Paul II, Angelus, December 30, 2001, 2.

23. De Sales, *Devout Life*, 44.

24. De Sales, *Devout Life*, 44.

25. Alphonsus de Liguori, *The Sermons of St. Alphonsus Liguori for All the Sundays of the Year, Sermon XVII*, Third Sunday in Lent (Rockford, IL: Tan Books, 1982), 136.

26. Teresa, *Collected Works of St. Teresa of Avila, Volume One* (Washington, DC: ICS Publications, 1976), 54.

27. Leo XIII, *Quamquam Pluries* (The Holy See, August 15, 1889), 3, www.vatican.va.

28. Teresa, *Collected Works*,1:54.

29. John Paul II, Homily, November 30, 1986, The Holy See, 4, www.vatican.va.

30. John A. Hardon, SJ, "The Role of Catholic Women Today: Hope of the Family for the Third Millennium," Real Presence Eucharistic Education and Adoration Association, http://www.therealpresence.org/archives/Family/Family_002.htm.

31. John Paul II, Homily, November 30, 1986, 7.

32. Thérèse, *Story of a Soul*, trans. John Clarke, OCD (Washington, DC: ICS Publications, 1996), 124.

33. John Paul II, *Redemptoris Custos* (The Holy See, August 15, 1989), 32, www.vatican.va.

34. Peter Julian Eymard, *Month of St. Joseph* (New York: Eymard League, 1948), 94.

35. Eymard, *Month of St. Joseph*, 106.

36. John Henry Newman, *Essays Critical and Historical, Vol 1. 4th Edition* (London, Basil Montagu Pickering, 1877), 23.

37. Eymard, *Month of St. Joseph*, 41.

38. Eymard, *Month of St. Joseph*, 60.

39. Quoted in Bernard LaFreniere, CSC, *Brother André According to Witnesses* (Montréal: St. Joseph's Oratory, 1997), 78–79.

40. John Paul II, *Redemptoris Custos*, 17.

41. John Paul II, "The Jubilee Pilgrimage to the Holy Land," Homily, March 25, 2000, The Holy See, 4, www.vatican.va.

42. Quoted in LaFreniere, *Brother André*, 78.

43. Bernardine of Siena, *English Translation of The Liturgy of the Hours*, "Feast of Joseph, Husband of Mary," March 19 (Washington, DC: International Commission on English in the Liturgy Corporation, 1974).

44. Bernardine of Siena, *Liturgy of the Hours*, "Feast of Joseph, Husband of Mary."

45. Benedict XVI, Homily, March 19, 2009, The Holy See, www.vatican.va.

46. Eymard, *Month of St. Joseph*, 104.

47. Catherine of Siena, *The Dialogue*, trans. Suzanne Noffke, OP (New York: Paulist Press, 1980), 145–146.

48. Donna-Marie Cooper O'Boyle, *Our Lady's Message to Three Shepherd Children and the World*, see Foreword by Andrew Apostoli, CFR (Manchester, NH: Sophia Institute Press, 2017), x.

49. Cooper O'Boyle, *Our Lady's Message*, x.

50. Sheen, *Way to Happiness*, 112.

51. John Paul II, "To the Bishops of the Ecclesiastical Provinces of Bombay, Goa, Hyderabad, Nagpur, and Verapoly on Their 'Ad Limina' Visit," Address, December 13, 1995, The Holy See, 2, www.vatican.va.

52. Josemaría Escrivá, *The Way* (New York: Scepter Publishers, 1982), 537.

53. John Paul II, *Redemptoris Custos*, 8.

54. John Paul II, *Redemptoris Custos*, 22.

55. Teresa, *Collected Works*, 1:34.

56. Benedict XVI, *Spe Salvi* (The Holy See, November 30, 2007), 50, www.vatican.va.

57. Benedict XVI, *Spe Salvi*, 50.

58. Benedict XVI, *Spe Salvi*, 50.

59. Benedict XVI, *Spe Salvi*, 50.

60. Benedict XVI, *Spe Salvi*, 50.

61. Sheen, *Way to Happiness*, 132.

62. Paul VI, *The Month of May* (The Holy See, April 29, 1965), 1, www.vatican.va.

63. Benedict XVI, *Spe Salvi*, 50.

64. Andrew Apostoli, CFR, *Fatima and the Triumph of Mary: Reflections on the Fatima Message* (Washington, NJ: World Apostolate of Fatima, 2016), 84.

65. "Hail Star of the Sea," author unknown.

66. Teresa of Calcutta, archives of The Mother Teresa Center, Missionaries of Charity.

67. Benedict XVI, Regina Caeli, April 30, 2006, The Holy See, www.vatican.va.

68. Benedict XVI, Regina Caeli, April 30, 2006.

69. Paul VI, *Month of May*, 1.

70. René Laurentin, *Bernadette Speaks: A Life of Saint Bernadette Soubirous in Her Own Words* (Boston: Pauline Books & Media, 2000), 34.

71. Teresa of Calcutta, archives of The Mother Teresa Center, Missionaries of Charity.

72. Louis de Montfort, *True Devotion to the Blessed Virgin Mary* (Staten Island: Society of St. Paul, 1962), 1.

73. De Montfort, *True Devotion*, 1.

74. Teresa of Calcutta, archives of The Mother Teresa Center, Missionaries of Charity.

75. John Paul II, General Audience, July 23, 1997, The Holy See, 5, www.vatican.va.

76. Gertrude, "Prayer to the Sacred Heart" (Adapted by Alphonsus de Liguori).

77. Pius XI, *Miserentissimus Redemptor*, 13, www.vatican.va.

78. John Paul II, "Devotion to the Sacred Heart of Jesus," Address, June 6, 1999, The Holy See, www.vatican.va.

79. Josemaría Escrivá, *Christ Is Passing By* (New Rochelle, NY: Scepter Publishers), 75.

80. John Paul II, *Ecclesia de Eucharistia* (The Holy See, April 17, 2003), 59, www.vatican.va.

81. Quoted in Émile Bougaud, *Life of Blessed Margaret Mary Alacoque*, trans. a Visitandine of Baltimore (New York: Benziger Brothers, 1890), 176.

82. Sheen, *Way to Happiness*, 134.

83. John Paul II, Homily, September 18, 1984, The Holy See, www.vatican.va.

84. Margaret Mary Alacoque, *The Letters of Saint Margaret Mary Alacoque*, trans. Clarence A. Herbst, SJ (Chicago: Henry Regnery Company, 1954), 151.

85. Leo XIII, "Prayer of Consecration to the Sacred Heart," issued with the Encyclical Letter *Annum Sacrum* (The Holy See, May 25, 1899), www.vatican.va.

86. Pius XII, *Haurietis Aquas* (The Holy See, May 15, 1956), 2, www.vatican.va.

87. Benedict XVI, General Audience, February 10, 2010, The Holy See, www.vatican.va.

88. Leo XIII, *Annum Sacrum*, 8.

89. Thérèse, *The Poetry of Saint Thérèse of Lisieux*, trans. Donald Kinney, OCD (Washington, DC: ICS Publications, 1996), 119.

90. Thérèse, *Poetry*, 120.

91. Jean Bainvel, "Devotion to the Sacred Heart of Jesus," in *The Catholic Encyclopedia* (New York: Robert Appleton Company, 1910), 7:164.

92. John Paul II, "His Heart Is the Heart of the Church," Solemnity of the Sacred Heart of Jesus, Homily, Warsaw, June 11, 1999, The Holy See, 6, www.vatican.va.

93. John Paul II, *Letter to the Elderly* (The Holy See, October 1, 1999), 10, www.vatican.va.

94. John Paul II, *Letter to the Elderly*, 14.

95. John A. Hardon, SJ, "The Mercy of God," Real Presence Eucharistic Education and Adoration Association, http://www.therealpresence.org/archives/Divine_Mercy/Divine_Mercy_001.htm.

96. John A. Hardon, SJ, "Quotes on the Most Blessed Sacrament," Real Presence Eucharistic Education and Adoration Association, http://www.therealpresence.org/eucharst/tes/quotes2.html.

97. Francis Xavier Nguyen van Thuan, *Testimony of Hope: The Spiritual Exercises of John Paul II* (Boston: Pauline Books & Media, 2000), 131.

98. Quoted in Alphonsus de Liguori, *The Glories of Mary* (Gastonia, NC: TAN Books, 2023), 608.

99. Personal letter from Mother Teresa to the author.

100. John A. Hardon, SJ, "Devotion to the Sacred Heart Today," Real Presence Eucharistic Education and Adoration Association, http://www.therealpresence.org/archives/Sacred_Heart/Sacred_Heart_002.htm.

101. Clement of Rome, "The Letter to the Corinthians," trans. Francis X. Glimm, 7:4, in *The Apostolic Fathers* (New York: Christian Heritage, Inc., 1947), 15.

102. John A. Hardon, SJ, "The Precious Blood of Christ," Real Presence Eucharistic Education and Adoration Association, December 26, 1987, http://www.therealpresence.org/archives/Christology/Christology_013.htm.

103. Hardon, "The Precious Blood of Christ."

104. De Liguori, *Glories of Mary*, 60–61.

105. Jesus Christ is both perfectly divine and perfectly human and has two complete and distinct natures at once (see *CCC* 464–469).

106. Hardon, "The Precious Blood of Christ."

107. Hardon, "The Precious Blood of Christ."

108. Some well-known Eucharistic miracles took place in Siena, Italy, 1730; Amsterdam, Holland, 1345; Blanot, France, 1331; Bolsena, Italy, 1264; and Lanciano, Italy, eighth century.

109. Fulton J. Sheen, in *Sermon in a Sentence: A Treasury of Quotations on the Spiritual Life*, ed. John P. McClernon (London: Baronius Press LTD, 2015), 150.

110. Quoted in Penny Hickey, OCDS, comp., *Drink of the Stream: Prayers of Carmelites* (San Francisco: Ignatius Press, 2002), 31–32.

111. Quoted in Hickey, *Drink of the Stream*, 31.

112. Lucia dos Santos, *Fatima in Lucia's Own Words: Sister Lucia's Memoirs*, ed. Louis Kondor, SVD, trans. Dominican Nuns of Perpetual Rosary (np: Fatima Postulation Center, 1976), 152.

113. Dos Santos, *Fatima in Lucia's Own Words*, 152, 154.

114. Anne Catherine Emmerich, *The Life of the Blessed Virgin Mary* (Rockford, IL: Tan Books, 1970), 31.

115. Hardon, "Devotion to the Sacred Heart Today."

116. Hardon, "Devotion to the Sacred Heart Today."

117. "Corpus Christi Novena," EWTN (website), accessed March 19, 2024, https://www.ewtn.com/catholicism/devotions/corpus-christi-novena-277.

118. John Paul II, Homily, December 10, 1978, The Holy See, 3, www.vatican.va.

119. Francis, "Feast of Sts. Joachim and Anne," Homily, July 26, 2022, The Holy See, www.vatican.va.

120. Teresa of Calcutta, archives of The Mother Teresa Center, Missionaries of Charity.

121. John XXIII, *Pacem in Terris* (The Holy See, April 11, 1963), 16, www.vatican.va.

122. Teresa of Calcutta, archives of The Mother Teresa Center, Missionaries of Charity.

123. John Paul II, *Mane Nobiscum Domine* (The Holy See, October 7, 2004), 18, www.vatican.va.

124. Teresa of Calcutta, archives of The Mother Teresa Center, Missionaries of Charity.

125. Pew Research Center, https://www.pewresearch.org/fact-tank/2019/08/05/transubstantiation-eucharist-u-s-catholics/.

126. Sheen, *Way to Happiness*, 139.

127. John Paul II, *Mane Nobiscum Domine*, 18.

128. John Paul II, *Mane Nobiscum Domine*, 18.

129. Mother Mectilde de Bar, "Text of our Foundress, Mother Mectilde de Bar," accessed March 25, 2024, https://www.service-des-moniales.cef.fr/en/monastery-of-the-immaculate-conception-at-craon/

130. John A. Hardon, SJ, "The Sacred Heart Is the Holy Eucharist," Real Presence Eucharistic Education and Adoration Association, February 15, 2016, http://www.therealpresence.org/eucharst/intro/sacred.htm.

131. "Text of our Foundress, Mother Mectilde de Bar."

132. "Text of our Foundress, Mother Mechtilde de Bar."

133. Francis (@Pontifex) X, July 31, 2014, 3:31 a.m., https://twitter.com/Pontifex/status/494762200456634370.

134. Paul VI, Vatican Council II, *Lumen Gentium, Dogmatic Constitution on the Church* (The Holy See, November 21, 1964), 69, www.vatican.va.

135. John Chrysostom, "Homily on Ephesians, XXI," in *Nicene and Post-Nicene Fathers of the Christian Church* (Grand Rapids: Wm B. Eerdmans, 1976), 13:156–157.

136. Personal letter from Mother Teresa to the author, March 7, 1989.

137. John Paul II, *Mane Nobiscum Domine*, 25.

138. John Paul II, *Mane Nobiscum Domine*, 15.

139. John Paul II, *Mane Nobiscum Domine*, 15.

140. De Liguori, *Glories of Mary*, 450.

141. Quoted by de Liguori, *Glories of Mary*, 399.

142. Quoted by de Liguori, *Glories of Mary*, 399.

143. Josemaría Escrivá, "Passionately Loving the World," in *Conversations with Monsignor Escrivá de Balaguer* (Manilla: Sinag-Tala Publishers, 1967), 192.

144. Sheen, *Sermon in a Sentence*, 114.

145. Quoted in de Liguori, *Glories of Mary*, 434.

146. Quoted in *The Roman Breviary*, book IV (London: Burns Oats & Washbourne, 1936), 477.

147. Paul VI, *Marialis Cultus*, 7.

148. Quoted in Abbe Francois Trochu, *The Curé d'Ars: Saint Jean-Marie-Baptiste Vianney*, trans. Dom Ernst Graf, OSB (Rockford, IL: TAN Books, 1977), 8.

149. Quoted in de Liguori, *Glories of Mary*, 406.

150. Quoted in de Liguori, *Glories of Mary*, 406.

151. Escrivá, *The Way*, 493.

152. Sheen, *Sermon in a Sentence*, 114.

153. Pius IX, *Ineffabilis Deus*, which proclaimed the dogma of the Immaculate Conception (The Holy See, December 8, 1854), final paragraph, www.vatican.va.

154. De Liguori, *Glories of Mary*, 399.

155. John Vianney, "Sermon for the Feast of the Nativity of Our Lady," in *Thoughts of the Curé d'Ars* (n.p.: Benziger Brothers, 1930), 64.

156. Fulton J. Sheen, *The World's First Love: Mary, Mother of God* (San Francisco: Ignatius Press, 1996), 259.

157. Pio of Pietrelcina, Letter to Padre Agostino, February 1, 1913, in *Secrets of a Soul: Padre Pio's Letters to His Spiritual Directors*, ed. Gianluigi Pasquale (Boston: Pauline Books & Media, 2003), 43.

158. John Paul II, Papal Visit, May 29, 1982, Wembley Stadium, The Holy See, 4, www.vatican.va.

159. De Liguori, *Glories of Mary*, 395.

160. De Liguori, *Glories of Mary*, 61.

161. Quoted in de Liguori, *Glories of Mary*, 399.

162. De Liguori, *Glories of Mary*, 425.

163. Quoted in de Liguori, *Glories of Mary*, 436.

164. Quoted in de Liguori, *Glories of Mary*, 447.

165. John Paul II, *Rosarium Virginis Mariae* (The Holy See, October 16, 2002), 24, www.vatican.va.

166. Thérèse, *The Prayers of Saint Thérèse of Lisieux: The Act of Oblation*, trans. Aletheia Kane, OCD (Washington, DC: ICS Publications, 1997), 75.

167. Thérèse, *Story of a Soul*, 243.

168. Gabriele Amorth, *Father Amorth: My Battle Against Satan*, trans. Charlotte J. Fasi (Manchester, NH: Sophia Institute Press, 2018), 35.

169. De Sales, *Devout Life*, 45.

170. "Fifteen Promises of the Blessed Mother," Rosary Center, https://rosarycenter.org/confraternity-obligations-benefits-and-promises.

171. "Fifteen Promises of the Blessed Mother" Rosary Center.

172. "Fifteen Promises of the Blessed Mother" Rosary Center.

173. "Fifteen Promises of the Blessed Mother" Rosary Center.

174. Louis de Montfort, *The Secret of the Rosary*, trans. Mary Barbour, TOP (Bay Shore, NY: Montfort Publications, 1988), 56.

175. "Fifteen Promises of the Blessed Mother" Rosary Center.

176. "Fifteen Promises of the Blessed Mother" Rosary Center.

177. "Fifteen Promises of the Blessed Mother" Rosary Center.

178. "Fifteen Promises of the Blessed Mother" Rosary Center.

179. John de Marchi, IMC, *Fatima from the Beginning*, trans. I.M. Kingsbury (Fatima, Portugal: Missoes, Consolata Fatima, 2006), 137.

180. "Fifteen Promises of the Blessed Mother" Rosary Center.

181. "Fifteen Promises of the Blessed Mother" Rosary Center.

182. Quoted in John Carr, CSSR, *Saint Gerard Majella* (Westminster, MD: The Newman Press, 1959), 136.

183. Quoted in Carr, *Saint Gerard Majella*, 178.

184. "Fifteen Promises of the Blessed Mother" Rosary Center.

185. "Fifteen Promises of the Blessed Mother" Rosary Center.

186. "Fifteen Promises of the Blessed Mother" Rosary Center.

187. "Fifteen Promises of the Blessed Mother" Rosary Center.

188. "Fifteen Promises of the Blessed Mother" Rosary Center.

189. John Paul II, *Rosarium Virginis Mariae*, 1.

190. John Paul II, *Rosarium Virginis Mariae*, 8.

191. Donald H. Calloway, MIC, *How to Pray the Rosary* (Stockbridge, MA: Marian Press, 2017), 14.

192. De Montfort, *Secret of the Rosary*, 27.

193. De Montfort, *Secret of the Rosary*, 93.

194. Sheen, *World's First Love*, 208.

195. De Montfort, *Secret of the Rosary*, 28–29.

196. Louis de Montfort, *God Alone: The Collected Writings of St. Louis de Montfort* (Bay Shore, NY: Montfort Publications, 1988), 93.

197. John Paul II, discussion with a select group of German Catholics, Fulda Germany, published in Stimme des Glaubens magazine, October 1981, https://fatima.org/pope-john-paul-ii-in-fulda-germany-1980/.

198. John Paul II, *Rosarium Virginis Mariae*, 2.

199. John Paul II, *Rosarium Virginis Mariae*, 3.

200. John Paul II, *Rosarium Virginis Mariae*, 6.

201. Michael Oguno, "The Power of the Rosary in the Battle Against the Forces of the Evil One," The Choice Flame (blog), May 2, 2020, https://choiceflame.com.ng/2020/05/02/the-power-of-the-rosary-in-the-battle-against-the-forces-of-the-evil-one/.

202. Oguno, "The Power of the Rosary in the Battle Against the Forces of the Evil One."

203. Calloway, *How to Pray the Rosary*, 15.

204. John Paul II, *Rosarium Virginis Mariae*, 41.

205. John Paul II, *Rosarium Virginis Mariae*, 6.

206. Miguel Marie Soeherman, MFVA, Homily at the Shrine of the Most Blessed Sacrament, Solemnity of All Saints, November 1, 2009, Hanceville, AL.

207. Soeherman, Homily at the Shrine of the Most Blessed Sacrament.

208. Apostoli, *Fatima and the Triumph of Mary*, 70.

209. Apostoli, *Fatima and the Triumph of Mary*, 70–71.

210. Benedict Groeschel, CFR, with John Bishop, *There Are No Accidents: In All Things Trust in God* (Huntington, IN: Our Sunday Visitor, 2004), 34.

211. Thérèse, *Story of a Soul*, 143.

212. Thérèse, *Story of a Soul*, 143–144.

213. Soeherman, "Homily at the Shrine of the Most Blessed Sacrament, Solemnity of All Saints."

214. Francis de Sales, Jane de Chantal, *Letters of Spiritual Direction* (New York: Paulist Press, 1988), 112.

215. De Sales, de Chantal, *Letters of Spiritual Direction*, 101.

216. Teresa, *Collected Works of St. Teresa of Avila, Volume Two* (Washington, DC: ICS Publications, 1980), 59.

217. Cardinal Angelo Sodano, "On the closing of the celebrations for the first centenary of the death of Saint Maria Goretti," Homily, April 25, 2003, The Holy See, www.vatican.va.

218. De Montfort, *Secret of the Rosary*, 68.

219. De Montfort, *Secret of the Rosary*, 68.

220. Augustine, *Confessions*, 186.

221. Quoted in The "Raccolta" or *Collection of Indulgenced Prayers and Good Works* (New York: Benziger Brothers, 1910), 61.

222. Gertrude of Helfta, *The Life and Revelations of Saint Gertrude* (Westminster, MD: The Newman Press, 1949), 410.

223. John Vianney, *Sermons of the Curé of Ars*, trans. Una Morrissy (Chicago: Henry Regnery Company, 1960), 134.

224. Pio of Pietrelcina, *Letters, Vol II Correspondence with Raffaelina Cerase, Noblewoman* (1914-1915) (San Giovanni Rotondo: n.p., 1987), 490.

225. René Laurentin, *Catherine Labouré: Visionary of the Miraculous Medal*, trans. Paul Inwood (Boston, MA: Pauline Books & Media), 42.

226. Groeschel, *There Are No Accidents*, 34.

227. Vianney, *Sermons of the Curé of Ars*, 92–93.

228. Laurentin, *Catherine Labouré*, 42.

229. Laurentin, *Catherine Labouré*, 47.

230. Donna-Marie Cooper O'Boyle, *The Miraculous Medal: Stories, Prayers, and Devotions* (Cincinnati: Servant Books, 2013), 70.

231. Cooper O'Boyle, *Miraculous Medal*, 70.

232. Pope John Paul II, "Letter of His Holiness Pope John Paul II for the Celebration of the Millennium of the Commemoration of All the Faithful Departed" (The Holy See, June 2, 1998), www.vatican.va.

233. Thérèse, *Story of a Soul*, 71.

234. Teresa, *Collected Works*, 2:145.

235. John Paul II, "Solemnity of the Immaculate Conception," Angelus, December 8, 2000, The Holy See, 1, www.vatican.va.

236. Francis de Sales, *The Love of God: A Treatise* (Westminster, MD: The Newman Press, 1962), 184.

237. Teresa, *Collected Works*, 2:98.

238. Antonio Valeriano, *Nican Mopohua Aquí se Cuenta/Here is Told*, trans. Mario Rojas Sánchez (Mexico: Pio Producciones, 2018), 43–44.

239. Teresa, *Collected Works*, 2:97.

240. Teresa, *Collected Works*, 2:101.

241. Teresa, *Collected Works*, 2:100.

242. Teresa, *Collected Works*, 2:100.

243. Teresa, *Collected Works*, 2:100.

244. John Paul II, Angelus, December 29, 1996, The Holy See, www.vatican.va.

245. Andrew Apostoli, CFR, "Heaven Is Real," Soul Magazine, Fall 2012.

246. Teresa of Calcutta, archives of The Mother Teresa Center, Missionaries of Charity.

247. Donna-Marie Cooper O'Boyle, *Advent with Our Lady of Fatima* (Manchester: Sophia Institute Press, 2018), 208.

248. Fulton J. Sheen, *Advent and Christmas with Fulton Sheen*, comp. Judy Bauer (Liguori: Liguori Publications, 2016), 7.

249. Augustine, *Sermons for Christmas and Epiphany* (Westminster, MD: The Newman Press, 1952), 74.

250. Vianney, *Sermons of the Curé of Ars*, 168.

251. Found in dos Santos, *Fatima in Lucia's Own Words*, 152.

252. Found in dos Santos, *Fatima in Lucia's Own Words*, 36.

253. *The Roman Missal*, English translation according to the Third Typical Edition (Totowa, NJ: Catholic Book Publishing, 2011), July 26, Saints Joachim and Anne, Parents of the Blessed Virgin Mary, Collect.

254. Bartolo Longo, quoted in John Paul II, *Rosarium Virginis Mariae*, 43.

255. *The Roman Missal*, December 12, Our Lady of Guadalupe, Collect.

About the Author

Donna-Marie Cooper O'Boyle is a Catholic wife, mother of five, and grandmother of two. She loves teaching the faith and has served as a catechist for close to forty years. She leads retreats and pilgrimages worldwide and is an award-winning best-selling author of forty books. Donna-Marie is also an award-winning journalist, international speaker, and the host and creator of three television series on EWTN.

Donna-Marie was blessed to know Saint Teresa of Calcutta for a decade and has received a special blessing on her writing of Mother Teresa from Saint John Paul II. Donna-Marie was invited by the Holy See to participate at a Vatican Congress and is an authority on the life of Saint Maria Faustina Kowalska and the General Editor and a contributor to the Divine Mercy Catholic Bible.

A good part of Donna-Marie's work is centered on the family, faith, the saints, angels, Divine Mercy, the Eucharist, and women's issues and spirituality. In addition to her own TV shows, she has appeared on Fox News, Zenit News, Vatican Insider, Rome Reports, Vatican Radio, EWTN News Nightly, and The Choices We Face, and is a frequent guest on EWTN's Bookmark, Women of Grace, and Sunday Night Prime, as well as on national radio and television. Her memoir is entitled *The Kiss of Jesus*, where she shares about her life in order to inspire hope in others.

Donna-Marie is also a photographer and a jewelry designer who dabbles in art. She lives with her family in rural New England, admiring God's creation. Learn more at Donna-Marie's website: www.donnacooperoboyle.com as well as on her social media platforms.

Thank You.

Your purchase of this book and engagement with our other projects supports us in the work we do as Daughters of St. Paul. This book is the fruit of our consecrated life, prayer, and mission of communicating God's love.

We hold you and all your intentions in our prayers. We invite you to connect with us or send us prayer intentions at pauline.org.

Advance praise for *Daily Devotions for Grandmothers*

"Steep, Act, Pray, Savor. This beautiful rhythm of prayer and devotion leads the way as you pray for your grandchildren throughout the year. Donna-Marie Cooper O'Boyle has crafted a meaningful, evergreen guide for grandparents who want to spiritually accompany the little ones (and big ones) they so ardently love. Well done!"

— Marge Steinhage Fenelon, award-winning author, international speaker, and Certified Discernment Coach

"For grandmothers longing to strengthen their faith and embrace their role with deeper love, this book offers a warm and comforting presence. Donna-Marie Cooper O'Boyle provides daily doses of wisdom, Scripture, and prayer, creating a treasured resource for grandmothers seeking spiritual guidance and joyful connection within their sacred calling. Grounded in Catholic teachings, it's a beautiful blend of heartfelt inspiration and practical support."

— Fr. Luke Mary Fletcher, CFR

"Donna-Marie Cooper O'Boyle's *Daily Devotions for Grandmothers* offers a calm harbor for the prayerful soul. Through grace-filled reflections, wise insights, uplifting prayers, and a myriad of her own loving remembrances, she reminds grandmothers (and grandfathers!) that their vocation is both a blessing and a mission. Each page invites a quiet conversation of gratitude with God, encouraging grandparents to see His presence in the simple, sacred moments with grandchildren in the midst of family life."

— Patrick Madrid, host of the daily "Patrick Madrid Show" on Relevant Radio

"I love that in this book, gifted author Donna-Marie Cooper O'Boyle acknowledges that there are many ways to be a grandmother. Just as our 'grandma name' may vary, the circumstances of our serving as a grandparent within our families are diverse. In her beautiful daily devotional, Donna-Marie reminds us that our greatest gift as grandmothers is to pray without ceasing for our families. She gives us a template to make this a practical and enjoyable daily priority. A must-have for the prayer corner of every Grandma, Nana, Mimi, or Abuelita!"

— Lisa M. Hendey, founder of CatholicMom.com

"Grandparenting may be the most crucial phase of our vocation as laypeople. Presumably, we're wiser than we were when we were mere parents—so we have more to give. But we also find ourselves living at a time when young people have fewer chances to encounter the faith. We need to make the most of the moments we have with our grandchildren, and this book helps us prepare for those moments with prayer."

— Mike Aquilina, co-founder, St. Paul Center for Biblical Theology

"For generations, grandparents have been vital in passing on the faith to their grandchildren. Yet, as fewer grandparents actively practice their faith, Donna-Marie Cooper O'Boyle offers a much-needed resource to rekindle their love for God and the Church. For faith-filled grandmothers, this book will deepen their devotion; for those seeking to grow in faith, it provides gentle guidance."

— Fr. Edward Looney, pastor, author, podcaster

"This daily handbook for holiness is filled with wisdom derived from everyone from Mother Teresa to Donna-Marie's own grandmother. The five-minute devotions are rich in theological content, helpful action items, and powerful prayers. Whether you call yourself a Nana, a Nonna, or a Grandma, chances are you will grow closer to Jesus and His beloved Mother Mary by diving into this devotional each day. This is a book that will truly make your soul sing!"

— Maria V. Gallagher, award-winning journalist, life coach, and author

"This book highlights the vitally important role grandmothers play in the life of a family. Donna-Marie, recognizing the wealth of knowledge and the breadth of life experience that grandmothers possess, offers these eloquent reflections that both underscore the distinctive grace of grandmas and provide spiritual nourishment for their souls. *Daily Devotions for Grandmothers* is a beautifully conceived book that truly honors the gifts and blessings of grandmothers who enrich the entire family, the Church of the home."

— Deacon Harold Burke-Sivers, author

"Donna-Marie Cooper O'Boyle has, in her wonderful book, *Daily Devotions for Grandmothers*, encapsulated so much about the deep desires and longings of all grandparents, but grandmothers in particular. Filled with poignant stories, effective recommendations, and provocative reflections, she provides the contemporary journey of grandmothers with the beauty, hope, and faithfulness so necessary in making an eternal difference."

— Dan Spencer, Founder & Executive Director of Legacy of Faith